Living by the Light of the Moon

2015 MOON BOOK

Beatrex Quntanna

Acknowledgments

I wish to acknowledge…

Jennifer Masters for the cover art and her ability to capture the nature of prosperity with her magical painting of Lakshmi, the goddess of abundance. Thank you Jennifer! Violet Canzonetta for her enthusiasm, teamwork, endless nights editing, and keeping me consistent. Michelenne Crab for her tech-support and personal support for the last 13 years. Michael Makay for the daily Tibetan Numerology intentions that inspire and direct us to make the most of our day. Jaime Lyerly for her research. I'd like to give additional recognition to Kathy Guy who continues to be the *Over-lighting Diva* for the *Moon Book*.

Special thanks to…

Katherine Sale for the astrological calculations for the entire year. Kaliani Devinne for contributing the Moon charts. Jill Estensen for sharing aspects from her *Dimensional Astrology* system, that add an innovative approach to experiencing the degrees and the polarity they create for each Moon phase. Last, but not least, deep gratitude to the countless students who come to Moon Class; without you guys this teaching would not exist.

Book Cover Art

Lakshmi: Dancing by the Light of the Moon by Jennifer Masters

Book Design & Art Direction

Jennifer Masters, artist and illustrator
www.jennifer-masters.fineartamerica.com
jennifer@new-temple.com

Dimensional Astrology

Jill Estensen's innovative translation for the Sabian Symbols
intuvision@roadrunner.com

Astrological Calculations

Katherine Sale, MSW, MAc, is an Intuitive Astrologer with a psycho-spiritual approach to counseling, focusing on Soul-Centered Astrology, with an emphasis on the integration of the Soul through the personality.
www.KatherineSale.com
StargazerKat@gmail.com

Copyright ©2014 by Beatrex Quntanna

All Rights Reserved. No part of this book may be reproduced or transmitted in any form or by any means without the written permission of the publisher, except for the inclusion of brief quotations in a review.

ISBN 978-0-9625292-5-2

Printed in the United States of America

ART ALA CARTE PUBLISHING
760-944-6020
beatrex@cox.net
www.mymoonbook.com
www.beatrex.com

This book is dedicated to the memory of Nancy Tappe my friend, mentor, master-teacher, and mystic who inspires the creation of this book year after year.

Table of Contents

The Importance of Cycles — 6
How to Use This Book — 7

January — 12
Full Moon in Cancer — 14
New Moon in Aquarius — 22

February — 30
Full Moon in Leo — 32
New Moon in Aquarius — 40

March — 48
Full Moon in Virgo — 50
New Moon in Pisces – Solar Eclipse — 58

April — 66
Full Moon in Libra – Lunar Eclipse — 68
New Moon in Aries — 76

May — 84
Full Moon in Scorpio — 86
New Moon in Taurus — 94

June — 102
Full Moon in Sagittarius — 104
New Moon in Gemini — 112

July — 120
Full Moon in Capricorn — 122
New Moon in Cancer — 130
Full Moon in Aquarius — 138

August — 146
New Moon in Leo — 148
Full Moon in Pisces — 156

September — 164
New Moon in Virgo – Solar Eclipse — 166
Full Moon in Aries – Lunar Eclipse — 174

October — 182
New Moon in Libra — 184
Full Moon in Taurus — 192

November — 200
New Moon in Scorpio — 202
Full Moon in Gemini — 210

December — 218
New Moon in Sagittarius — 220
Full Moon in Cancer — 228

About the Author — 236
Other Works by This Author — 237

The Importance of Cycles

Each moon cycle offers a different combination of energies. These energies pour down to the Earth, giving us a chance to grow harmoniously into wholeness. The key is to remember that this is a study in light. Following the luminaries, the Sun and the Moon, through the zodiac and noting the cycles of illumination and reflection can bring you to a deeper creative experience of life. The Moon is the great cosmic architect, the builder and dissolver of form and foundation. The Full Moon is about dissolving, and the New Moon is about building. The *2015 Moon Book* is a workbook will assist you in knowing what to build and when, and what to dissolve and when.

Over the years Beatrex has developed a valuable connection of knowledge about how to use the moon cycles to enhance the quality of your life. This workbook is filled with activities to do during each moon cycle, in its specific zodiac sign and time, for the entire year. Life, at the highest spiritual level, moves beyond time and uses cycles to increase your ability to actualize your full potential for living. Cycles are in charge of your personal development; while time is in charge of the change in direction that happens when you take the risk to grow and begin to trust in Divine Timing.

The *2015 Moon Book* synthesizes techniques that allow for the power of development and direction to occur in the entire spectrum of wholeness. Each zodiac sign holds the knowledge necessary to integrate an aspect of yourself in order to become whole. As the Moon and Sun travel around our planet each month, a different aspect of self-development is presented to you via the constellation (zodiac sign) it is visiting. For centuries, the Moon has been the keeper of the secrets of life. If used appropriately, the Moon sets the stage for successful living. This workbook reveals those secrets and supports you in learning them.

We are now in The Fifth World, a time for co-creation. In order to co-create, we must live in the moment, stay in our truth, accept what is without judgment, and live love. This requires adjustment and a re-calibration down to the core of our beings. It also provides us with newfound freedom that requires us to give up our devotion to our past in order to embark on new frontiers. This year the workbook is set up with a support structure that easily guides you towards co-creation and freedom so that the power of acceptance can become your reality in 2015.

When the Moon is Full

When the Moon is full, it's in direct opposition to the Sun and time to set yourself free. This polarity provides a disintegrating effect that presents the best possible opportunity to dissolve anything that stands in the way of your personal freedom. Several hours before a Full Moon you may experience a tension that happens when the Sun and Moon come into an opposing position. This aspect asks you to learn to understand opposite natures without feeling the need to separate them. As a matter of fact, they are designed to teach you how to find the middle ground and integrate these opposites so that you cannot be manipulated by polarity. Integration creates unity, which then creates harmony. The identifying polarity themes are provided for you on the appropriate Full Moon pages. Use the astrological theme and freedom ideas as inspiration to write your list of ways to be free.

Once your list is written, light a candle, and read your list out loud. Then, place it under a circle-shaped mirror, and put your candle on top of the mirror. You might put the candle, wishes, and mirror outside in the moonlight or in a special place in your home. Let the candle burn out. For your protection, make sure to use a candle that is in glass, such as a votive or seven-day candle. When your candle has finished burning, your freedom list will be in operation. Remember that being free is as important as co-creating. It is the empty space that makes room for co-creation to occur. Before writing your freedom list you might want to look over the trigger points on the previous page and see if there is anything you might want to let go of before writing your freedom list. Remember to be free is to live without resistance.

Please note: All times listed in the book are local to the Pacific time zone. Add or subtract hours accordingly to adjust times for your time zone. It is best to do your creation and freedom ceremonies at the specific time noted, except during a "dropping moon." When a new or full moon peaks at the same time as it goes void, this is called a dropping moon. At these times it is very important for you to write your co-creation list or freedom list half an hour before the designated time. Visit www.mymoonbook.com for mirrors.

When the Moon is New

When the Moon is new, it is in the same sign as the Sun. This unites the power of the magnetic and dynamic fields that are in perfect resonance for co-creating. This is a potent time to make your desires known to yourself and to the Universe by writing a personal co-creation list. Use the astrological theme and co-creation ideas as inspiration to write your list of what you wish to manifest. Think about your list like a kid does when writing to Santa Claus. Let yourself become comfortable, while extending the boundaries beyond what you believe is possible. You might consider writing the following words at the end of your co-creation list, "This, or something better than this, comes to me in an easy and pleasurable way for the good of all concerned."

Once your list is written, light a candle, and read your list out loud. Then, place it under an eight-sided mirror, and put your candle on top of the mirror. You might put the candle, wishes, and mirror outside in the moonlight or in a special place in your home. For your protection, make sure to use a candle that is in glass, such as a votive or seven-day candle. Let the candle burn out. By the time the candle burns out, your co-creations are in place and ready to come true.

Please note: All times listed in the book are local to the Pacific time zone. Add or subtract hours accordingly to adjust times for your time zone. It is best to do your creation and freedom ceremonies at the specific time noted, except during a "dropping moon." When a new or full moon peaks at the same time as it goes void, this is called a dropping moon. At these times it is very important for you to write your co-creation list or freedom list half an hour before the designated time. Visit www.mymoonbook.com for mirrors.

How to Use This Book

These Sections Will Help You to Live by the Light of the Moon

Astrological Highlights

This section explains the planets and how they will affect your life each month. It does not contain all of the aspects; it simply highlights points of interest that promote personal growth during each month. If you are interested in more study, take an astrology class. If you are an astrologer and want more information, we have provided a chart for each moon phase for your convenience.

The Monthly Calendar

This section provides you with a monthly overview and keeps you connected to the lunar, solar, and planetary cycles. It lets you know when the Moon is void-of-course, when it moves into a new sign, when the Sun and planets change signs, and when a planet goes retrograde or stationary direct (shown by the $\frac{S}{D}$ symbol). The calendar also has the Tibetan Numerology of the Day, along with an affirmation, to help you align with the energy and set your intentions for the day.

Void Moon

When the Moon is void-of-course, it has made its last major aspect in a sign and stays void until it enters the next sign. When the Moon is void-of-course, you will see the icon V/C on the calendar. This is not a good time to start new projects, relationships, or to take trips, unless you intend to never follow through. When the Moon ☽ enters a new sign, you will see this arrow ➡ It will be followed by the symbol for the new sign and the time that the Moon enters it.

Super-Sensitivity ▲

This happens when the Moon travels across the sky, hits the center of the galaxy, and connects with a fixed star. When this happens the atmosphere becomes chaotic. An extra amount of energy pours down in a spiral at a very fast speed making it difficult to focus. This fragility can make you depressed, anxious, dizzy, and accident-prone. It is a good idea to keep your thought process away from this energy. This is global, not personal.

Low-Vitality ▼

This happens when the Moon is directly opposite the center of the galaxy. When this fixed-star opposition occurs, the Earth becomes very fragile and gets depleted. This leads to exhaustion in our physical bodies and is a sign for us to nurture ourselves by resting. The depletion can create Earth changes. Endings can also happen and resistance to these completions will bring on exhaustion. Best to detach and let go.

The Sun

Each month you will see the icon for the Sun ☉ with an arrow ➡ indicating when the Sun enters a new sign. When the Sun changes signs, the climate of energy takes on a new theme for your personal development. Look for the Sun icon, with an arrow followed by an astrological sign, to indicate sign change and time.

Planets

Planets also change signs and move in retrograde and direct motions. Retrograde planets are next to the date in each day's box followed by retrograde icon ℞. In the middle of each box is information about planetary changes of time and direction.

Please note: All times are given for the Pacific time zone. Add or subtract hours accordingly to adjust times for your time zone.

Choice Points: Motivation – Resistance

These are a part of Dimensional Astrology presenting a pre-scribed action and resistance for each of the 360-degrees on the astrology wheel. The object of Dimensional Astrology is to depolarize and neutralize motivation and resistance. Each degree for the Moon and it's house are described to better enhance your understanding of the phase and its effects on you and your world. The gift comes when you integrate and combine the motivation and the resistance without judgment. For example, in the New Moon in January, the motivation is ambition and the resistance is mediocrity. You will find yourself being driven to be more ambitious. If you resist, you will fall into mediocrity.

"I" Statements

These statements align the Self with the characteristics of the astrological sign and the house the sign lives in.

Body Mind Spirit

Each astrological sign rules a body part, a mental trait or attitude, and a spiritual condition. This section is provided to increase understanding of the tendencies and patterns that are activated during the moon transit.

Elements

Each Moon Cycle has a primary element (earth, air, fire or water) attached to the constellation to which it is assigned that brings you more awareness of what to work on during the cycle.

House Themes

Each House the moon lands in brings a focus for that moon as a baseline for self-development during the moon phase.

Karmic Awakenings

Every once in a while the chart for the Moon will show an intercepted astrological sign in a house on the chart. This indicates a karmic pattern is in operation on that day.

Gods and Goddesses

When the Moon enters a new zodiac sign, a changing of guardians occurs. Deep within each sign lives a god or goddess who is the keeper of this cyclical domain. This archetype's assignment is to hold the space for an aspect of wholeness to actualize.

On Your Altar

An altar is an outer focus for inner work. Esoteric coordinates such as tarot cards, flowers, colors, gemstones, fragrances, and numerology are provided as an enhancement to better assist you in working with each moon phase. Perhaps you are working on a love theme; you might want to add six hearts, six flowers, and six gemstones on your altar with your co-creation list and candle. The coordinating tarot card can be used as a visual activation. Flowers, colors, and gemstones accent your intentions. The fragrance provides a special connection to Spirit. You may want to burn candles of this scent, spritz your aura or your altar with the fragrance, or simply sniff the fragrance to awaken your olfactory system. Visit www.mymoonbook.com for moon mists.

Co-Creation List

Write down what you want to create and manifest in your life.

Freedom List

Write down what you want to move beyond in order to set yourself free.

List Ideas

Use these ideas to jump start your own lists. Let your imagination take off from here.

Clearing the Slate for Freedom

This is the first step to freedom and releasing during the Full Moon Cycle. Each section is filled with trigger points that are specific to the astrological sign where the moon resides. See if any of them feel familiar. Acknowledge what's familiar and then follow the instructions by forgiving, releasing, and letting go.

Meditation

This section focuses on the freedom part of the moon cycle.

Challenges and Victories

These are sets of affirmations designed to say out loud during a specific moon cycle to determine a motivational tone for your self-discovery. After saying all of them out loud, you will know which statement applies to you. Circle the one that is yours and use it as a personal mantra daily during the moon phase.

The Astro Wheel

Western astrological charts are placed within a circle or wheel. The wheel is a picture of the sky from a particular place and time on Earth. It is divided into 12 parts called houses. Each house deals with a particular area of life. Key concepts for each house are written outside the wheel. Compare the wheel in the book to your very own chart and discover the theme that you will be living personally during the moon phase.

Cosmic Check-In

"I" statements are designed specifically to keep you in touch with all of the signs and their houses each time the Moon is new or full. Fill in the blanks to complete each statement during each full and new moon phase to activate all parts of your birth chart and keep you in touch with Oneness. Have fun noticing how different you are during each cycle.

Blank Pages

Between each moon phase blank pages are provided for journaling.

Heavenly Bodies

☉	Sun	Outer personality, potential, director, the most obvious traits of the consciousness projection
☽	Moon	Emotion, feelings, memory, unconsciousness, mother's influence, ancestors, home life
☿	Mercury	The way you think, the intention beneath your thoughts, communication, academia (lower mind)
♀	Venus	Beauty, value, romantic love, sensuality, creativity, social, fun, femininity
♂	Mars	Action, change, variety, sex drive, ambition, warrior, ego, athletics, masculinity
♃	Jupiter	Benevolent, jovial, excessive, expansive, optimistic, abundance, good fortune, extravagant
♄	Saturn	Teacher, karma, disciplined, restrictive, father's influence
♅	Uranus	Liberated, revolutionary, explosive, spontaneous, breakthrough, innovation, technology
♆	Neptune	Mystical, charming, sensitive, addictive, glamor, deceptive, illusions
♇	Pluto	Money, wealth, transformation, secrets, hidden information, sexuality, psychic power
⚷	Chiron	Wounded healer, healing, holistic therapies
☊	North Node	This represents where you are headed in this lifetime. In other words, it represents the direction your life will take you, your future focus. In Eastern astrology, this is sometimes called the "head of the dragon."
☋	South Node	This represents what you brought with you this lifetime and what you are moving away from. It is sometimes called the "tail of the dragon" in Eastern astrology.

Astrological Signs

Each sign of astrology has a particular quality or tone that is described in more detail with the moons.

Sign		"I" Statement		Element	Key Words
♈	Aries	I Am	Sign of the Ram Ruled by Mars ♂ Aries begins the zodiac year with the Spring Equinox	Fire	Ego, identity, championship, leadership, action-oriented, warrior, and self-first.
♉	Taurus	I Have	Sign of the Bull Ruled by Venus ♀	Earth	Self-value, abundant, aesthetic, business, sensuous, art, beauty, flowers, gardens, collector, and shopper.
♊	Gemini	I Communicate	Sign of the Twins Ruled by Mercury ☿	Air	Versatile, expressive, restless, travel-minded, short trips, flirt, gossip, "nose for news," and messenger.
♋	Cancer	I Feel	Sign of the Crab Ruled by the Moon ☽ Cancer begins with the Summer Solstice	Water	Emotional, nurturing, family-oriented, home, mother, cooking, security-minded, ancestors, builder of form and foundation.
♌	Leo	I Love	Sign of the Lion Ruled by the Sun ☉	Fire	Willful, dramatic, loyal, children, child-ego state, love affairs, decadent, royal, show-stopper, theatre, adored and adoring.
♍	Virgo	I Heal	Sign of the Virgin Ruled by Mercury ☿	Earth	Gives birth to divinity, perfectionist, discernment, scientific, analytical, habitual, work-oriented, body maintenance, earth connection, attention to detail, service-oriented, earth healer, herbs, and judgmental.
♎	Libra	I Relate	Sign of the Scales Ruled by Venus ♀ Libra begins with the Autumnal Equinox	Air	Relationship, social, harmony, industry, the law, diplomacy, morality, beauty, strategist, logical, and over-active mind.
♏	Scorpio	I Transform	Sign of the Scorpion Ruled by Pluto ♀ and Mars ♂	Water	Intense, passionate, sexual, powerful, focused, controlling, deep, driven, and secretive.
♐	Sagittarius	I Seek	Sign of the Archer Ruled by Jupiter ♃	Fire	Optimistic, generous, preacher-teacher, world traveler, higher knowledge, goal-oriented, philosophy, culture, publishing, extravagance, excessive, exaggerator, and good fortune.
♑	Capricorn	I Produce	Sign of the Goat Ruled by Saturn ♄ Capricorn begins at the Winter Solstice	Earth	Ambitious, concretive, responsible, achievement, business, corporate structure, world systems, and useful.
♒	Aquarius	I Know	Sign of the Water Bearer Ruled by Uranus ♅	Air	Inventive, idealistic, utopian, rebellion, innovative, technology, community, friends, synergy, group consciousness, science, magic, trendy, and future-orientation.
♓	Pisces	I Trust	Sign of the Fishes Ruled by Neptune ♆	Water	Sensitive, creative, empathetic, theatre, addiction, escape artist, glamor, secretive, divinely guided, healer, medicine.

The Astrology Wheel

Western astrological charts are placed within a circle or wheel. The wheel is a picture of the sky from a particular place and time on Earth. It is divided into 12 parts called houses. Each house deals with a particular area of life. Below are some key concepts for each house.

	Statement	Ruling Sign		Key Notes
1st House	I Am	♈	Aries	Your outer appearance, the way you present yourself, the way you dress, the way you enter a room, and what you leave behind when you leave the room.
2nd House	I Have	♉	Taurus	The way you make your money and the way you spend your money.
3rd House	I Communicate	♊	Gemini	How you get the word out and the message behind the words.
4th House	I Feel	♋	Cancer	The way your early environmental training was and how that set your foundation for living, and why you chose your mother.
5th House	I Love	♌	Leo	The way you love and how you want to be loved.
6th House	I Heal	♍	Virgo	The way you manage your body and its appearance.
7th House	I Relate	♎	Libra	One-on-one relationships, defines your people attraction, and how you work in relationships with the people you attract.
8th House	I Transform	♏	Scorpio	How you share money and other resources, what you keep hidden regarding sex, death, real estate, and regeneration.
9th House	I Seek	♐	Sagittarius	The way you approach spirituality, philosophy, journeys, higher knowledge, and aspiration.
10th House	I Produce	♑	Capricorn	Your approach to status, career, honor, and prestige, why you chose your Father.
11th House	I Know	♒	Aquarius	Your approach to friends, social consciousness, teamwork, community service, and the future.
12th House	I Trust	♓	Pisces	Determines how you deal with your karma, unconscious software, and what you will experience in order to attain mastery by completing your karma. It is also about the way you connect to the Divine.

Tibetan Numerology of the Day

2	Balance	Be decisive and move past vacillation.
3	Fun	Have a party. Take on a creative project. Express the "Disneyland" side of yourself.
4	Structure	Take the day to organize. Get the job done. Work and you will sail through the day.
5	Action, exercise, travel	Exercise—join a gym, take a dance class, play tennis, go for a walk. Travel—go for a drive, travel the world, visit your travel agent. Make a change.
6	Love	Go out for a night of romance. Work on beauty in your home. Nurture yourself and take care of your health.
7	Research	Read a book. Learn something new and get smart. Take a class.
8	Money	Have a business meeting. Meet with your accountant. Make a sales call. Start a new business.
9	Connecting with the Divine	Meditate. Take part in a humanitarian project. Do community service.
10	Seeing the "big picture"	Take an innovative idea and run with it today!
11	Completion	Do what it takes to be complete.

Planetary Highlights

Jupiter is Retrograde in Leo Until April 8

The courage to love every day is here now. It's time to open your heart and be brave enough to go for prosperity on all levels, especially in relationship, home, health, and beauty. Take a look at where you were 12 years ago and see how far you have come.

Mercury goes Retrograde in Aquarius on January 21 Until February 11

Expect the mind to work overtime rehashing undelivered communications from the past. It's time to allow yourself the privilege of living in the moment, so update your mind.

January 3 – Venus Moves into Aquarius

You might find yourself attracting a new kind of love interest; if so, let it happen. It's time to let go of the same cookie-cutter attraction and go for something new.

January 4 – Mercury Moves into Aquarius

Conversations should be quite inspiring right now. Get out your notepad and write down the ideas that flow into your head; the genius is at work here. Innovation is in the air. Find your team and use it to make the world a better place.

January 4 – Full Moon in Cancer

The influence of Pluto and the Sun make this a transformational moon cycle. If there is anything hanging around your life that needs to be released, now is the time. The global systems and familiar structures will be undergoing a major reworking. The key here is to let it happen so that the new order can emerge and we evolve.

January 4-20 – Mercury and Venus are Coupled in Aquarius

Here is a reminder to make decisions based on love, creativity, and joy, rather than reason. Allow the power of the Aquarian mind to show you a new direction.

January 4 – Uranus, North, and South Nodes are in Opposition in Aries and Libra

This instills a desire to activate a new paradigm for relationships to include freedom as a part of the love equation. The goal here is to be free to love without conflict or entrapment.

January 12 – Mars Moves into Pisces

Yikes! Hold onto your hat; your emotional body is up for a steam-cleaning.

January 20 – Neptune and Mars Conjunct in Pisces

Mars is dynamic and forceful with an ironclad will. Neptune hides behind the veil of illusion and has a way of confusing issues with masks of personality that hide under the radar. This can be a confusing transit.

January 20 – New Moon in Aquarius

Expect a re-arrangement of plans. Learn to live spontaneously! Open yourself to new ideas and new people.

January 20 – The Sun Moves into Aquarius

This is a time when the mind advances to a higher octave. Let your thought waves fly into the higher realms as high, or higher than, the sky. This time is about becoming aware of the new potential for the year. Get your butterfly net and capture a thought that can make your future better.

January 27 – Venus Moves into Pisces

Expect to dive deeply into the place where romance lives. Have fun dreaming and playing with your beloved.

Low-Vitality – January 2-3, 29-30

This happens when a planet, the Sun, or the Moon hits a degree that dissipates energy from the center of the Earth. The result is exhaustion on a physical level. The advice here is to stay close to home, let go of resistance, and allow endings to happen. Do what you can to find a way to nurture yourself on these days.

Super-Sensitivity – January 17-18

This happens as the Sun, the Moon or a planet crosses the center of the galaxy and activates the atmosphere to become chaotic. If you personalize this activity, you may feel a bit dizzy, overly sensitive, confused, ungrounded, moody, or depressed. The advice here is to become aware that this energy is available and work to keep good boundaries to avoid the chaos. Avoid crowds, daydreaming, and meditation on these days.

♈ Aries	♋ Cancer	♐ Sagittarius	☽ Moon	♄ Saturn	☊ North Node	V/C Void-of-Course
♉ Taurus	♌ Leo	♑ Capricorn	☿ Mercury	♅ Uranus	☋ South Node	▲ Super-Sensitivity
♊ Gemini	♍ Virgo	♒ Aquarius	♀ Venus	♆ Neptune	➡ Enters	▼ Low-Vitality
	♎ Libra	♓ Pisces	♂ Mars	♇ Pluto	℞ Retrograde	
	♏ Scorpio	☉ Sun	♃ Jupiter	⚷ Chiron	S/D Stationary Direct	

January

Sunday	Monday	Tuesday	Wednesday	Thursday	Friday	Saturday
				1 ♃℞ Happy New Year ☽ V/C 4:18AM ☽→♊ 9:08AM 10. Today is a new beginning.	**2** ♃℞ ▼ 11. You are part of the Universe.	**3** ♃℞ ▼ ☽ V/C 3:54AM ☽→♋ 5:07PM ♀→♒ 6:49AM 3. A playful heart has joy.
4 ♃℞ ☽ V/C 8:53PM ○ 14°♋31' 8:53PM ☿→♒ 5:09PM 4. Create your own structure.	**5** ♃℞ 5. Remember to exercise.	**6** ♃℞ ☽→♌ 3:02AM 6. Tell someone you care.	**7** ♃℞ 7. Read something enlightening.	**8** ♃℞ ☽ V/C 9:04AM ☽→♍ 2:57PM 8. Gratitude creates abundance.	**9** ♃℞ 9. Know you are divinely blessed.	**10** ♃℞ ☽ V/C 7:45AM 10. Begin each day with a prayer.
11 ♃℞ ☽→♎ 3:56AM 2. Decide what is best for you.	**12** ♃℞ ♂→♓ 2:21AM 3. Learn from your experience today.	**13** ♃℞ ☽ V/C 1:46AM ☽→♏ 3:43PM 4. Organize your work space.	**14** ♃℞ 5. Take a different direction.	**15** ♃℞ ☽ V/C 3:51PM 6. Flowers can make a difference.	**16** ♃℞ ☽→♐ 12:00AM 7. Choose wisely; then act.	**17** ♃℞ ▲ ☽ V/C 11:25AM 8. Joyfully share what you have.
18 ♃℞ ▲ ☽→♑ 4:04AM 9. Pray for enlightenment.	**19** ♃℞ Martin Luther King ☽ V/C 2:51AM 10. Make sure you have a dream.	**20** ♃℞ ☽→♒ 4:59AM ● 0°♒09' 5:13AM ☉→♒ 1:44AM 11. Strive for what is right.	**21** ♃☿℞ ☽ V/C 5:45PM ☿℞ 17°♒05' 7:55AM 3. Find humor in your day.	**22** ♃☿℞ ☽→♓ 4:47AM 4. Be loyal and independent.	**23** ♃☿℞ ☽ V/C 3:12AM 5. Variety is the spice of life.	**24** ♃☿℞ ☽→♈ 5:31AM 6. Your heart knows the truth.
25 ♃☿℞ 7. Trust your inner knowing.	**26** ♃☿℞ ☽ V/C 6:23AM ☽→♉ 8:37AM 8. Be a leader without followers.	**27** ♃☿℞ ☽ V/C 6:18PM ♀→♓ 7:01AM 9. Help someone spiritually.	**28** ♃☿℞ ☽→♊ 2:36PM 10. Replace a worn out item.	**29** ♃☿℞ ▼ 2. Remember to stay in balance.	**30** ♃☿℞ ▼ ☽ V/C 1:24AM ☽→♋ 11:08PM 3. Enjoy some playful music.	**31** ♃☿℞ 4. Know what works best for you.

January 4th
8:53 PM

Full Moon in Cancer

Dropping Moon
This happens when a new or full moon peaks at the same time as it goes void. During a "dropping moon" it becomes very important for you to write your co-creation list or your freedom list half an hour before the designated time.

Degree Choice Points
14° Cancer 30'

Motivation Love of Life

Resistance Deprivation

Gift Return other energies that you have collected.

Statement I Feel
Body Stomach
Mind Worry
Spirit Nurturing

Element
Water – Motion without resistance, gateway to all things hidden (conscious and unconscious), a need for emotional nourishment.

Eleventh House Moon
5° Cancer 26'

Eleventh House Umbrella Theme
I Know/I Feel – Your approach to friends, social consciousness, teamwork, community service, and the future.

Motivation Comfort

Resistance Expendable

Gift Yield to angelic or inspired direction.

The Sun is Opposite the Moon

Full Moons are always in opposition to the Sun. This creates a feeling of tension between where you want to shine and how your feelings are flowing on a sensory level about the Sun's directive. The two forces seem like they are working against each other, yet they are on the same team displaying different techniques to attain the same mission. The Cancer/Capricorn polarity creates tension about being at home with family versus being at work positioning yourself for success.

Cancer Goddess

Demeter is the Goddess of Nature's Abundance. When her family was disrupted and her child taken, she withheld nourishment from the Earth, and Nature stopped producing. The people weren't nourished and withheld their honoring of the Gods. As a result, an agreement was struck between Heaven and Earth. Demeter agreed to let go and release full control of her child and restored Nature's abundance in exchange for a new, balanced relationship with her daughter. When the Moon is full in Cancer it is time to look at your mother/child issues and release what is no longer nurturing you.

On Your Altar

Colors Shades of gray and milky, creamy colors

Numerology 4 – Create your own structure

Tarot Card The Chariot – The ability to move forward

Gemstones Pearl, moonstone, ruby

Plant remedy Shooting Star – The ability to move straight ahead

Fragrance Peppermint – The essence of the Great Mother

Meditation

The freedom themes are provided by the zodiac sign and can be from this lifetime or other lifetimes. These meditations assist in dissolving blocks and opening pathways to new frontiers.

When the Moon is in Cancer, it is time to reconcile with past events. Sit quietly and breathe in and out until you are settled. Ask for an Angel of Records to show you a time when your need was not fulfilled. It is important to listen to your emotional nature and take time out to be nurtured. Reflection and illumination are the main themes while sinking deeply into the subconscious memory. During the Cancer Moon, it is time to research your Soul's records to release past memories of wrongs enacted against you so you can move beyond any attachment to self-pity.

Cancer Challenges and Victories

Say all of the statements in this section out loud. Then, underline the phrase that means the most to you. Use the phrase as your special affirmation for manifesting and co-creating throughout this phase of the moon.

Today, I take advantage of my ability to take action and position myself for success. I clearly know that the road to success is before me, and all I need to do is move forward. I am aware that when I take action and move forward, the Universe fills in the dots. Whether I move left, right, or straight ahead doesn't matter—what matters is that I am in movement. Today, I release indecisiveness that keeps me stuck. Today, I let go of vacillation that exhausts my mind. Today, I take my foot off of the brakes and find the gas pedal. I allow movement to occur, even if I don't know where I am going. When I take action, I trust the guideposts will appear. I am aware that action leads me to my new direction. Today, I know and GO! I remember that Karma comes to the space of non-action, while success comes through action. Action brings me to my victory. Standing still leads to regret, resentment, and chaos. I am aware that action can be as simple as taking a walk on the beach, buying fresh flowers to add a new dimension to my home, or simply going to a new restaurant for lunch. I take action today to break up a crystallized pattern and, in so doing, my life begins to show me newfound awareness and light to guide me.

Cancer Homework

It's now time to conquer pride and ambition, overcome fear of loneliness, release the need for money, security, and possessions, discover the value of emotions, and connect to beauty. Submerge yourself in a tub of water, relax, and let the clean water flow through your cells to wash away all of your hurts, resentments, and history that keep you trapped in the past. Pull the plug and let the spiral of water carry away your pain. Be prepared to boldly claim your presence in the present. Look around your kitchen and throw away the pots and pans that continue to feed your past, rather than vitalizing your life now.

January 4th
8:53 PM

Full Moon in Cancer

Clearing the Slate for Freedom

Remember a time when you experienced the following trigger points. Write down what happened, forgive yourself, release it, and let it go to clear your slate for freedom.

Blame

- Forgive
- Release
- Let Go

Attachment to Things

- Forgive
- Release
- Let Go

Emotional Attachment to the Past

- Forgive
- Release
- Let Go

Self-Pity

- Forgive
- Release
- Let Go

Broken Promises

- Forgive
- Release
- Let Go

My Freedom List

Say this statement out loud three times before writing your freedom list!

I am a free spiritual being and it is my desire to be free to think and to express myself fully.

I am now free and ready to make choices beyond survival!

Cancer Freedom List Ideas

Now is the time to set myself free from self-pity, defensive behavior,
nurturing everyone else but me, living in the past, being a mother, and having a mother.

January 4th
8:53 PM

Full Moon in Cancer

How to Use the Moon Book With Your Chart

Fill in the blanks on the Cosmic Check-In page. Then look up the degree of the moon on the chart below. Take note of the "I" statement on the outside of the wheel where the moon is located. Now, locate the same degree on your own chart and make a note of the house and corresponding "I" statement. Go back to the Cosmic Check-In page and circle the two statements from the charts and read what you wrote. This will give you an idea about what to expect from this moon phase on a personal level.

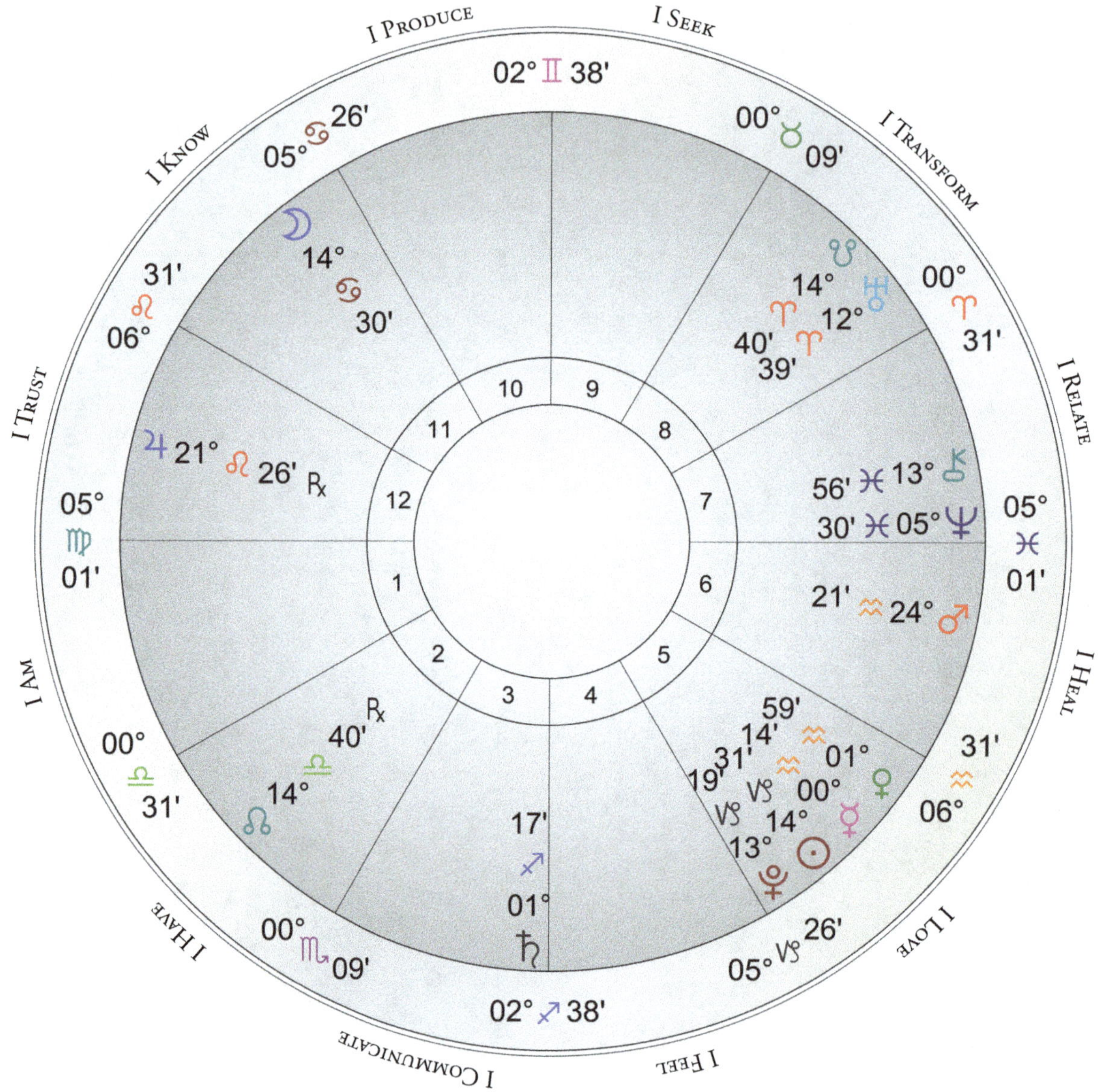

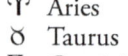

♈ Aries	♋ Cancer	♐ Sagittarius	☽ Moon	♄ Saturn	☊ North Node	V/C Void-of-Course
♉ Taurus	♌ Leo	♑ Capricorn	☿ Mercury	♅ Uranus	☋ South Node	▲ Super-Sensitivity
♊ Gemini	♍ Virgo	♒ Aquarius	♀ Venus	♆ Neptune	➡ Enters	▼ Low-Vitality
	♎ Libra	♓ Pisces	♂ Mars	♇ Pluto	℞ Retrograde	
	♏ Scorpio	☉ Sun	♃ Jupiter	⚷ Chiron	S/D Stationary Direct	

Cosmic Check-In

Take a moment to write a brief phrase for each "I" statement.
This activates all areas of your life for this creative cycle.

♋ I Feel

♌ I Love

♍ I Heal

♎ I Relate

♏ I Transform

♐ I Seek

♑ I Produce

♒ I Know

♓ I Trust

♈ I Am

♉ I Have

♊ I Communicate

January 20th
5:13 AM

New Moon in Aquarius

Degree Choice Points
0° Aquarius 8'

Motivation Endurance

Resistance Intolerance

Gift Pay attention to your body, it is your auto-pilot.

Statement I Know
   Body Ankles
   Mind True Genius
   Spirit Vision

Element
Air – Inspiration, the breath of life, allows the mind to achieve new insights and fresh perspectives, active and abstract dreaming, freedom from attachments.

First House Moon
4° Capricorn 12'

First House Umbrella Theme
I Am/I Know – Your outer appearance, the way you present yourself, the way you dress, the way you enter a room, and what you leave behind when you leave the room.

Motivation Utilize

Resistance Exploit

Gift New experiences create fresh realities.

When the Sun is in Aquarius

This is a time when the higher octave of the mind comes into play and one is given the power of vision. The Aquarian energies promote knowing by being a wellspring of knowledge. They expand the radius of contact by going beyond the known in areas of communication and cooperation. Now is the time to be initiated into greater awareness to serve the fields of human endeavors. Connect and combine magic with science and become a creative influence. When the sun is in Aquarius we must unify with our team players and collect innovative ideas to advance the world to a better place.

Aquarius Goddess

The Aquarian goddess, Star Woman, is also known as Hathor, the keeper of the light who gives birth to insight. All goddesses are born from the stars. Star Woman is in charge of directing the light bodies through the void of Creation to the point of insight, which occurs when the radiance is instilled in the memory of creation. She instills the light of the world into your own being so you can become in service to the souls who have lost their way.

On Your Altar

Colors Violet, neon, crystalline rainbow tints

Numerology 11 – Strive for what is right

Tarot Card The Star – Golden opportunities for the future

Gemstones Aquamarine, blue topaz, peacock pearls

Plant Remedy Queen of the Night Cactus – Ability to see light in the dark

Fragrance Myrrh – Healing the nervous system

My Co-Creation List

This or something better than this comes to me in an easy and pleasurable way, for the good of all concerned. Thank you, Universe!

Aquarius Co-Creation Ideas

Now is the time to focus on manifesting vision, invention, technology, freedom, friends, community, personal genius, higher awareness, teamwork, science, and magic.

January 20th
5:13 AM

New Moon in Aquarius

Aquarius Challenges and Victories

Say all of the statements in this section out loud. Then, underline the phrase that means the most to you. Use the phrase as your special affirmation for manifesting and co-creating throughout this phase of the moon.

Today, I chart my course for my new direction. My future is set on a new, fresh evolutionary course. I am guided by a higher source and trust in that guidance. I know my life has value and I am willing to contribute to the pool of consciousness by experiencing my life and living my life to the fullest view of possibility. Today, I know my possibilities are endless. My Spirit and my Soul are connected to Heaven and to Earth and this knowing brings me to the awareness that I can add to the higher qualities of life because I am connected to the whole. My being is far-reaching and immeasurable. I contribute to existence simply by knowing. All of the guideposts are connected for me today to see my way to a profound new future. My vision is clear and I can clearly set my sights on this new course. Golden opportunities come with this new vision and I trust in my guidance to bring me to this new level of manifesting power. I check in with my inner lights, each day, by meditating and asking for all seven of the energy centers in my body to come into alignment with the outer symbols of guidance. I do this by becoming still and breathing until I feel the stillness. Then, I place my hand on each center in my body, one center at a time, to be activated by light. Next, I ask out loud for each center in my body to let me know what its energetic contribution to the new direction is and how best to use the energy to move forward on my new course of action. I write down each statement and connect each statement to the guiding star in the sky. I am now linked up physically and spiritually and ready to navigate my total self towards my new evolutionary direction.

Aquarius Homework

Aquarians co-create a storehouse of information through innovative telecommunications, technology, social networking and media, and global communication. They are typically found in the fields of psychology, science fiction authoring or film-making, speech writing, and aerospace engineering.

Consider these three Aquarian gifts:

- Opportunity – Become a creative influence
- Enlightenment – When you become aware that you are light
- Brotherhood – Separation doesn't exist anymore

Where do you see these occurring in your life?

Without Acknowledgment Progress Cannot Occur

Acknowledgement creates space for victory and gratitude, which automatically brings you to a level of completion so a new cycle of opportunity can occur in your life. When you celebrate your wins and acknowledge your victories with gratitude, you update your cells so that your ability to move forward is not hindered by a cellular holographic pattern that is stuck in the past. Cellular lag creates resistance and makes moving forward most difficult. The key is to stay continuously updated by acknowledging yourself for what you did do at the end of each day, rather than heading off to sleep thinning about what you did not do. By acknowledging what you did not do, you play into your karmic storage bank and keep your progress at bay. When you acknowledge yourself and your manifestations you are complete, and more cycles of opportunity become available to you in each new day. Be prepared for miracles!

Victory List

When a creation result is acknowledged it seals the deal. This makes room for more magnificence to expand into your life and increases your abundance factor adding to your ability to receive. As each aspect of your co-creation list arrives in your life, spend time allowing, acknowledging, and accepting it with the true gusto of gratitude! Keep your victory list active here.

Gratitude List

This fulfills the relationship between the giver and the receiver, which completes the cycle with the Universe so that a new beginning can be established.

January 20th
5:13 AM

New Moon in Aquarius

How to Use the Moon Book With Your Chart

Fill in the blanks on the Cosmic Check-In page. Then look up the degree of the moon on the chart below. Take note of the "I" statement on the outside of the wheel where the moon is located. Now, locate the same degree on your own chart and make a note of the house and corresponding "I" statement. Go back to the Cosmic Check-In page and circle the two statements from the charts and read what you wrote. This will give you an idea about what to expect from this moon phase on a personal level.

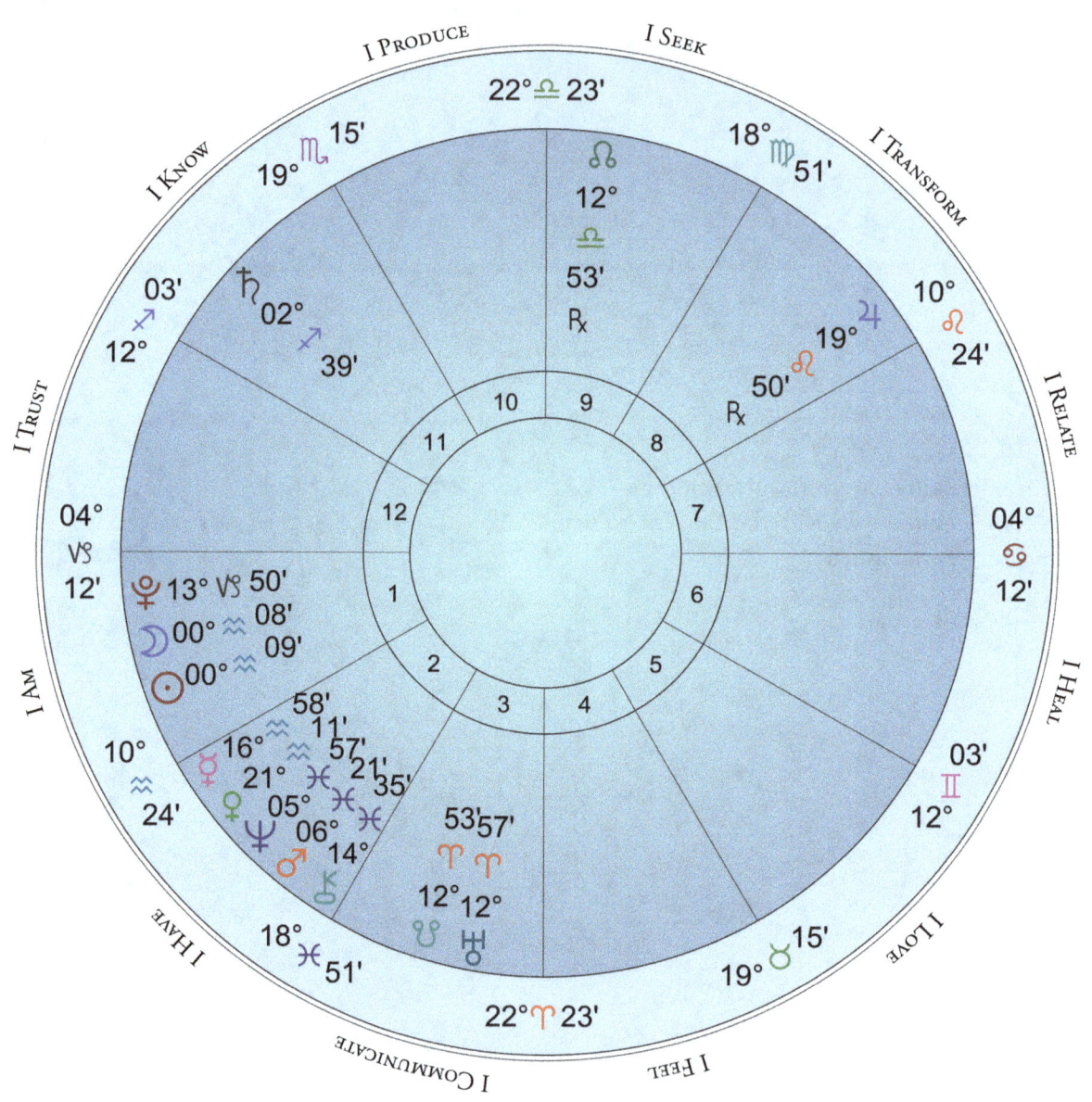

♈ Aries	♋ Cancer	♐ Sagittarius	☽ Moon	♄ Saturn	☊ North Node	V/C Void-of-Course
♉ Taurus	♌ Leo	♑ Capricorn	☿ Mercury	♅ Uranus	☋ South Node	▲ Super-Sensitivity
♊ Gemini	♍ Virgo	♒ Aquarius	♀ Venus	♆ Neptune	➡ Enters	▼ Low-Vitality
	♎ Libra	♓ Pisces	♂ Mars	♇ Pluto	℞ Retrograde	
	♏ Scorpio	☉ Sun	♃ Jupiter	⚷ Chiron	S/D Stationary Direct	

26

Cosmic Check-In

Take a moment to write a brief phrase for each "I" statement.
This activates all areas of your life for this creative cycle.

♒ I Know

♓ I Trust

♈ I Am

♉ I Have

♊ I Communicate

♋ I Feel

♌ I Love

♍ I Heal

♎ I Relate

♏ I Transform

♐ I Seek

♑ I Produce

Planetary Highlights

Mercury is Retrograde in Aquarius Until February 11

The mind works overtime looking for wider horizons ... the wider the better. Avoid details and just let expansion be your guide. Complete old business, but avoid signing any contracts. Wait until after the 11th to look for new technology.

Jupiter is Retrograde in Leo Until April 8

Review the year 2003 to check on any leftover relationship issues that are coming forward to be addressed and completed. Remember what the climate was around your home and home life in 2003. Resolve, recalibrate, and update yourself to now.

February 3 – Full Moon in Leo

This freedom moon is asking us to do a clean sweep on love issues that are not part of the present. Now is the time to open a doorway into a new kind of loving that has truth and freedom as its natural expression. Freedom comes to those that know they are loved.

February 3 – Jupiter and the Moon are Conjunct in Leo and Opposing the Sun in Aquarius

If you have a tendency to cling to what is familiar, emotional attachment to the past could be a problem here. Let your emotions guide you toward the issues that are in need of releasing. Let yourself look at where you let love keep you from feeling free and set an intention to work on this without rebellion.

February 3 – Mars and Chiron are Conjunct in Pisces

Places that need healing in your life will become heated or irritated. If you use this irritation wisely, you will know what is ready to heal.

February 3 – Venus and Neptune are Dancing in the Sky

Deep love and playful love are happening simultaneously. Don't miss out on the bliss that is available for the next few days!

February 3 – Uranus and the South Node in Aries are Conjunct and Opposing the North Node in Libra

This oxymoronic configuration will be laced in and out of the fiber of life all year. It brings up a question about how to be in a love relationship and consider yourself first.

February 18 – Venus and Mars are Dancing in Pisces

Expect some hot, sizzling, passionate lovemaking to occur during these days. This attraction force is huge, so enjoy every minute. Make love, not war.

February 18 – New Moon in Aquarius

It's time to manifest new friends, new causes, and new technology. This is a very strong moon for groups to gather and create a field of awareness that will manifest good for the future by infusing the wellspring with new knowledge. Set the stage for your future potential to grow toward actualization. Become a Light Creator!

February 18 – The Sun Enters Pisces

When the Sun is in Pisces we are all given a glance into our relationship with the Divine. We have a great opportunity to get clear on our purpose and direction as it applies to our spiritual pathway. Pisces rules our feet, the symbolic meaning of feet is understanding, so it is their job to keep us on a pathway that best serves our understanding through learning to trust.

February 19 – Chinese New Year – Enter the Sheep

The sheep is the 8th animal in the order of the Chinese zodiac. The number 8 is an auspicious number and is considered a sign of peace and prosperity. The lesson of the Sheep Year has to do with seizing the moment so that the manifestations presented will not be lost. The challenge is not to let the mind wander.

February 19 – Mars Enters Aries

This is an auspicious time to reacquaint yourself with the part of you that is a champion. Mars rules action. It's now time to ignite what you desire for yourself. Go for it NOW!

Super-Sensitivity – February 13-14

Be aware that chaos is in the air and it is global, not personal. Avoid meditation, going out of your body, or daydreaming of any kind.

Low-Vitality – February 26-27

The Earth is at a low right now and so is your body. Stay close to home and nurture yourself.

♈ Aries	♋ Cancer	♐ Sagittarius	☽ Moon	♄ Saturn	☊ North Node	V/C Void-of-Course
♉ Taurus	♌ Leo	♑ Capricorn	☿ Mercury	♅ Uranus	☋ South Node	▲ Super-Sensitivity
♊ Gemini	♍ Virgo	♒ Aquarius	♀ Venus	♆ Neptune	➡ Enters	▼ Low-Vitality
	♎ Libra	♓ Pisces	♂ Mars	♇ Pluto	℞ Retrograde	
	♏ Scorpio	☉ Sun	♃ Jupiter	⚷ Chiron	S/D Stationary Direct	

February

Sunday	Monday	Tuesday	Wednesday	Thursday	Friday	Saturday
1 ♃☿℞ ☽ V/C 5:36AM 5. Try something different for dinner.	**2** ♃☿℞ ☽→♌ 9:40AM 6. Light a candle in someone's memory.	**3** ♃☿℞ ☽ V/C 9:30PM ○14°♌48' 3:08PM 7. Open your mind to new ideas.	**4** ♃☿℞ ☽→♍ 9:45PM 8. Pay someone's way just for fun.	**5** ♃☿℞ 9. See the good in everyone.	**6** ♃☿℞ ☽ V/C 2:09PM 10. Start anew and don't look back.	**7** ♃☿℞ ☽→♎ 10:43AM 11. Let the vastness be inspiring.
8 ♃☿℞ 3. Set a play date with a friend.	**9** ♃☿℞ ☽ V/C 3:58AM ☽→♏ 11:05PM 4. Restructure what isn't working.	**10** ♃☿℞ 5. Embrace the joy of change.	**11** ♃℞ ☽ V/C 9:32PM ☿D—1°♒18' 6:58AM 6. Plan and execute a dinner party.	**12** ♃℞ ☽→♐ 8:46AM 7. Take a class in something new.	**13** ♃℞ ▲ 8. Praise the efforts of a co-worker.	**14** ♃℞ ▲ Valentine's Day ☽ V/C 7:14AM ☽→♑ 2:24PM 9. Celebrate the joy of loving.
15 ♃℞ 10. Update an old appliance.	**16** ♃℞ President's Day ☽ V/C 12:16PM ☽→♒ 4:13PM 2. Move forward with your decision.	**17** ♃℞ 3. Make it a fun day.	**18** ♃℞ Ash Wednesday ☽ V/C 3:47PM ☽→♓ 3:47PM ●29°♒59' 3:47PM ☉→♓ 3:51PM 4. Loyalty generates trust.	**19** ♃℞ Chinese New Year Enter the Sheep ☽ V/C 3:01PM ♂→♈ 4:12PM 5. Take a risk and be adventurous.	**20** ♃℞ ☽→♈ 3:12PM ♀→♈ 12:07PM 6. Just for fun; send someone a card.	**21** ♃℞ ☽ V/C 4:35PM 7. Combine wisdom with knowledge.
22 ♃℞ ☽→♉ 4:28PM 8. Being rich isn't just about money.	**23** ♃℞ ☽ V/C 6:57PM 9. Donate to a favorite charity.	**24** ♃℞ ☽→♊ 8:53PM 10. Plan a long awaited trip.	**25** ♃℞ 2. Look at both sides of an issue.	**26** ♃℞ ▼ ☽ V/C 12:43AM 3. Take pride in what you create.	**27** ♃℞ ▼ ☽→♋ 4:49AM 4. Show someone you are dependable.	**28** ♃℞ ☽ V/C 9:53AM 5. Change is good for the spirit.

February 3rd
3:08 PM

Full Moon in Leo

Degree Choice Points
14° Leo 47'

Motivation Solidarity

Resistance Disruption

Gift Experience with unfamiliar energy intelligence requires a translator.

Statement I Love
  Body Heart
  Mind Self-Confidence
  Spirit Generosity

Element
Fire – Passion, enthusiasm, being centered in personal identity, ability to direct will, arrogance, self-centered, all-consuming.

Second House Moon
9° Leo 13'

Second House Umbrella Theme
I Have/I Love – The way you make your money and the way you spend your money.

Motivation Intuitive Logic

Resistance Dark Night of the Soul

Gift Meet YOUR needs first, the rest will follow.

The Sun is Opposite the Moon

Full Moons are always in opposition to the Sun. This creates a feeling of tension between where you want to shine and how your feelings are flowing on a sensory level about the Sun's directive. The two forces seem like they are working against each other, yet they are on the same team displaying different techniques to obtain the same mission. The Leo/Aquarius polarity creates tension about the need to be adored and the need to be free.

Leo God

Apollo, the god of light, is gifted with extraordinary beauty and insight. Despite his magnificent beauty, he never experienced the true heart-connection in love. He took the name of the Sun god; however, he has never performed his duties as such. He is personified as the ideal male, standing for order and reason. The gateway of his temple is inscribed with a statement, "Know Thyself." He attracted many adoring people because of his beauty, yet they never entered the realm of his heart. During the Full Moon in Leo, we must set ourselves free from the facets of emptiness that come from the desire to be adored rather than to be loved and loving.

On Your Altar

Colors Royal purple, gold, orange

Numerology 7 – Open your mind to new ideas

Tarot Card Strength – Passion for all of life

Gemstones Amber, emerald, pyrite, citrine, yellow topaz

Plant remedy Sunflower – Standing tall in the center of life

Fragrance Jasmine – Remembering your Soul's original intention

Meditation

The freedom themes are provided by the zodiac sign and can be from this lifetime or other lifetimes. These meditations assist in dissolving blocks and opening pathways to new frontiers.

When the Moon is in Leo, we have the opportunity to see the records of our Soul's original intent. Close your eyes and take in a few deep breaths. Then, ask to make contact with an Angel of Records. Once that has been established, ask to be shown a time when you lost your original intent and replaced it with self-appointed authority. Honesty is the key to the Leo Moon. Ask for help to set yourself free from the self-appointed authority and accept the grace that reconnects you to your original intention. The Leo Full Moon connects solar power to your power, and the angel brings a refreshment of grace.

Leo Challenges and Victories

Say all of the statements in this section out loud. Then, underline the phrase that means the most to you. Use the phrase as your special affirmation for manifesting and co-creating throughout this phase of the moon.

I no longer feel the need to be in control and dominated by my mind telling me that it is appropriate to repress my feelings. I am going to claim my dominion today and feel the power of life running through me. I accept the privilege of being fully human and fully alive. I look to see where I lack courage to connect to what is natural for me. I see where I have been stubborn and turn to face my resistance. I become aware of when my higher self says "Go" and my lower self says "No." I am aware that my lower self (my body) is a creature of habit and will sabotage me with the idea that change takes too much energy. I take responsibility for the part of me that is a creature of habit and talk to my body about coming into alignment with my new intention to become fully passionate and fully alive. I remember today that in order to get the body to move forward with me, I need two-thirds of my cells to align with my request. First, I become aware of the part of myself that is trying to control all of my outcomes and keep me a slave to those outcomes, rather than trusting in the evolution of nature and the concept of Divine Order. I give up the fight today knowing that this struggle is dissipating all my energy and making me exhausted. In order for my body to respond, I need to awaken my cells through sound and touch. So, today I rub my body and speak out loud by sharing my request for connection, revitalization, rejuvenation, passion, and support. Today, I celebrate the idea that I can connect to my wholeness by activating my cells to support my commitment to my aliveness. I can now stand tall in the center of life and grow in self-confidence.

Leo Homework

Review your memorabilia and see what no longer matches your current love nature, your creative nature, and your loving self. Set your heart free while chanting, "Love is all you need." Become a part of the new consciousness on the Earth that brings a more abundant life when we expand the radius of our love. Live Love Every Day!

February 3rd
3:08 PM

Full Moon in Leo

Clearing the Slate for Freedom

Remember a time when you experienced the following trigger points. Write down what happened, forgive yourself, release it, and let it go to clear your slate for freedom.

Impatience

- Forgive
- Release
- Let Go

Feeling Superior

- Forgive
- Release
- Let Go

Controlling

- Forgive
- Release
- Let Go

"Off with Their Heads" Syndrome

- Forgive
- Release
- Let Go

Brat Attacks (Being Childish)

- Forgive
- Release
- Let Go

My Freedom List

Say this statement out loud three times before writing your freedom list!

I am a free spiritual being and it is my desire to be free to think and to express myself fully.

From this day forward I resolve to be true – first to myself and my highest self, and then to the highest self in me which is the Source of Love That I Am.

Leo Freedom List Ideas

Now is the time to set myself free from the need to be the center of attention, obstacles to generosity, false pride and false identity, blocks to confidence and creativity, excuses that keep me from quality time with my children, blocks to knowing that I am loved and lovable, and the idea that everyone needs to be devoted to me in all situations.

February 3rd
3:08 PM

Full Moon in Leo

How to Use the Moon Book With Your Chart

Fill in the blanks on the Cosmic Check-In page. Then look up the degree of the moon on the chart below. Take note of the "I" statement on the outside of the wheel where the moon is located. Now, locate the same degree on your own chart and make a note of the house and corresponding "I" statement. Go back to the Cosmic Check-In page and circle the two statements from the charts and read what you wrote. This will give you an idea about what to expect from this moon phase on a personal level.

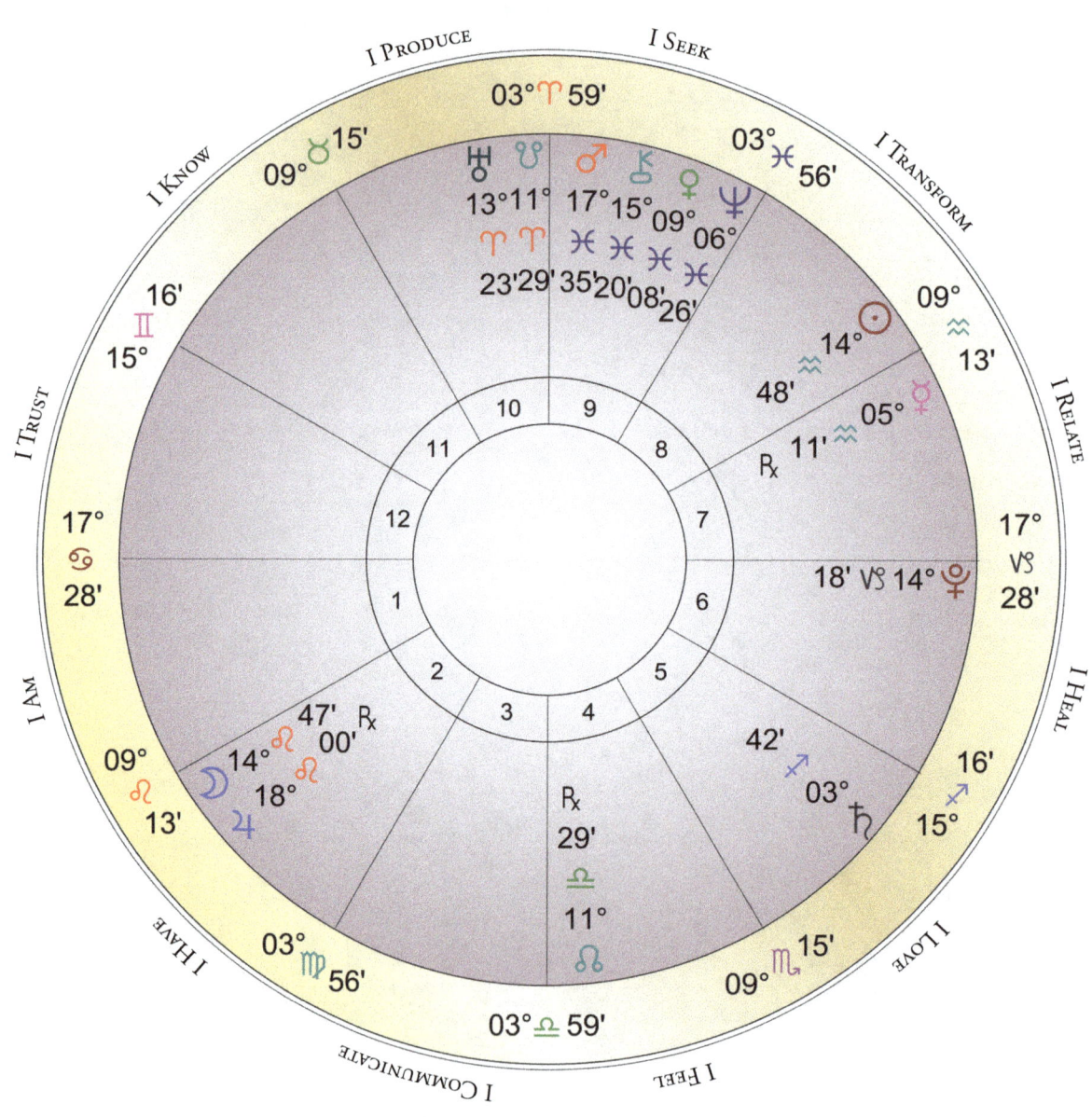

♈ Aries	♋ Cancer	♐ Sagittarius	☽ Moon	♄ Saturn	☊ North Node	V/C Void-of-Course
♉ Taurus	♌ Leo	♑ Capricorn	☿ Mercury	♅ Uranus	☋ South Node	▲ Super-Sensitivity
♊ Gemini	♍ Virgo	♒ Aquarius	♀ Venus	♆ Neptune	➡ Enters	▼ Low-Vitality
	♎ Libra	♓ Pisces	♂ Mars	♇ Pluto	℞ Retrograde	
	♏ Scorpio	☉ Sun	♃ Jupiter	⚷ Chiron	S/D Stationary Direct	

Cosmic Check-In

Take a moment to write a brief phrase for each "I" statement.
This activates all areas of your life for this creative cycle.

♌ I Love

♍ I Heal

♎ I Relate

♏ I Transform

♐ I Seek

♑ I Produce

♒ I Know

♓ I Trust

♈ I Am

♉ I Have

♊ I Communicate

♋ I Feel

February 18th
3:47 PM

New Moon in Aquarius

Dropping Moon
This happens when a new or full moon peaks at the same time as it goes void. During a "dropping moon" it becomes very important for you to write your co-creation list or your freedom list half an hour before the designated time.

Degree Choice Points
29° Aquarius 59'

Motivation	Ancient Wonders
Resistance	Scapegoating
Gift	Give form to the formless!
Statement	I Know
Body	Ankles
Mind	True Genius
Spirit	Vision

Element
Air – Inspiration, the breath of life, allows the mind to achieve new insights and fresh perspectives.

Seventh House Moon
8° Aquarius 2'

Seventh House Umbrella Theme
I Relate/I Know – It's all about your people attraction and how you work in relationship with the people you attract.

Motivation	Accomplishment
Resistance	Pretentious
Gift	Raise the bar for yourself and others.

Karmic Awakening: Aries/Libra
You may experience this karma if the need to initiate action comes up and you assert your own desire. Avoid the karma by sharing the need to maintain harmony with others. With Pisces on the cusp of Aries, it will become necessary to translate your idealism into action to avoid the karma. Virgo is on the cusp of Libra, demonstrating that analytical work must be put at the service of others to avoid the karma. Your lesson is to know that the results of your efforts must be shared.

When the Sun is in Aquarius
This is a time when the higher octave of the mind comes into play and one is given the power of vision. The Aquarian energies promote knowing by being a wellspring of knowledge. They expand the radius of contact by going beyond the known in areas of communication and cooperation. Now is the time to be initiated into greater awareness to serve the fields of human endeavors. Connect and combine magic with science and become a creative influence.

Aquarius Goddess
The Aquarian goddess, Star Woman, is also known as Hathor, the keeper of the light who gives birth to insight. All goddesses are born from the stars. Star Woman is in charge of directing the light bodies through the void of Creation to the point of insight, which occurs when the radiance is instilled in the memory of creation. She instills the light of the world into your own being so you can become in service to the souls who have lost their way.

On Your Altar
Colors Violet, neon, crystalline rainbow tints

Numerology 4 – Loyalty generates trust

Tarot Card The Star – Golden opportunities for the future

Gemstones Aquamarine, blue topaz, peacock pearls

Plant Remedy Queen of the Night Cactus – Ability to see light in the dark

Fragrance Myrrh – Healing the nervous system

February 19 – Chinese New Year – Enter the Sheep
The Year of the Sheep is all about Peace and Prosperity. It will be important to live in the moment and do what it takes to keep your mind from wandering.

My Co-Creation List

This or something better than this comes to me in an easy and pleasurable way, for the good of all concerned. Thank you, Universe!

Aquarius Co-Creation Ideas

Now is the time to focus on manifesting vision, invention, technology, freedom, friends, community, personal genius, higher awareness, teamwork, science, and magic.

February 18th
3:47 PM

New Moon in Aquarius

Aquarius Challenges and Victories

Say all of the statements in this section out loud. Then, underline the phrase that means the most to you. Use the phrase as your special affirmation for manifesting and co-creating throughout this phase of the moon.

Today, I chart my course for my new direction. My future is set on a new, fresh evolutionary course. I am guided by a higher source and trust in that guidance. I know my life has value and I am willing to contribute to the pool of consciousness by experiencing my life and living my life to the fullest view of possibility. Today, I know my possibilities are endless. My Spirit and my Soul are connected to Heaven and to Earth and this knowing brings me to the awareness that I can add to the higher qualities of life because I am connected to the whole. My being is far-reaching and immeasurable. I contribute to existence simply by knowing. All of the guideposts are connected for me today to see my way to a profound new future. My vision is clear and I can clearly set my sights on this new course. Golden opportunities come with this new vision and I trust in my guidance to bring me to this new level of manifesting power. I check in with my inner lights, each day, by meditating and asking for all seven of the energy centers in my body to come into alignment with the outer symbols of guidance. I do this by becoming still and breathing until I feel the stillness. Then, I place my hand on each center in my body, one center at a time, to be activated by light. Next, I ask out loud for each center in my body to let me know what its energetic contribution to the new direction is and how best to use the energy to move forward on my new course of action. I write down each statement and connect each statement to the guiding star in the sky. I am now linked up physically and spiritually and ready to navigate my total self towards my new evolutionary direction.

Aquarius Homework

Aquarians co-create a storehouse of information through innovative telecommunications, technology, social networking and media, and global communication. They are typically found in the fields of psychology, science fiction authoring or film-making, speech writing, and aerospace engineering.

Consider these three Aquarian gifts:

- Opportunity – Become a creative influence
- Enlightenment – When you become aware that you are light
- Brotherhood – Separation doesn't exist anymore

Where do you see these occurring in your life?

Without Acknowledgment Progress Cannot Occur

Acknowledgement creates space for victory and gratitude, which automatically brings you to a level of completion so a new cycle of opportunity can occur in your life. When you celebrate your wins and acknowledge your victories with gratitude, you update your cells so that your ability to move forward is not hindered by a cellular holographic pattern that is stuck in the past. Cellular lag creates resistance and makes moving forward most difficult. The key is to stay continuously updated by acknowledging yourself for what you did do at the end of each day, rather than heading off to sleep thinning about what you did not do. By acknowledging what you did not do, you play into your karmic storage bank and keep your progress at bay. When you acknowledge yourself and your manifestations you are complete, and more cycles of opportunity become available to you in each new day. Be prepared for miracles!

Victory List

When a creation result is acknowledged it seals the deal. This makes room for more magnificence to expand into your life and increases your abundance factor adding to your ability to receive. As each aspect of your co-creation list arrives in your life, spend time allowing, acknowledging, and accepting it with the true gusto of gratitude! Keep your victory list active here.

Gratitude List

This fulfills the relationship between the giver and the receiver, which completes the cycle with the Universe so that a new beginning can be established.

February 18th
3:47 PM

New Moon in Aquarius

How to Use the Moon Book With Your Chart

Fill in the blanks on the Cosmic Check-In page. Then look up the degree of the moon on the chart below. Take note of the "I" statement on the outside of the wheel where the moon is located. Now, locate the same degree on your own chart and make a note of the house and corresponding "I" statement. Go back to the Cosmic Check-In page and circle the two statements from the charts and read what you wrote. This will give you an idea about what to expect from this moon phase on a personal level.

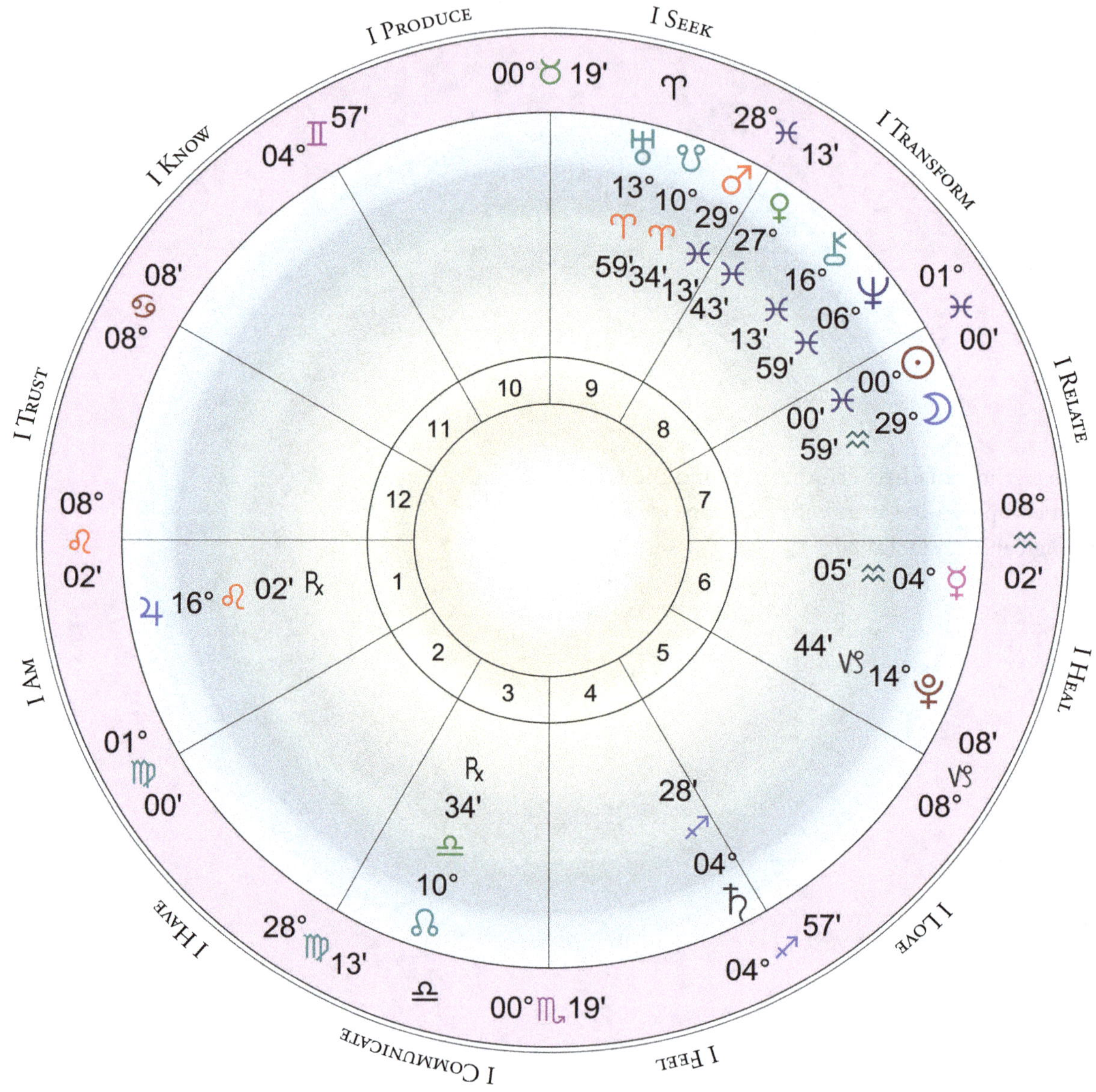

♈ Aries	♋ Cancer	♐ Sagittarius	☽ Moon	♄ Saturn	☊ North Node	V/C Void-of-Course
♉ Taurus	♌ Leo	♑ Capricorn	☿ Mercury	♅ Uranus	☋ South Node	▲ Super-Sensitivity
♊ Gemini	♍ Virgo	♒ Aquarius	♀ Venus	♆ Neptune	➡ Enters	▼ Low-Vitality
	♎ Libra	♓ Pisces	♂ Mars	♇ Pluto	℞ Retrograde	
	♏ Scorpio	☉ Sun	♃ Jupiter	⚷ Chiron	S/D Stationary Direct	

Cosmic Check-In

Take a moment to write a brief phrase for each "I" statement.
This activates all areas of your life for this creative cycle.

♒ I Know

♓ I Trust

♈ I Am

♉ I Have

♊ I Communicate

♋ I Feel

♌ I Love

♍ I Heal

♎ I Relate

♏ I Transform

♐ I Seek

♑ I Produce

Planetary Highlights

Jupiter is Retrograde in Leo Until April 8

It is time to look at the issue of adoration. Look within to see how much adoration you really want in your life and how much resentment you have about the fact that it isn't happening. Ask yourself, "How can I manifest attention in a positive way, rather than creating brat attacks to get attention?" Learn that attention comes when you ask for it in an appetizing way, and that you accept it with grace when it arrives.

March 14 – Saturn goes Retrograde in Sagittarius Until August 1

Saturn is our teacher asking for discipline and practicality. Sagittarius rules our spiritual focus and the expansion of our quest for knowledge. With Saturn's influence here, we will need to accept the idea that our spirituality will be put to the test.

March 5 – Full Moon in Virgo

Make a breakthrough here to relieve yourself from habits, related to your body, that keep you from being at the top of your game. Watch out for destructive thinking patterns. Get a good plan of action to move yourself to a new standard of excellence.

March 5 – Venus, Uranus, South Node, Chiron, and the Sun are all Clustered in Aries and Pisces – Opposite the Virgo Moon

Hold on to your hats … this a recipe for integrating several aspects of the known you and the unknown you all at the same time. Do your best not to freeze-frame yourself on any aspect too soon. Simply let it all happen and you will have all the tools you need for your personal evolution to actualize.

March 5 – Jupiter in Leo and Mercury in Aquarius are Opposite Each Other

This is a major expanded thought pattern; *The Great Gatsby* of the mind. Pay attention and see how the genius of the Aquarian mind can capture the grandeur of this thought and put it into action for innovation.

March 12 – Mercury Enters Pisces

Prepare for your thinking pattern to get cloudy and even murky. This is a time to express your Divinity, not your mind. Meditate, create, and listen to the voice within.

March 17 – Venus Enters Taurus

Celebration is in the atmosphere. Go dancing, have a party, surround yourself with beauty, get juicy, and don't forget to go shopping! Live love, share love, and receive love!

March 20 – Spring Equinox – The Sun Enters Aries

This is the Astrological New Year. The spark of Spring is awakening us from our Winter sleep. Dreamtime is over; come alive and discover your new 2015 identity.

March 20 – Solar Eclipse – New Moon in Pisces

If you let yourself become aware of where you were in 1996, the theme for this moon will unfold in a very positive way. Ask yourself, "Where was I living? Who were the important people in my life at that time? What were the spiritual principals that I was following?" Expect a revelation to happen and know that this backdrop will be cleared.

March 20 – Neptune and Mercury Conjunct in Pisces

"Smoke and Mirrors" could cloud your thinking right now. Do not make any decisions or go forward with any plans for the next few days. Wait for the smoke to clear. Reality checks will be important!

March 30 – Mercury Enters Aries

Everything will move at the speed of lightning. The green light is on. Go! Go! Go! Now is your time to make it all happen.

March 31 – Mars Enters Taurus

Open yourself to a slower pace right now. Pushing could bring on an accident or two. Take time out to see the whole picture and delight in the beauty that surrounds you.

Super-Sensitivity – March 12-13

The center of the Universe is pouring down debris, adding chaos to the atmosphere. Just remember, it doesn't belong to you.

Low-Vitality – March 25-26

The Earth is depleted right now. Take extra care of yourself and get rest. Pushing leads to exhaustion.

Aries	Cancer	Sagittarius	Moon	Saturn	North Node	V/C Void-of-Course
Taurus	Leo	Capricorn	Mercury	Uranus	South Node	Super-Sensitivity
Gemini	Virgo	Aquarius	Venus	Neptune	Enters	Low-Vitality
	Libra	Pisces	Mars	Pluto	Retrograde	
	Scorpio	Sun	Jupiter	Chiron	Stationary Direct	

March

Sunday	Monday	Tuesday	Wednesday	Thursday	Friday	Saturday
1 ♃℞ ☽→♌ 3:34PM 6. Understanding is the key to love.	**2** ♃℞ 7. Learn something more in-depth.	**3** ♃℞ ☽ V/C 12:47AM 8. Acknowledge your abundance.	**4** ♃℞ ☽→♍ 3:57AM 9. Use your intuitive awareness.	**5** ♃℞ ☽ V/C 10:36AM ○14°♍50' 10:05AM 10. Make room for new in your life.	**6** ♃℞ ☽→♎ 4:52PM 2. A sense of wellbeing brings balance.	**7** ♃℞ 3. Create with your heart's desire.
8 ♃℞ Pacific Day Light Time Begins ☽ V/C 6:23PM 4. An organized approach is best.	**9** ♃℞ ☽→♏ 6:09AM 5. See all the ways to do the same thing.	**10** ♃℞ 6. Love the new people around you.	**11** ♃℞ ☽ V/C 12:46PM ☽→♐ 4:30PM 7. If you think it, you can do it.	**12** ♃℞ ▲ ♀→♓ 8:53PM 8. Follow the urge to manifest.	**13** ♃℞ ▲ ☽ V/C 4:11PM ☽→♑ 11:39PM 9. Ask your spiritual teachers.	**14** ♃♄℞ ♄℞ 4°♐55' 8:03PM 10. Choose to move beyond limits.
15 ♃♄℞ 3. You are creative and abundant.	**16** ♃♄℞ ☽ V/C 1:01AM ☽→♒ 3:13AM 4. Revise a plan for a new foundation.	**17** ♃♄℞ St. Patrick's Day ☽ V/C 11:18AM ♀→♉ 3:16AM 5. Everything you do affects the world.	**18** ♃♄℞ ☽→♓ 3:57AM 6. There is unity in community.	**19** ♃♄℞ 7. Use research to move you forward.	**20** ♃♄℞ Spring Equinox ☉→♈ 3:46PM ☽ V/C 2:36AM ☽→♈ 3:27AM ●29°♓27' 2:36AM Solar Eclipse 2:46AM 8. Accept leadership.	**21** ♃♄℞ ☽ V/C 3:50PM 9. Be willing to express emotions.
22 ♃♄℞ ☽→♉ 3:40AM 10. When it's over, let it be.	**23** ♃♄℞ ☽ V/C 7:24AM 2. Back your decisions with action.	**24** ♃♄℞ ☽→♊ 6:22AM 3. Let your imagination soar.	**25** ♃♄℞ ▼ 4. Tolerate the opinions of others.	**26** ♃♄℞ ▼ ☽ V/C 5:34AM ☽→♋ 12:45PM 5. Truth is constantly changing.	**27** ♃♄℞ 6. Expect a heartfelt experience.	**28** ♃♄℞ ☽ V/C 6:58PM ☽→♌ 10:47PM 7. Truth comes from knowing.
29 ♃♄℞ 8. Know you are a manifestor.	**30** ♃♄℞ ☽ V/C 6:56AM ☿→♈ 6:45PM 9. Choose happiness; it is a choice.	**31** ♃♄℞ ☽→♍ 11:12AM ♂→♉ 9:28AM 10. Live fully in the now.				

March 5th
10:05 AM

Full Moon in Virgo

Karmic Awakening: Scorpio/Taurus

Karma will raise its head when you feel the need to get tangible results that produce something of value rather than combining resources and having a transformational experience. In simpler terms, the karmic challenge will go head-to-head when the need to accumulate has trouble letting go of outcomes. Aries is on the cusp of Taurus, so you may be seen as a leader, but the Taurus side asks you to create something long-lasting. Libra on the cusp of Scorpio requires diplomacy and may overshadow your inner power and intensify karma that could rob you of the chance to create change.

The Sun is Opposite the Moon

Full Moons are always in opposition to the Sun. This creates a feeling of tension between where you want to shine and how your feelings are flowing on a sensory level about the Sun's directive. The two forces seem like they are working against each other, yet they are on the same team displaying different techniques to obtain the same mission. The Virgo/Pisces polarity creates tension between doing your work and finding your path.

Virgo Goddess

Gaia gave birth to herself out of Chaos. After her own birth, she immediately gave birth to Uranus, the King of the Universe. Gaia is the creator of Heaven and Earth. She is the symbol for all that is natural. Unlike her counterpart Uranus, who rules the sky, she rules the womb and enclosed spaces. Gaia is the Earth, giving birth to all of life and all organisms that shape the Earth's biosphere. When the Moon is full in Virgo, we are given the opportunity to look at what we have birthed within ourselves and set ourselves free from what is no longer giving us energy. Virgo sees Divinity in the details, so take a close look at what needs to be released to restore your physical energy.

On Your Altar

Colors Green, blue, earth tones

Numerology 10 – Make room for new in your life

Tarot Card The Hermit – Knowing your purpose and sharing it with the world

Gemstones Emerald, sapphire

Plant remedy Sage – The ability to hold and store light

Fragrance Lavender – Management and storage of energy

Degree Choice Points
14° Virgo 50'

Motivation Gracefulness

Resistance Trivial Pursuits

Gift Look for similarities rather than differences.

Statement I Heal
  Body Intestines
  Mind Critical
  Spirit Divinity in the Details

Element
Earth – Devic communication, green thumb, DNA healing, security, practical.

Fifth House Moon
14° Virgo 46'

Fifth House Umbrella Theme
I Love/I Heal – The way you love and how you want to be loved.

Motivation Gracefulness

Resistance Trivial Pursuits

Gift Look for similarities rather than differences.

Meditation

The freedom themes are provided by the zodiac sign and can be from this lifetime or other lifetimes. These meditations assist in dissolving blocks and opening pathways to new frontiers.

When the Moon is in Virgo, the nighttime is sleepless and restless due to mental anxiety coming face-to-face with the thought world. Sit quietly and close your eyes. Breathe in and breathe out. It is a time to discover truth through action, and to detach from pain-producing thinking patterns which lead us to addiction. Ask for an Angel of Records to take you to a moment in time when you chose self-destructive behavior to mask anxiety. Release the addictive thinking patterns that control you. Ask for help from the Angel to see a way to accept the depth of your feelings.

Virgo Challenges and Victories

Say all of the statements in this section out loud. Then, underline the phrase that means the most to you. Use the phrase as your special affirmation for manifesting and co-creating throughout this phase of the moon.

Today I take time to go within to be silent. I imagine myself on a country road moving towards a beautiful mountain. I bask in the glory of the power of the mountain and know that it is calling me to the top. I find a pathway to the top and begin to climb. As I climb I become aware of a presence guiding me and empowering me to keep going, creating a sense of peacefulness within me.

I become aware of my own power in this silent journey to the top and revel in the serenity that nature and silence bring me. At last I am about to reach the summit and, just before I do, I feel the power drawing me to go within on a deeper level. I stop for a moment and look back at the path I have just climbed and know that my life's path is a remarkable gift. I connect to the center of the Earth and feel an inner glow.

The top of the mountain calls to me and, as I reach the top, a voice says to me, "Take in the view and look in all directions." As I turn 360-degrees, I sense a light igniting me in every direction. Then the voice says, "Look up!" Now, my awareness shifts and I see that I have become an illuminating light glowing in all six directions. Next I hear, "Sit in your silence and take in the vastness of who you are. Who you are is immeasurable." I sit, feeling the glow of light within me, and become aware of a greater plan for my life. I allow myself to receive this plan. I accept this assignment and slowly walk down the mountain, knowing that I can be a shining light for myself and others. I know I must take my light out to the world and share what I know to be my truth. Today, I become a messenger for the light.

Virgo Homework

Become integrated so that the light of your personality becomes soul-infused. When you are soul-infused and are in service to your higher self, you radiate love and light through the power of the inner self through all activities, thoughts, and emotions and become more magnificent. Learn the art of detachment and let your soul take control.

March 5th
10:05 AM

Full Moon in Virgo

Clearing the Slate for Freedom

Remember a time when you experienced the following trigger points. Write down what happened, forgive yourself, release it, and let it go to clear your slate for freedom.

Judgment

- Forgive
- Release
- Let Go

Habitual Actions

- Forgive
- Release
- Let Go

Avoiding the Big Picture by being Obsessed with Details

- Forgive
- Release
- Let Go

Being Stubborn

- Forgive
- Release
- Let Go

Letting "Being Perfect" Stop Your Action

- Forgive
- Release
- Let Go

My Freedom List

Say this statement out loud three times before writing your freedom list!

I am a free spiritual being and it is my desire to be free to think and to express myself fully.

I hereby fully and completely free my mind from all adhesions to outdated philosophies, habits, relationships, groups of people, man-made laws, moral codes, all rules, set ideas and set ways of thinking, traditions, organizations, duty-motivated activities, guilt, judgment, and being misunderstood!

Virgo Freedom List Ideas

Now is the time to set myself free from finding fault with myself, my addiction to perfection, my addiction to detail, over-indulging in image management, pain-producing thinking patterns, judgment of others, resistance to being healthy, and destructive behaviors.

March 5th
10:05 AM

Full Moon in Virgo

How to Use the Moon Book With Your Chart

Fill in the blanks on the Cosmic Check-In page. Then look up the degree of the moon on the chart below. Take note of the "I" statement on the outside of the wheel where the moon is located. Now, locate the same degree on your own chart and make a note of the house and corresponding "I" statement. Go back to the Cosmic Check-In page and circle the two statements from the charts and read what you wrote. This will give you an idea about what to expect from this moon phase on a personal level.

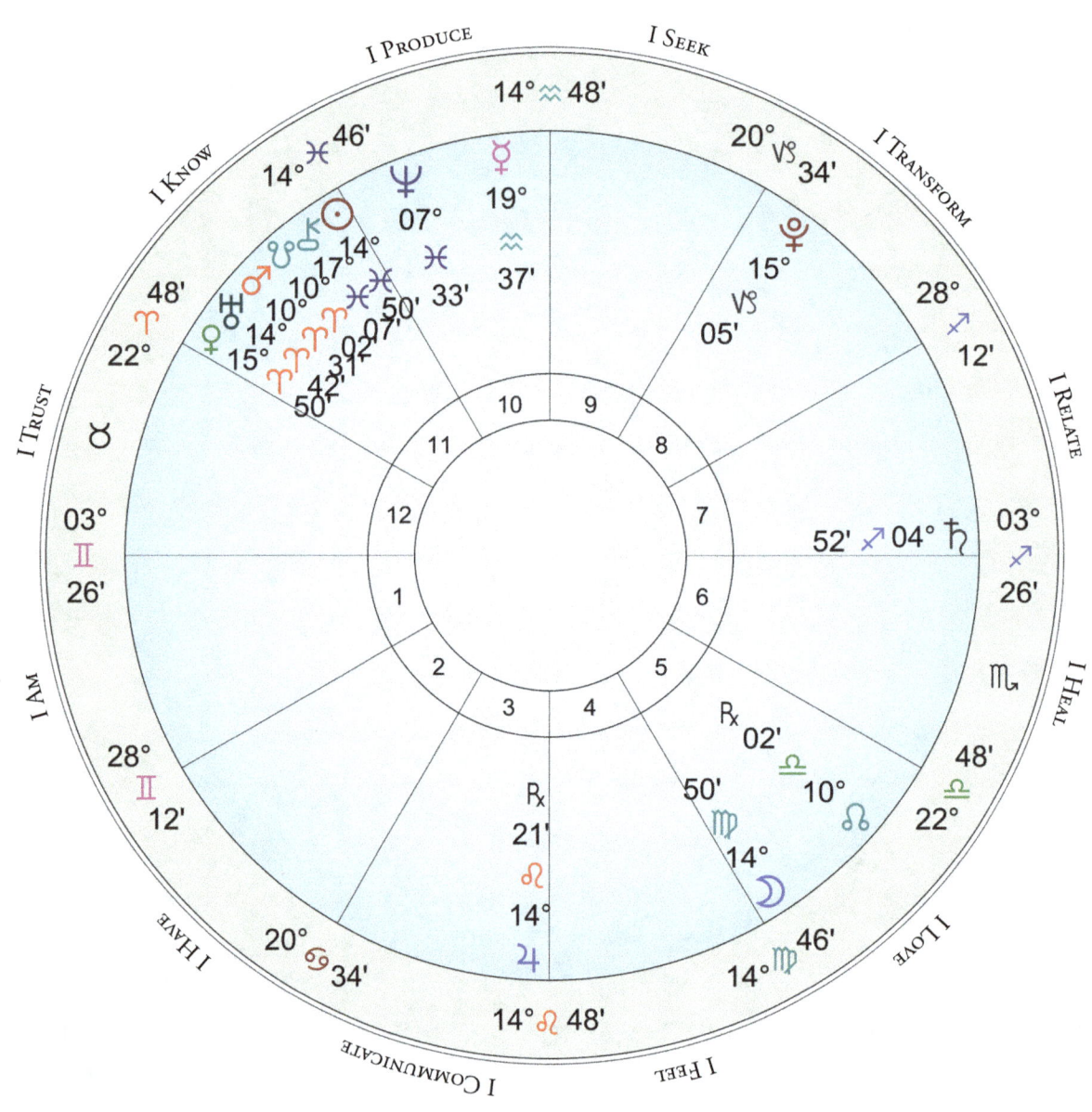

♈ Aries	♋ Cancer	♐ Sagittarius	☽ Moon	♄ Saturn	☊ North Node	V/C Void-of-Course
♉ Taurus	♌ Leo	♑ Capricorn	☿ Mercury	♅ Uranus	☋ South Node	▲ Super-Sensitivity
♊ Gemini	♍ Virgo	♒ Aquarius	♀ Venus	♆ Neptune	➡ Enters	▼ Low-Vitality
	♎ Libra	♓ Pisces	♂ Mars	♇ Pluto	℞ Retrograde	
	♏ Scorpio	☉ Sun	♃ Jupiter	⚷ Chiron	S/D Stationary Direct	

Cosmic Check-In

Take a moment to write a brief phrase for each "I" statement.
This activates all areas of your life for this creative cycle.

♍ I Heal

♎ I Relate

♏ I Transform

♐ I Seek

♑ I Produce

♒ I Know

♓ I Trust

♈ I Am

♉ I Have

♊ I Communicate

♋ I Feel

♌ I Love

Solar Eclipse
March 20th
2:36 AM

New Moon in Pisces

Dropping Moon
This happens when a new or full moon peaks at the same time as it goes void. During a "dropping moon" it becomes very important for you to write your co-creation list or your freedom list half an hour before the designated time.

Degree Choice Points
29° Pisces 27'

Motivation   Culmination of Efforts

Resistance   Inarticulate

Gift   Focus positive energies in your own yard – beautify your environment.

Statement   I Trust
Body   Feet
Mind   Super-sensitive
Spirit   Mystical

Element
Water – Grace, rhythm, cycles of awareness, Divine Feminine

Third House Moon
23° Pisces 20'

Third House Umbrella Theme
I Communicate/I Trust – How you get the word out and the message behind the words.

Motivation   Cultivation

Resistance   Pollution

Gift   Completing a blueprint requirement.

When the Sun is in Pisces

This is a time when you come in contact with your most Divine essence. It is a time to meditate and connect to your higher purpose. Let your intuition guide you to a program of service. Let your Soul take control and connect to a space beyond your ego. In order to do this, you must become free of your habits, hang ups, and fantasies. Compassion frees you from the slavery of self-interest and the lure of your personality's blind urges, emotional traps, and mental crystallizations. When the Soul takes control, you unite your personality with Divine essence and radiate the light needed to find your true pathway.

Pisces Goddess

Pisces goddess, Kuan Yin, is the embodiment of all that is compassionate. She guides us to the abyss, a place known as emptiness. This place is called the Great Unknown, where the ego drops and there is only the truth of one's nature. Kuan Yin protects us and holds us when we let go, surrender, and evolve. She is the goddess of emptiness. She helps to constantly empty the self from the limitations of the ego—fear, doubt, guilt, shame, and denial. In exchange, we gain beauty, light, and service. She is often pictured riding on the head of a dragon. It is the breath of the dragon that pierces the veil of illusion.

On Your Altar

Colors   Turquoise, blue, green, aqua

Numerology   8 – Accept leadership

Tarot Card   The Moon – The inner journey, reflection, illumination

Gemstones   Amethyst, opal, jade, turquoise

Plant Remedy   Passion flower – The ability to live in the here and now

Fragrance   Lotus – Connecting to the Divine without arrogance

My Co-Creation List

This or something better than this comes to me in an easy and pleasurable way, for the good of all concerned. Thank you, Universe!

Pisces Co-Creation Ideas

Now is the time to focus on manifesting connection with the Divine, creativity, healing powers, psychic abilities, sensitivity, compassion, and service.

Solar Eclipse
March 20th
2:36 AM

New Moon in Pisces

Pisces Challenges and Victories

Say all of the statements in this section out loud. Then, underline the phrase that means the most to you. Use the phrase as your special affirmation for manifesting and co-creating throughout this phase of the moon.

I see my path clearly now. I know I must walk by myself on this journey into the deepest part of my Soul. It is time to clear the way and look beneath the surface to discover the parts of myself that I have placed in the unconscious world to be worked on at a later date. That later date is now. I am aware that the postponement of my inner reality can no longer be delayed.

Evolution is pulling me and it has become greater than my distractions, my fear, my denial, and my refusal to face what I have hidden from myself and others. I am aware of outside influences that pull me away from facing my inner realms. I know, without a doubt, that I am only as sick as the secrets I keep from myself and others. I see clearly how these distractions, illusions, and secrets need to be recognized so I can find the separated parts of myself that have been left in the dark, obscured from the light. I know that it is time to bring myself into wholeness and bring my shadow side to the light of my awareness.

I begin by closing my eyes and experiencing darkness. I imagine walking on a lonely road, in the dark, by myself. I pay particular attention to the sensations in my body and allow for the body to guide me to the places of dullness, numbness, fear, and anxiety. I simply allow for the intelligence of the body to coordinate the feeling with an image, person, or an event. I stay still and know, from the depth of my being, that recognition is all that is required of me right now. When recognition occurs, the light of awareness is ignited and the conscious world will take care of the rest. I know that the road to enlightenment requires me to first take the road into the dark side of my Soul.

Pisces Homework

Pisces co-creates by using her psychic powers for counseling, therapy, hypnosis, the ministry, and creating spiritual schools or healing centers. She is also successful in visionary arts, acting, music, medical and pharmaceutical fields, and oceanography.

Take time to go within to discover where new pathways are open for advancement. Blessings pour forth to those who move toward these pathways in the spirit of service. Be open to these pathways and consider the ones that benefit our planet with new ideas, creative expression, and expanded views that lead people to higher levels of service.

Without Acknowledgment Progress Cannot Occur

Acknowledgement creates space for victory and gratitude, which automatically brings you to a level of completion so a new cycle of opportunity can occur in your life. When you celebrate your wins and acknowledge your victories with gratitude, you update your cells so that your ability to move forward is not hindered by a cellular holographic pattern that is stuck in the past. Cellular lag creates resistance and makes moving forward most difficult. The key is to stay continuously updated by acknowledging yourself for what you did do at the end of each day, rather than heading off to sleep thinning about what you did not do. By acknowledging what you did not do, you play into your karmic storage bank and keep your progress at bay. When you acknowledge yourself and your manifestations you are complete, and more cycles of opportunity become available to you in each new day. Be prepared for miracles!

Victory List

When a creation result is acknowledged it seals the deal. This makes room for more magnificence to expand into your life and increases your abundance factor adding to your ability to receive. As each aspect of your co-creation list arrives in your life, spend time allowing, acknowledging, and accepting it with the true gusto of gratitude! Keep your victory list active here.

Gratitude List

This fulfills the relationship between the giver and the receiver, which completes the cycle with the Universe so that a new beginning can be established.

Solar Eclipse
March 20th
2:36 AM

New Moon in Pisces

How to Use the Moon Book With Your Chart

Fill in the blanks on the Cosmic Check-In page. Then look up the degree of the moon on the chart below. Take note of the "I" statement on the outside of the wheel where the moon is located. Now, locate the same degree on your own chart and make a note of the house and corresponding "I" statement. Go back to the Cosmic Check-In page and circle the two statements from the charts and read what you wrote. This will give you an idea about what to expect from this moon phase on a personal level.

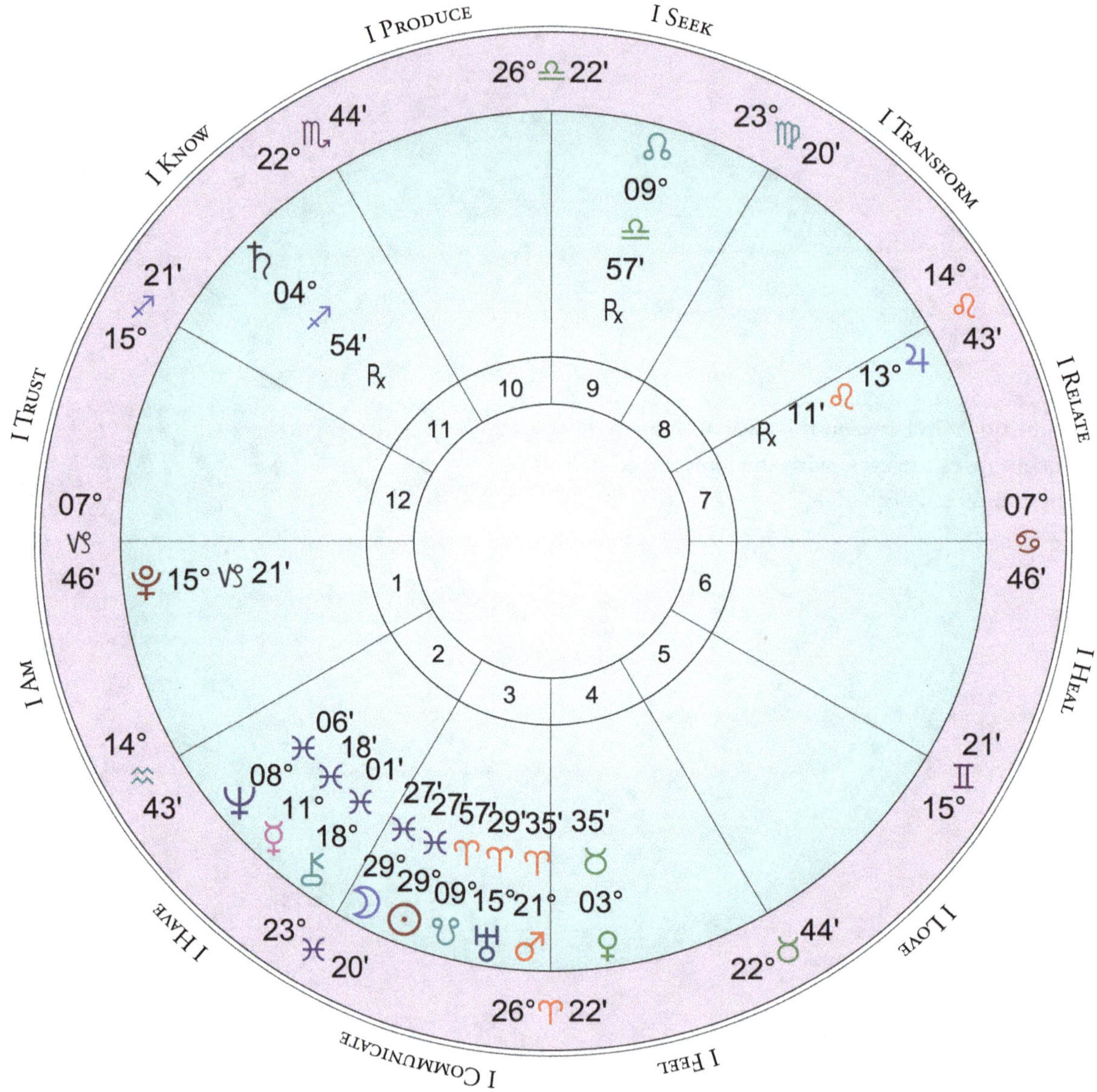

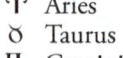

♈ Aries	♋ Cancer	♐ Sagittarius	☽ Moon	♄ Saturn	☊ North Node	V/C Void-of-Course
♉ Taurus	♌ Leo	♑ Capricorn	☿ Mercury	♅ Uranus	☋ South Node	▲ Super-Sensitivity
♊ Gemini	♍ Virgo	♒ Aquarius	♀ Venus	♆ Neptune	➡ Enters	▼ Low-Vitality
	♎ Libra	♓ Pisces	♂ Mars	♇ Pluto	℞ Retrograde	
	♏ Scorpio	☉ Sun	♃ Jupiter	⚷ Chiron	S/D Stationary Direct	

Cosmic Check-In

Take a moment to write a brief phrase for each "I" statement.
This activates all areas of your life for this creative cycle.

♓ I Trust

♈ I Am

♉ I Have

♊ I Communicate

♋ I Feel

♌ I Love

♍ I Heal

♎ I Relate

♏ I Transform

♐ I Seek

♑ I Produce

♒ I Know

Planetary Highlights

Jupiter is Retrograde in Leo Until April 8

Expect a blast of good fortune to come your way. Be aware that this transit brings joy and prosperity to those who have the courage to accept what is ahead. Celebrate the quality of your life expanding in ways that you never imagined. Optimism is the key to making this happen. Be willing!

Saturn is Retrograde in Sagittarius Until August 1

This could activate many people preaching what they know. If you don't let yourself be reality-based in your belief systems, snake oil could bite you. Make it known to your higher power that you will follow your heart and not get caught up in what looks good.

April 16 – Pluto goes Retrograde in Capricorn Until September 24

Just when things get going strong and quantum leaps are happening, Pluto comes in and gets your fear going by taking something away. Remember, Pluto is here to transmute everything that doesn't work in the new world. If you accept the unknown world and accept what is being placed in the past for your highest and best good, fear won't happen. Be willing to go beyond fear and know that your survival depends on accepting what is new right now.

April 4 – Lunar Eclipse – Full Moon in Libra

This moon is about releasing love patterns, from 1996, that didn't work. Pay attention to what didn't work and let it go.

April 14 – Mercury Enters Taurus

Slow down and smell the roses. The energy here is sluggish; accept this and something wonderful might manifest right into your lap. If you try to push or rush, a missed opportunity could occur.

April 18 – New Moon in Aries

Manifesting your new identity is happening now. Use this moment in time to get a fix on your new identity and celebrate this reflection into actualization.

April 18 – The Planetary Cluster Continues in Aries

This cluster is proving itself to be committed to your future. It's a time of self-growth and integration without questioning or resisting. Mars (action), Mercury (communication), the Sun (potential), Moon (reflection), and Uranus (the future) are connecting to you all at once. Accept this infusion to determine the new you.

April 18 – Venus in Gemini and Saturn in Sagittarius Oppose Each Other for a Few Days

Venus does her best flirting when in Gemini. However, with Saturn breathing down her neck and watching her every move, she might have to behave for a few days. Expect a brat attack or two.

April 20 – The Sun Moves into Taurus

It's time to manifest! Look around your physical arena and honor the beauty. If the energy is not reading beauty, do what it takes to make it so. All of the flowers are blooming right now inspiring you to bloom and grow!

April 30 – Mercury Moves into Gemini

Expect mental alignment to come into action. Conversations will be at the peak of any moment. Enjoy the exchange of ideas. Make that sales pitch you have been waiting to make. Now is the time to write the marketing letter and get your project out there.

Super-Sensitivity – April 9-10

Do what you can to realize there is chaos in the air and don't make it personal. Slow down and avoid travel if possible!

Low-Vitality – April 21-22

The Earth is at a low right now. Earth changes are possible. Gather together and honor the Earth by drumming. Avoid rushing or pushing the envelope ... simply be still.

♈ Aries	♋ Cancer	♐ Sagittarius	☽ Moon	♄ Saturn	☊ North Node	V/C Void-of-Course
♉ Taurus	♌ Leo	♑ Capricorn	☿ Mercury	♅ Uranus	☋ South Node	▲ Super-Sensitivity
♊ Gemini	♍ Virgo	♒ Aquarius	♀ Venus	♆ Neptune	➡ Enters	▼ Low-Vitality
	♎ Libra	♓ Pisces	♂ Mars	♇ Pluto	℞ Retrograde	
	♏ Scorpio	☉ Sun	♃ Jupiter	⚷ Chiron	S/D Stationary Direct	

April

Sunday	Monday	Tuesday	Wednesday	Thursday	Friday	Saturday
			1 ♃♄℞ April Fool's Day 2. Make a clear decision.	2 ♃♄℞ ☽ V/C 2:00AM 3. Find joy in your experience.	3 ♃♄℞ Passover ☽→♎ 12:07AM 4. Don't get boxed in.	4 ♃♄℞ ☽ V/C 8:58 AM ○ 14°♎24' 5:05AM Lunar Eclipse 5:01AM 5. Exercise in a happy way.
5 ♃♄℞ Easter ☽→♏ 12:04PM 6. Invite someone to dinner.	6 ♃♄℞ 7. Do your research carefully.	7 ♃♄℞ ☽ V/C 1:41PM ☽→♐ 10:08PM 8. Willingness helps you manifest.	8 ♄℞ ♃D -12°♌35' 9:58AM 9. The Divine force supports you.	9 ♄℞ ▲ ☽ V/C 10:41AM 10. Make room for something new.	10 ♄℞ ▲ ☽→♑ 5:46AM 2. Let your choices bring balance.	11 ♄℞ ♀→♊ 8:30AM 3. Bring a playful energy into the day.
12 ♄℞ ☽ V/C 1:14AM ☽→♒ 10:43AM 4. Follow the blue-print you created.	13 ♄℞ 5. Physical move-ment is key.	14 ♄℞ ☽ V/C 12:44PM ☽→♓ 1:11PM ☿→♉ 3:53PM 6. Embrace what makes you feel good.	15 ♄℞ ☽ V/C 2:36PM 7. Dispense your knowledge.	16 ♄♇℞ ☽→♈ 1:59PM ♇℞→ 15°♑32' 8:52PM 8. Abundance has no limits.	17 ♄♇℞ 9. Know you are on a spiritual journey.	18 ♄♇℞ ● 28°♈25' 11:56AM ☽ V/C 11:56AM ☽→♉ 2:31PM 10. Be clear with your intentions.
19 ♄♇℞ ☽ V/C 4:06PM 2. Once you know, then decide.	20 ♄♇℞ ☽→♊ 4:27PM ☉→♉ 2:43AM 3. Life is easy if you let it be.	21 ♄♇℞ ▼ ☽ V/C 10:37PM 4. Learn how a spe-cific system works.	22 ♄♇℞ ▼ Earth Day ☽→♋ 9:25PM 5. Change it up today.	23 ♄♇℞ 6. Give with an unbiased heart.	24 ♄♇℞ ☽ V/C 10:03AM 7. Share freely what you know.	25 ♄♇℞ ☽→♌ 6:12AM 8. Our cells manifest what is right for us.
26 ♄♇℞ 9. Ask Spirit for what you desire.	27 ♄♇℞ ☽ V/C 7:12AM ☽→♍ 6:07PM 10. Leave the past in the past.	28 ♄♇℞ 2. Make a decision, then act.	29 ♄♇℞ 3. Bring some fun into your life.	30 ♄♇℞ ☽ V/C 5:23AM ☽→♎ 7:02AM ☿→♊ 7:01PM 4. Move beyond your boundaries.		

Lunar Eclipse
April 4th
5:05 AM

Full Moon in Libra

Degree Choice Points
14° Libra 23'

Motivation
Cyclical Opportunities

Resistance Mental Looping

Gift Be a harmonizer, offer a light-hearted or profound truth.

Statement I Relate
Body Kidneys
Mind Social
Spirit Peace

Element
Air – Need for new insights, active dreaming, freedom from attachments, forgiveness.

Seventh House Moon
9° Virgo 59'

Seventh House Umbrella Theme
I Relate/I Heal – It's all about your people attraction and how you work in relationship with the people you attract.

Motivation Intelligence

Resistance Fragmentation

Gift Obscurity maintains the integrity of your commitment.

The Sun is Opposite the Moon

Full Moons are always in opposition to the Sun. This creates a feeling of tension between where you want to shine and how your feelings are flowing on a sensory level about the Sun's directive. The two forces seem like they are working against each other, yet they are on the same team displaying different techniques to obtain the same mission. The Libra/Aries polarity creates tension between the idea of "We" versus "Me."

Libra Goddess

Athena was born out of her father's head. She was the first woman who incorporated logic into her consciousness. Her keen ability to combine logic and intuition gave birth to strategy. Because of her strategic concepts, she became a consort to all of the great warriors. Unlike Aries, who is the Warrior, Libra is the General. When the Moon is full in Libra, you must look at how strategy is working in your life. Has strategy become out of balance? Are you too removed from your "troops in the field?" It is time to balance your head with your heart.

On Your Altar

Colors Pink, green

Numerology 5 – Exercise in a happy way

Tarot Card Justice – The ability to stay in the center of polarity

Gemstones Rose quartz, jade

Plant remedy Olive trees – Stamina

Fragrance Eucalyptus – Clarity of breath

Meditation

The freedom themes are provided by the zodiac sign and can be from this lifetime or other lifetimes. These meditations assist in dissolving blocks and opening pathways to new frontiers.

When the Moon is in Libra, the ego undergoes a research program looking for motives behind all action. Sit quietly and close your eyes. Breathe in and breathe out. Ask the Angel of Records to take you to a moment in time of perceived errors, miscarriage of justice, or false sense of self-guilt. Ask to be anointed by a cloister of Heavenly Saints so that false guilt can be removed and exchanged for forgiveness. Then, a full expression of feelings can flow in a friendly manner toward yourself and others.

Libra Challenges and Victories

Say all of the statements in this section out loud. Then, underline the phrase that means the most to you. Use the phrase as your special affirmation for manifesting and co-creating throughout this phase of the moon.

I am awakened to the reality of the Law of Cause and Effect. I take time out today to see what is coming back to me. I know my actions, my words, and my thoughts have life and manifest in a pattern that returns to me. Today, I am in a place where I can clearly see the results of my words, my actions, and my thoughts. I am aware that it is time for a review and, in so doing, I am given the opportunity to balance, integrate and redistribute these results in a more productive way. When I truly know and experience the Law of Cause and Effect (what I send out comes back to me), I can take responsibility for my actions, words, and thoughts, and set myself free of blame. When blame is gone from my thought pattern (self-inflicted or circumstantial), I am able to benefit from my review rather than wasting energy justifying or defending my position. I now accept the idea that I am free to reconcile with whatever I have labeled as an injustice in my life. I take the time to re-route my thinking towards making life a beneficial experience. Today, I accept that in changing my language I can change my life. Today, I prepare to take actions toward beneficial experiences. Today, I release the need to be right and accept the right to be. Today, I stop judging life and start living life.

Libra Homework

Let the fresh air blow away mental stagnation related to times when you let others' interests supersede your own. Drink an excess amount of water to alert your kidneys that the freedom process has commenced. It's time to deepen your intention to be one with the light, promoting restoration on Earth.

Lunar Eclipse
April 4th
5:05 AM

Full Moon in Libra

Clearing the Slate for Freedom

Remember a time when you experienced the following trigger points. Write down what happened, forgive yourself, release it, and let it go to clear your slate for freedom.

Guilt

- Forgive
- Release
- Let Go

Need to Justify

- Forgive
- Release
- Let Go

Feeling Wrong

- Forgive
- Release
- Let Go

Defending

- Forgive
- Release
- Let Go

Avoiding the Moment Due to Spending Time Strategizing

- Forgive
- Release
- Let Go

My Freedom List

Say this statement out loud three times before writing your freedom list!

I am a free spiritual being and it is my desire to be free to think and to express myself fully.

I hereby fully and completely free my mind from all adhesions to outdated philosophies, habits, relationships, groups of people, man-made laws, moral codes, all rules, set ideas and set ways of thinking, traditions, organizations, duty-motivated activities, guilt, judgment, and being misunderstood!

Libra Freedom List Ideas

Now is the time to set myself free from situations that are not balanced, people-pleasing and the need to be liked, sorrow over past relationships, unsupportive relationships, the need to be right, false accusations, and being misunderstood.

Lunar Eclipse
April 4th
5:05 AM

Full Moon in Libra

How to Use the Moon Book With Your Chart

Fill in the blanks on the Cosmic Check-In page. Then look up the degree of the moon on the chart below. Take note of the "I" statement on the outside of the wheel where the moon is located. Now, locate the same degree on your own chart and make a note of the house and corresponding "I" statement. Go back to the Cosmic Check-In page and circle the two statements from the charts and read what you wrote. This will give you an idea about what to expect from this moon phase on a personal level.

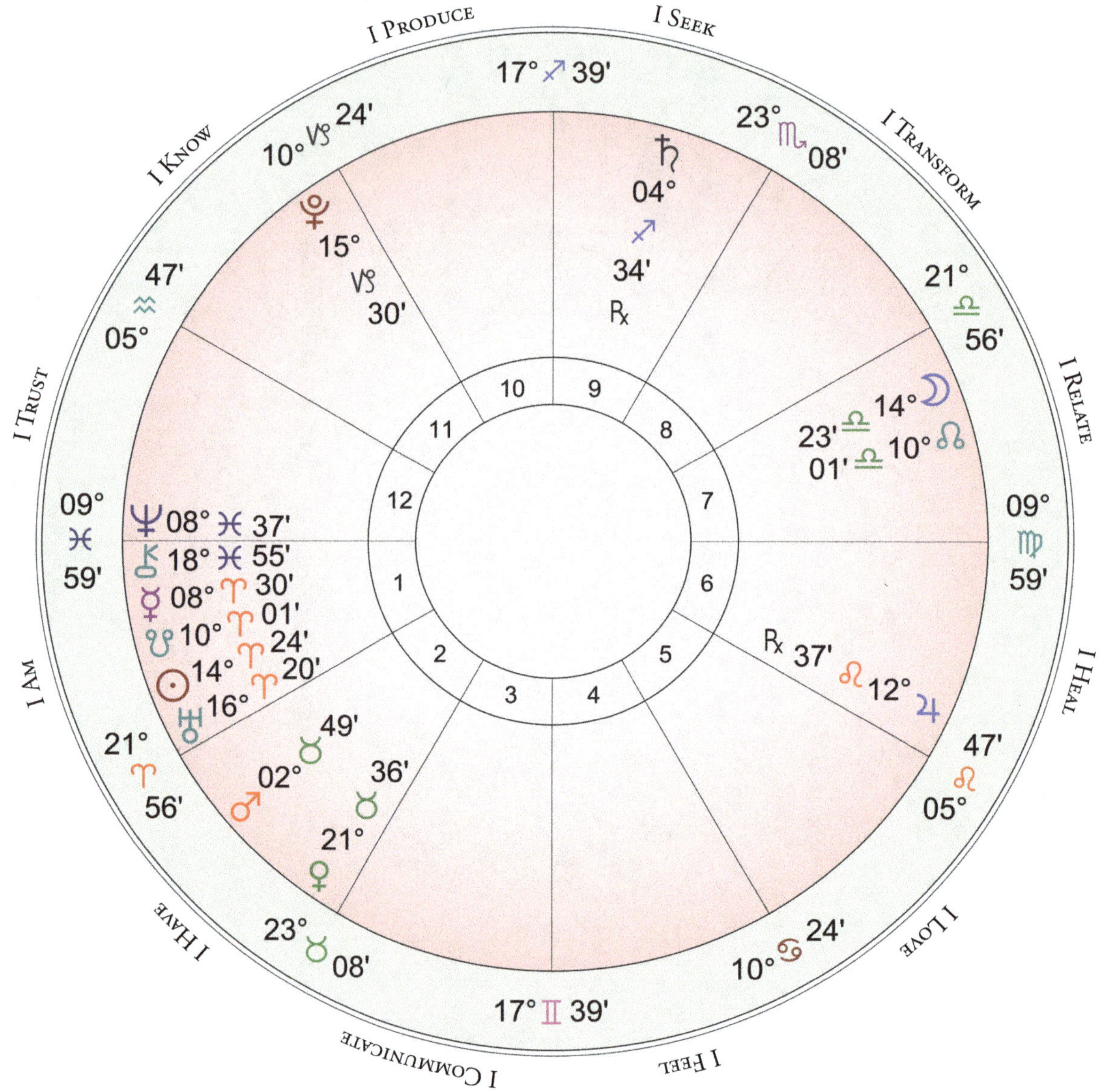

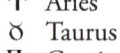

♈ Aries	♋ Cancer	♐ Sagittarius	☽ Moon	♄ Saturn	☊ North Node	V/C Void-of-Course
♉ Taurus	♌ Leo	♑ Capricorn	☿ Mercury	♅ Uranus	☋ South Node	▲ Super-Sensitivity
♊ Gemini	♍ Virgo	♒ Aquarius	♀ Venus	♆ Neptune	➡ Enters	▼ Low-Vitality
	♎ Libra	♓ Pisces	♂ Mars	♇ Pluto	℞ Retrograde	
	♏ Scorpio	☉ Sun	♃ Jupiter	⚷ Chiron	S/D Stationary Direct	

Cosmic Check-In

Take a moment to write a brief phrase for each "I" statement.
This activates all areas of your life for this creative cycle.

♎ I Relate

♏ I Transform

♐ I Seek

♑ I Produce

♒ I Know

♓ I Trust

♈ I Am

♉ I Have

♊ I Communicate

♋ I Feel

♌ I Love

♍ I Heal

April 18th
11:56 AM

New Moon in Aries

Dropping Moon
This happens when a new or full moon peaks at the same time as it goes void. During a "dropping moon" it becomes very important for you to write your co-creation list or your freedom list half an hour before the designated time.

Degree Choice Points
28° Aries 24'

Motivation Cosmic Direction

Resistance Flattery

Gift Observe without judgment.

Statement I Am
    Body Head
    Mind Impulsive
    Spirit Initiation

Element
Fire – Championship energy, serving self-first, Divine Masculine, all-consuming.

Tenth House Moon
14° Aries 34'

Tenth House Umbrella Theme
I Produce/I Am – Your approach to status, career, honor, and prestige, and why you chose your Father.

Motivation Artful Expression

Resistance Bored with Routine

Gift When in balance, your life is easily managed.

When the Sun is in Aries

Aries awakens the dreamer from Winter sleep and represents the raw energy of Spring, when the new shoots of life burst forth. Aries is the fundamental, straightforward approach to life. There is no challenge that is too great, no obstacle too daunting, and no rival too powerful for the Aries. Aries symbolizes initiation, leadership, strength, and potency. Competition and achievement are very important to Aries. Now is the time to be a pioneer and break all barriers to become the winner you are.

Aries Goddess

Aries goddess, Tara, is the goddess of sublime realization. She assists us in dispelling our fears in order to receive the gifts life has available to us. She was born from a star, sparking life into the dark waters of Winter, becoming the first incarnation of water and fire. Thus, the birth of Spring emerges. Legend says that Buddha placed her in the deepest part of the forest to guarantee life and light to all. He claimed her as the Mother of all Buddhas, to be reborn countless lifetimes to guarantee enlightenment and compassion to all women. The Dalai Lama calls her the first "Women's Libber" because she is the symbol of the rebirth of the feminine and gives birth to enlightenment, as does Aries on the equinox.

On Your Altar

Colors Red, black, white

Numerology 10 – Be clear with your intentions

Tarot Card Emperor – Success on all levels

Gemstones Diamond, red jasper, coral, obsidian

Plant Remedy Pomegranates, oak – Planting new life and rooting new life

Fragrance Ginger – The ability to ingest and digest life

My Co-Creation List

This or something better than this comes to me in an easy and pleasurable way, for the good of all concerned. Thank you, Universe!

Aries Co-Creation Ideas

Now is the time to focus on manifesting personality power, leadership, strength, self-acceptance, winning, courage, personal appearance, and advancing to new frontiers.

April 18th
11:56 AM

New Moon in Aries

Aries Challenges and Victories

Say all of the statements in this section out loud. Then, underline the phrase that means the most to you. Use the phrase as your special affirmation for manifesting and co-creating throughout this phase of the moon.

I am the author of my life. I accept that I am a winner and, in so doing, all doors are open to me. I hold the world in the palm of my hand and I know that there is not a mountain that I cannot climb. My ability to respond to life is in operation today and I direct my intention to bring me to the next level of self-determined achievement. The world and its systems are available for me to use as tools for my success and I use them with true excellence. I am organized and all systems are in place for me to make my mark on the world. I accept that my structured ground state and my dynamic energy are ready to make headway using pure determination, action, planning, and power. I will manage this plan and know that the sequence of events provided support me to make a breakthrough today.

I am willing to make my plan and take action on it. I gather my support team together today to focus on the appropriate action and encourage each person in their area of excellence and production. I am a great leader and my dynamic power is a good resource for others to determine their own success formula. I am aware that all parts of my team are important and place value on all areas of performance required to manifest in the world. I know how to place people in their best areas of expertise, so they can experience their own unique talent manifesting. Today, I honor my father for what he taught me by what he did, or didn't do, to encourage my ability to perform. I am the producer. I am the protector. I am the provider. I am the promoter. I am power. I am the author of my life.

Aries Homework

Aries co-creates best as a professional athlete, personal trainer or coach, martial arts expert, military professional, demolitions expert, fireworks manufacturer, wardrobe consultant, and through sales and promotions.

Merge your light and dark forces so balance can occur. Then, give shape to your feelings through creative forms and learn to live in the duality of your Soul and watch your spirit soar! The embodiment of this duality connects you to the Unity, a requirement for these times.

Without Acknowledgment Progress Cannot Occur

Acknowledgement creates space for victory and gratitude, which automatically brings you to a level of completion so a new cycle of opportunity can occur in your life. When you celebrate your wins and acknowledge your victories with gratitude, you update your cells so that your ability to move forward is not hindered by a cellular holographic pattern that is stuck in the past. Cellular lag creates resistance and makes moving forward most difficult. The key is to stay continuously updated by acknowledging yourself for what you did do at the end of each day, rather than heading off to sleep thinning about what you did not do. By acknowledging what you did not do, you play into your karmic storage bank and keep your progress at bay. When you acknowledge yourself and your manifestations you are complete, and more cycles of opportunity become available to you in each new day. Be prepared for miracles!

Victory List

When a creation result is acknowledged it seals the deal. This makes room for more magnificence to expand into your life and increases your abundance factor adding to your ability to receive. As each aspect of your co-creation list arrives in your life, spend time allowing, acknowledging, and accepting it with the true gusto of gratitude! Keep your victory list active here.

This fulfills the relationship between the giver and the receiver, which completes the cycle with the Universe so that a new beginning can be established.

Gratitude List

April 18th
11:56 AM

New Moon in Aries

How to Use the Moon Book With Your Chart

Fill in the blanks on the Cosmic Check-In page. Then look up the degree of the moon on the chart below. Take note of the "I" statement on the outside of the wheel where the moon is located. Now, locate the same degree on your own chart and make a note of the house and corresponding "I" statement. Go back to the Cosmic Check-In page and circle the two statements from the charts and read what you wrote. This will give you an idea about what to expect from this moon phase on a personal level.

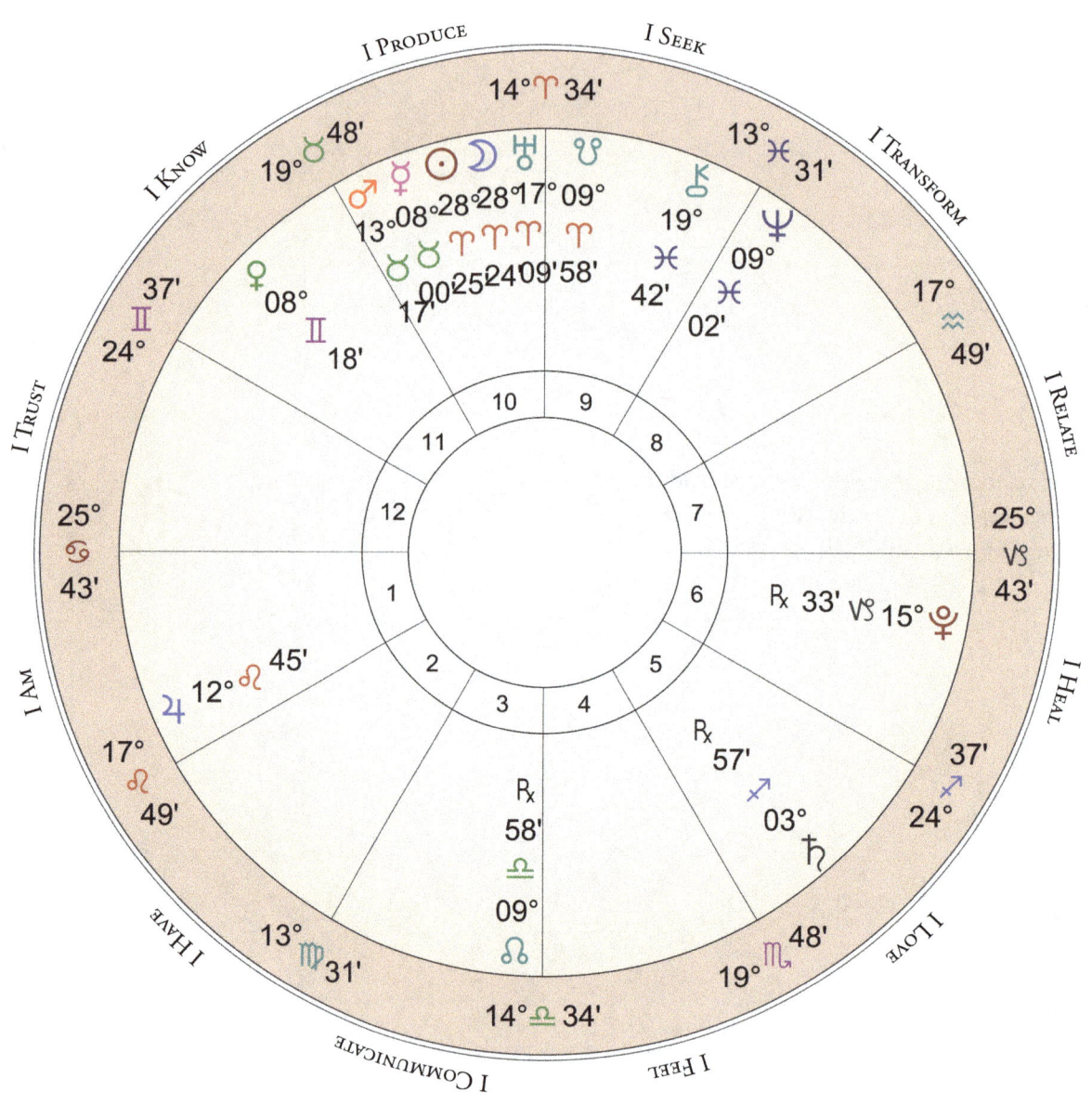

♈ Aries	♋ Cancer	♐ Sagittarius	☽ Moon	♄ Saturn	☊ North Node	V/C Void-of-Course
♉ Taurus	♌ Leo	♑ Capricorn	☿ Mercury	♅ Uranus	☋ South Node	▲ Super-Sensitivity
♊ Gemini	♍ Virgo	♒ Aquarius	♀ Venus	♆ Neptune	➡ Enters	▼ Low-Vitality
	♎ Libra	♓ Pisces	♂ Mars	♇ Pluto	℞ Retrograde	
	♏ Scorpio	☉ Sun	♃ Jupiter	⚷ Chiron	S/D Stationary Direct	

80

Cosmic Check-In

Take a moment to write a brief phrase for each "I" statement.
This activates all areas of your life for this creative cycle.

♈ I Am

♉ I Have

♊ I Communicate

♋ I Feel

♌ I Love

♍ I Heal

♎ I Relate

♏ I Transform

♐ I Seek

♑ I Produce

♒ I Know

♓ I Trust

Planetary Highlights

Saturn is Retrograde in Sagittarius until August 1

"Curb your enthusiasm" is the theme here. This month watch out for exaggeration or stretching the story to make it sound better by adding some extra flair for drama or for humor. Saturn will force you to see where you need to tell your stories based in reality, rather than with some extra fringe. So, it becomes a time to put yourself on a mission to discover the answer to your tall stories and step it down a bit.

Pluto is Retrograde in Capricorn Until September 24

Now is the time to make a written list of the changes you need to make in your life that you have been avoiding. The avoidance is related to some fear of survival. This is an oxymoron. In truth, that which you are holding on to will be your downfall, not the other way around. Re-route your thinking and get the new mantra working in your head that says, "What I let go of, brings me a pot of gold."

May 18 – Mercury goes Retrograde in Gemini Until June 11

It's time to rewind your thinking. This retrograde will have double the power because Mercury is in its own sign. Pay special attention to your software and any machinery. Avoid miscommunications by thinking twice before speaking. If possible, avoid ALL travel. The best action here is to finish up old projects, unclutter your mind, files, and your desk. Catch up on old correspondence. Clean up misunderstandings.

May 3 – Full Moon in Scorpio

This Moon assists us in releasing any secrets that we have kept hidden related to shared resources, money, sex, power, and death. Pay attention to any triggers that may occur in these areas and use your awareness to bring them to the light to be worked on consciously.

May 7 – Venus Enters Cancer

Expect to be overloaded with feelings about love. If used wisely, you actually may get your needs met here. Nurturing comes to the foreground and that, added to Venus' inescapable need for love, could make for a deep connection. This is a good time to have parties with family, especially if everyone brings their favorite recipe. It is also a good time to bring a new vibration of beauty into your home.

May 11 – Mars Enters Gemini

Hold on to your hat! You are on a fast-track to wherever you place your focus. Now is a great time to take a trip, especially if it includes adventure. The marketplace is waiting for your dynamic energy, so go now and make yourself known. It's also a great time to get involved in a sport, exercise program, or anything that you have been waiting to do that includes a change. Go! Go! Go!

May 17 – New Moon in Taurus

Manifestation is the name of the game here. This is the "Santa Claus Moon," so make your list filled with all of the goodies, dreams, and inspirations that you have always wanted to receive, but were afraid to ask. Now is the time!

May 17 – Saturn in Sagittarius Opposite Mars in Gemini

This could be a safety valve for the extreme speed involved with Mars in Gemini. If you feel or hear a voice in your head saying slow down ... please do so with caution. It may be letting you know that you have left out an important detail.

May 21 – The Sun Enters Gemini

This is a time when you are called on to live your polarity. The key here is to integrate your opposite natures, instead of separating them. The more you know your opposite side, the better your experience of life becomes.

Super-Sensitivity – May 6-7

Chaos is in the atmosphere; take it slow in order to avoid accidents and depression. The energy is mental, so keep your thinking under control to keep from experiencing a spiraling mind.

Low-Vitality – May 5-6, 19-20

Earth changes are possible; stay close to home. Don't push – if something is going to end, let it happen. Pay attention to your body, get a massage, a foot bath, or just hang out and rest.

♈ Aries	♋ Cancer	♐ Sagittarius	☽ Moon	♄ Saturn	☊ North Node	V/C Void-of-Course
♉ Taurus	♌ Leo	♑ Capricorn	☿ Mercury	♅ Uranus	☋ South Node	▲ Super-Sensitivity
♊ Gemini	♍ Virgo	♒ Aquarius	♀ Venus	♆ Neptune	➡ Enters	▼ Low-Vitality
	♎ Libra	♓ Pisces	♂ Mars	♇ Pluto	℞ Retrograde	
	♏ Scorpio	☉ Sun	♃ Jupiter	⚷ Chiron	S/D Stationary Direct	

May

Sunday	Monday	Tuesday	Wednesday	Thursday	Friday	Saturday
					1 ♄♀℞ May Day 5. Treat yourself to a body massage.	2 ♄♀℞ ☽ V/C 7:03AM ☽→♏ 6:47PM 6. Be sure to check any health issues.
3 ♄♀℞ ○ 13°♏23′ 8:42PM 7. Live what you study.	4 ♄♀℞ ☽ V/C 6:49PM 8. Give from a generous heart.	5 ♄♀℞ ▼ ☽→♐ 4:12AM 9. Spiritual balance = inspiration.	6 ♄♀℞ ▲ ▼ 10. Move beyond your past.	7 ♄♀℞ ▲ ☽ V/C 10:51AM ☽→♑ 11:16AM ♀→♋ 3:53PM 2. Do not overthink the situation.	8 ♄♀℞ 3. Express yourself.	9 ♄♀℞ ☽ V/C 1:35PM ☽→♒ 4:21PM 4. Loyalty is a sign of stability.
10 ♄♀℞ Mother's Day 5. Change is your friend.	11 ♄♀℞ ☽ V/C 3:36AM ☽→♓ 7:53PM ♂→♊ 7:41PM 6. Give your home some love.	12 ♄♀℞ 7. Respect the knowledge of others.	13 ♄♀℞ ☽ V/C 9:54AM ☽→♈ 10:13PM 8. Celebrate your abundance.	14 ♄♀℞ 9. Pray for someone who is sick.	15 ♄♀℞ ☽ V/C 5:03AM 10. Do something on your bucket list.	16 ♄♀℞ ☽→♉ 12:02AM 2. Keep your balance without extremes.
17 ♄♀℞ ☽ V/C 9:13PM ● 26°♉56′ 9:13PM 3. Is it your belief or someone else's?	18 ☿♄♀℞ ☽→♊ 2:27AM ☿℞-13°♊08′ 6:50PM 4. Structure your life on knowing.	19 ☿♄♀℞ ▼ ☽ V/C 10:57AM 5. Be sure the tires on your car are safe.	20 ☿♄♀℞ ▼ ☽→♋ 6:55AM 6. Lend an ear to someone in need.	21 ☿♄♀℞ ☽ V/C 5:36PM ☉→♊ 1:46AM 7. Sharing what you know brings joy.	22 ☿♄♀℞ ☽→♌ 2:42PM 8. Give people credit for what they do.	23 ☿♄♀℞ 9. Focus on your intention of prayer.
24 ☿♄♀℞ ☽ V/C 3:49AM 10. Make planning for the future joyful.	25 ☿♄♀℞ Memorial Day ☽→♍ 1:51AM 2. Move at a steady pace.	26 ☿♄♀℞ ☽ V/C 7:21PM 3. Live, love, and laugh with a friend.	27 ☿♄♀℞ ☽→♎ 2:41PM 5. Do not hesitate to make a change.	28 ☿♄♀℞ 6. Your home is your sanctuary.	29 ☿♄♀℞ ☽ V/C 1:20PM 7. Past life insights have value.	30 ☿♄♀℞ ☽→♏ 2:33AM 8. Be willing to question authority.
31 ☿♄♀℞ 9. Listen to your teachers and guides.						

May 3rd
8:42 PM

Full Moon in Scorpio

Degree Choice Points
13° Scorpio 22'

Motivation
Networking

Resistance
Control with Fear

Gift
Dissolve a mental partition with your imagination.

Statement
I Transform
- **Body** Sex Organs
- **Mind** Intensity
- **Spirit** Transformation

Element
Water – Seeks lowest ground to be contained, emotions that consume, need for Soul nourishment, sensitivity to others.

Twelfth House Moon
6° Scorpio 24'

Twelfth House Umbrella Theme
I Trust/I Transform – Determine how you deal with your karma, unconscious software, and what you will experience in order to attain mastery by completing your karma. It is also about the way you connect to the Divine.

Motivation Profound Insight

Resistance Isolation

Gift Change your vision to change your reality.

Karmic Awakening: Capricorn/Cancer

Karma will appear when the need for emotional growth and security steps on the toes of a goal focused on achievement and social status. Gemini is on the cusp of Cancer, so you may have a mental approach that creates difficulty confronting and dealing with emotions. The other side of the coin is that Sagittarius is on the cusp of Capricorn, which may create a challenge trying to figure out how and when to stop expanding and defining appropriate limits making it difficult to build something solid.

The Sun is Opposite the Moon

Full Moons are always in opposition to the Sun. This creates a feeling of tension between where you want to shine and how your feelings are flowing on a sensory level about the Sun's directive. The two forces seem like they are working against each other, yet they are on the same team displaying different techniques to obtain the same mission. The Scorpio/Taurus polarity creates tension between sharing resources and living abundantly for yourself.

Scorpio God

Pluto was one of the three remaining sons of Saturn who were not consumed by his wrath. The three brothers looked at the elements that Time could not consume: Air, Water, and Death. The three brothers chose their non-consumable domains. Jupiter took the air, Neptune the water, and Pluto the grave or the underworld. Pluto means wealth in the Greek language and is defined as "invisible fullness." Pluto is the god of wealth. Hidden assets belong to the underworld and cannot be consumed until they are brought above the ground. When the Moon is full in Scorpio, you are given the opportunity to shine the light on your own underworld and see what you are hiding on an unconscious level. Subjects that Pluto tends to keep hidden are death, taxes, money, legacies, and sex. Look deep within yourself to see what resentments, fears, or hidden agendas you might be harboring in these areas. Bring them forward above the ground and into the light of day.

On Your Altar

Colors Indigo, deep purple, scarlet

Numerology 7 – Live what you learn

Tarot Card Death – The ability to make changes

Gemstones Topaz, tanzanite, onyx, obsidian

Plant remedy Manzanita – Prepares the body for transformation

Fragrance Sandalwood – Awakens your sensuality

Meditation

The freedom themes are provided by the zodiac sign and can be from this lifetime or other lifetimes. These meditations assist in dissolving blocks and opening pathways to new frontiers.

When the Moon is in Scorpio, it is time to contact an Angel of Transformation to move you beyond the unruly representatives of your lower nature, such as retaliation, revenge, dominance, and misappropriated sexual focus.

Sit down quietly. Breathe in and breathe out. Ask for clarification of purpose and dedication without deviation. Work with the Angel of Transformation to assist you in freeing yourself from any judgment attached to indiscretions, and replace your field of awareness with appropriate focus, determination, and drive.

Scorpio Challenges and Victories

Say all of the statements in this section out loud. Then, underline the phrase that means the most to you. Use the phrase as your special affirmation for manifesting and co-creating throughout this phase of the moon.

I will not compromise myself today. I know that transformation occurs when I stand tall in my truth, even if everything around me needs to die. I see death as a new beginning and know that in death comes new aliveness. I am willing to embrace transformation and open to the idea that change is in my favor. I know that in letting go, I give new life to myself. I am willing to accept that life is ever-changing and in a constant state of renewal; one cannot occur without the other.

Releasing is easy when I offer myself something new. When I allow for the motion of change to stay alive, I let go with one hand and receive with the other hand. The ever-present flow and motion keeps me alive and connected to the revitalizing power of Nature. When the power of Nature becomes apparent to me, I become aware that Nature abhors a vacuum. Rejuvenation is mine when I embrace change.

Scorpio Homework

The Scorpio Moon creates the urge within us to make life happen. Pay attention to these urges so you can prepare yourself for greater action, intention, and purpose.

May 3rd
8:42 PM

Full Moon in Scorpio

Clearing the Slate for Freedom

Remember a time when you experienced the following trigger points. Write down what happened, forgive yourself, release it, and let it go to clear your slate for freedom.

Secrets

- Forgive
- Release
- Let Go

Sharing Money

- Forgive
- Release
- Let Go

Sexual Indiscretions

- Forgive
- Release
- Let Go

Control Dramas

- Forgive
- Release
- Let Go

Revenge

- Forgive
- Release
- Let Go

My Freedom List

Say this statement out loud three times before writing your freedom list!

I am a free spiritual being and it is my desire to be free to think and to express myself fully.

I am now free and ready to make choices beyond survival!

Scorpio Freedom List Ideas

Now is the time to set myself free from resentment, jealousy, revenge, joint financial situations, vendettas, betrayals, blocks to transformation, destructive relationships, resistance to changing paradigms, obstacles to having a healthy sex life, and karma relating to all issues of power.

May 3rd
8:42 PM

Full Moon in Scorpio

How to Use the Moon Book With Your Chart

Fill in the blanks on the Cosmic Check-In page. Then look up the degree of the moon on the chart below. Take note of the "I" statement on the outside of the wheel where the moon is located. Now, locate the same degree on your own chart and make a note of the house and corresponding "I" statement. Go back to the Cosmic Check-In page and circle the two statements from the charts and read what you wrote. This will give you an idea about what to expect from this moon phase on a personal level.

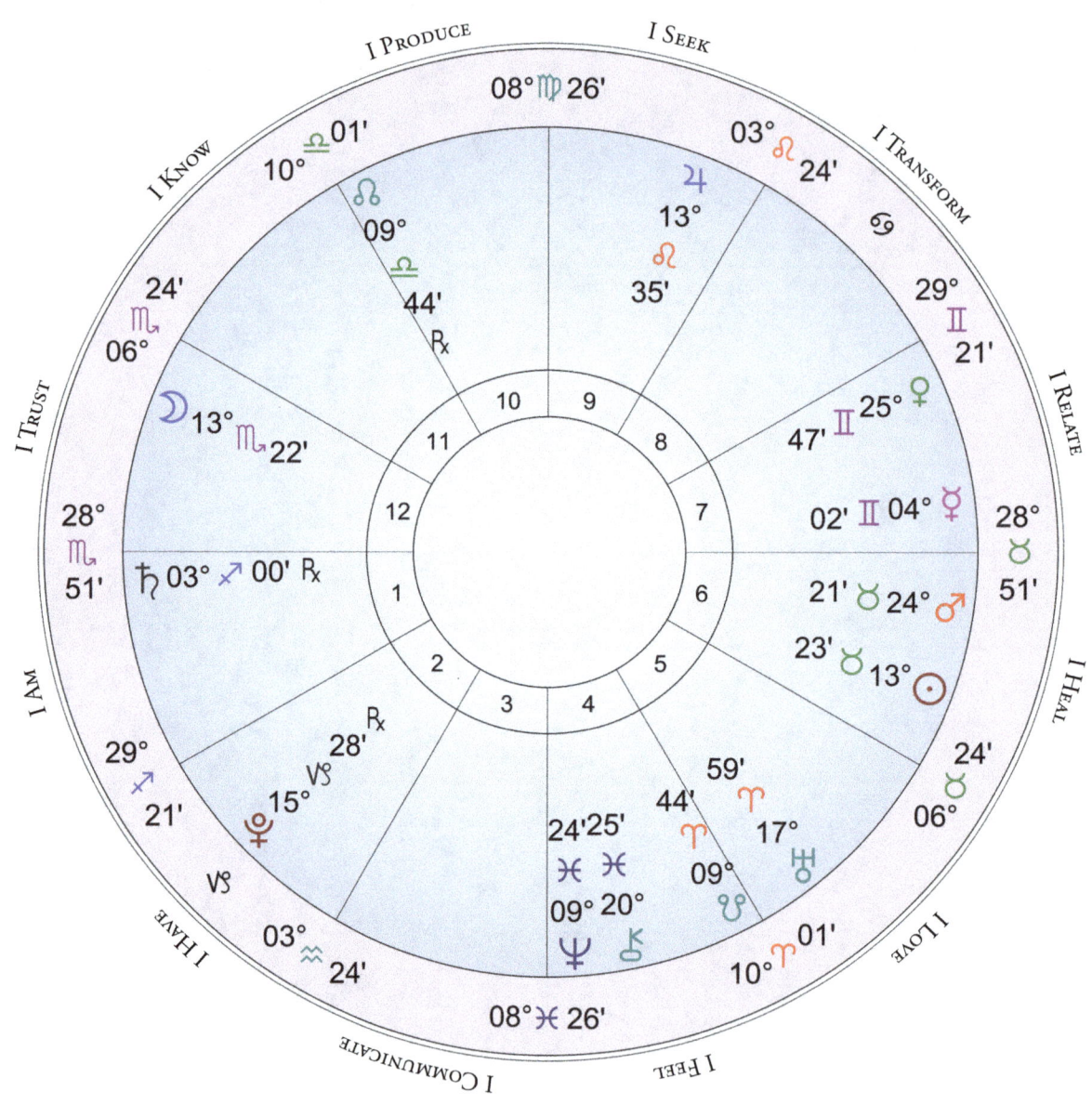

♈ Aries	♋ Cancer	♐ Sagittarius	☽ Moon	♄ Saturn	☊ North Node	V/C Void-of-Course
♉ Taurus	♌ Leo	♑ Capricorn	☿ Mercury	♅ Uranus	☋ South Node	▲ Super-Sensitivity
♊ Gemini	♍ Virgo	♒ Aquarius	♀ Venus	♆ Neptune	➡ Enters	▼ Low-Vitality
	♎ Libra	♓ Pisces	♂ Mars	♇ Pluto	℞ Retrograde	
	♏ Scorpio	☉ Sun	♃ Jupiter	⚷ Chiron	S/D Stationary Direct	

Cosmic Check-In

Take a moment to write a brief phrase for each "I" statement.
This activates all areas of your life for this creative cycle.

♏ I Transform

♐ I Seek

♑ I Produce

♒ I Know

♓ I Trust

♈ I Am

♉ I Have

♊ I Communicate

♋ I Feel

♌ I Love

♍ I Heal

♎ I Relate

May 17th
9:13 PM

New Moon in Taurus

Dropping Moon
This happens when a new or full moon peaks at the same time as it goes void. During a "dropping moon" it becomes very important for you to write your co-creation list or your freedom list half an hour before the designated time.

Degree Choice Points
26° Taurus 55'

Motivation	Hidden Talents/Skills
Resistance	Underestimate
Gift	You agreed to be a bridge between the past, present, future, and probable.
Statement	I Have
Body	Neck
Mind	Collector
Spirit	Accumulation

Element
Earth – Acquisition, increasing and creating abundance, practicing generosity.

Sixth House Moon
25° Taurus 24'

Sixth House Umbrella Theme
I Heal/I Have – The way you manage your body and its appearance.

Motivation	Storyteller/Bard/Poet
Resistance	Groveler (Bottom Feeder)
Gift	Organize your ideas to understand how they can be applied to the world.

Karmic Awakening: Pisces/Virgo

Karma will activate if the need to analyze and perfect the self comes into play, thus stopping the intention to be of service. The lesson here is to accept things the way they are, let go, and experience trust. When Leo is on the cusp of Virgo, you may be seen as stable, but inside, self-doubt will stand in the way of you being useful. On the other hand, when Aquarius is on the cusp of Pisces, your uniqueness could leave you feeling misunderstood.

When the Sun is in Taurus

Taurus is the time when we see the true manifesting power, as the plants move to a higher aspiration of life and bloom. Once again, we become connected to the essence of beauty as a symbol of our divinity. Taurus is the connection between humanity and divinity. Taurus' job is to infuse matter with light through accumulating layers of substance. This is why they are such good shoppers and collectors. The more they accumulate, the more divinity they experience. This process brings about a sense of self-value which is directly commensurate to the amount of money they manifest. Personal resources are part of the pattern. Discover your value at this time.

Taurus Goddess

Taurus goddess, Lakshmi, is the goddess of wealth, abundance, and luxury. Lakshmi is the embodiment of power, fortune, and beauty. She was born out of an ocean of milk. When churned, the alchemy of manifestation turned the milk to butter and a symbol of wealth came into being. She sits on the lotus to remind us to be aware of the stages of evolution required for manifestation, infusing matter with light. Her hands are filled with symbols that show the four stages of manifestation: purpose, wealth, bodily pleasures, and beatitude. The more attention you give Lakshmi in the form of prayer, the wealthier you become.

On Your Altar

Colors Green, pink, deep red, earth tones

Numerology 3 – Is it your belief or someone else's?

Tarot Card Hierophant – The ability to listen, inner-knowing

Gemstones Topaz, agate, smoky quartz, jade, rose quartz

Plant Remedy Angelica – Connecting Heaven and Earth

Fragrance Rose – Opening the heart

My Co-Creation List

This or something better than this comes to me in an easy and pleasurable way, for the good of all concerned. Thank you, Universe!

Taurus Co-Creation Ideas

Now is the time to focus on manifesting success, money, property, luxury, beauty, personal value, and pleasure.

May 17th
9:13 PM

New Moon in Taurus

Taurus Challenges and Victories

Say all of the statements in this section out loud. Then, underline the phrase that means the most to you. Use the phrase as your special affirmation for manifesting and co-creating throughout this phase of the moon.

Everything is possible for me today. My possibilities are endless. I have the power within me to make all of my dreams come true. I have the tools to make my talent a reality. I have the power to identify with my talent. Today, I focus my attention and intention on manifesting with my talent and, in so doing, I transform my ideas into reality. I recognize the part of me that is connected to the cosmic source of ideas and I express that source within me to manifest my creative power. I see my possibilities and act on them today. I am the creative power. I am all-knowing. I am an individual. There is no one else like me. I can manifest anything I desire. I intend it, I allow it, so be it.

Rules for Manifesting

Know what you want. Write it down. Say it out loud. Recognize that because you thought it, it can be so. Release your limiting beliefs. Override your limiting beliefs with power statements. Act as if you have already manifested your idea. Lastly, value yourself!

Taurus Homework

Taurus co-creates best when buying, selling, and owning real estate, gardening and landscaping, selling and collecting art, manufacturing and selling fine furniture, singing or acting, and as a restaurateur, antique dealer, or interior designer.

The Moon in Taurus asks us to infuse light into form and, in so doing, the bridge between humanity and divinity is manifested and we can assume our stewardship in the physical world. When we release Spirit into matter, we become open to the idea that accumulation and actualization set us free to experience the abundance available to us here on Earth. Go shopping!

Without Acknowledgment Progress Cannot Occur

Acknowledgement creates space for victory and gratitude, which automatically brings you to a level of completion so a new cycle of opportunity can occur in your life. When you celebrate your wins and acknowledge your victories with gratitude, you update your cells so that your ability to move forward is not hindered by a cellular holographic pattern that is stuck in the past. Cellular lag creates resistance and makes moving forward most difficult. The key is to stay continuously updated by acknowledging yourself for what you did do at the end of each day, rather than heading off to sleep thinning about what you did not do. By acknowledging what you did not do, you play into your karmic storage bank and keep your progress at bay. When you acknowledge yourself and your manifestations you are complete, and more cycles of opportunity become available to you in each new day. Be prepared for miracles!

Victory List

When a creation result is acknowledged it seals the deal. This makes room for more magnificence to expand into your life and increases your abundance factor adding to your ability to receive. As each aspect of your co-creation list arrives in your life, spend time allowing, acknowledging, and accepting it with the true gusto of gratitude! Keep your victory list active here.

This fulfills the relationship between the giver and the receiver, which completes the cycle with the Universe so that a new beginning can be established.

Gratitude List

May 17th
9:13 PM

New Moon in Taurus

How to Use the Moon Book With Your Chart

Fill in the blanks on the Cosmic Check-In page. Then look up the degree of the moon on the chart below. Take note of the "I" statement on the outside of the wheel where the moon is located. Now, locate the same degree on your own chart and make a note of the house and corresponding "I" statement. Go back to the Cosmic Check-In page and circle the two statements from the charts and read what you wrote. This will give you an idea about what to expect from this moon phase on a personal level.

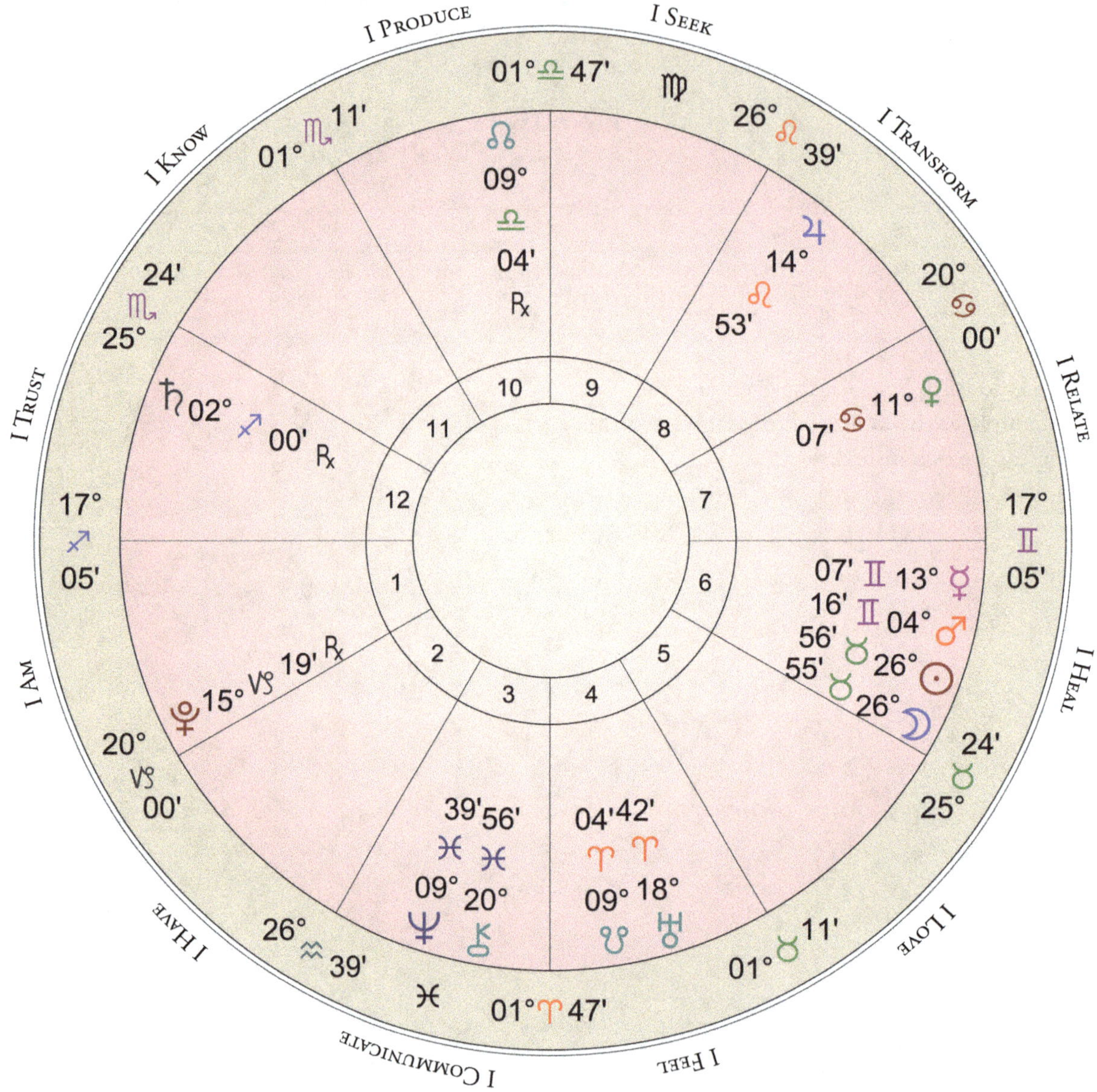

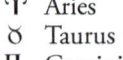

♈ Aries	♋ Cancer	♐ Sagittarius	☽ Moon	♄ Saturn	☊ North Node	V/C Void-of-Course
♉ Taurus	♌ Leo	♑ Capricorn	☿ Mercury	♅ Uranus	☋ South Node	▲ Super-Sensitivity
♊ Gemini	♍ Virgo	♒ Aquarius	♀ Venus	♆ Neptune	➡ Enters	▼ Low-Vitality
	♎ Libra	♓ Pisces	♂ Mars	♇ Pluto	℞ Retrograde	
	♏ Scorpio	☉ Sun	♃ Jupiter	⚷ Chiron	S/D Stationary Direct	

Cosmic Check-In

Take a moment to write a brief phrase for each "I" statement.
This activates all areas of your life for this creative cycle.

♉ I Have

♊ I Communicate

♋ I Feel

♌ I Love

♍ I Heal

♎ I Relate

♏ I Transform

♐ I Seek

♑ I Produce

♒ I Know

♓ I Trust

♈ I Am

Planetary Highlights

Mercury Retrograde in Gemini Until June 11

Get all old correspondence out and done before the 11th. Look at times when you withheld love, do a re-take.

Saturn Continues to be Retrograde in Sagittarius and Backs into Scorpio on June 14 Until August 1

Work on the concept of excess as it relates to your home by using the refinement power of Saturn to assist you. Expect to review areas of deviated focus where money, sex, creativity and death are involved. Bring these issues to the light and move on.

June 12 – Neptune goes Retrograde in Pisces Until November 18

The concept of trust could become a theme here. Expect some feelings of disappointment to happen, especially as it relates to fair-weather friends.

Pluto is Retrograde in Capricorn Until September 24

It is time to look at your fear of living a prosperous life. It takes courage to accept wealth and all of its trappings. See if you can remember when you judged someone for living in abundance to rationalize your lack.

June 24 – Chiron goes Retrograde in Pisces Until November 27

This brings potential for spiritual transformation! How can you release creative healing energy without getting stuck in unnecessary suffering? Time to heal the suffering, rather than the actual wound.

June 2 – Full Moon in Sagittarius

It is time to face your excessive nature and see where you have allowed your extravagance to get out of balance. See if you can accept that "less is more," without feeling a sense of loss.

June 2 – Mars, The Sun, and Mercury Tripled in Gemini are Opposite the Moon and Saturn in Sagittarius

You will be able to see how your ego is working, or not working, by watching what is reflected back to you. Expect your dynamic personality to be working overtime; it may need a little tempering.

June 5 – Venus Moves into Leo

Dance the dance of life. Total bliss, love, and prosperity are here; get your bells on and dance! It is good to be adored, just remember to be adoring as well.

June 14 – Saturn Retrograde Backs into Scorpio

It's one last chance to have the grand teacher, Saturn, show us what we forgot to learn in the first round. Look for remnants of resentment, betrayal, or passive aggression that need to be re-created into the light of consciousness. Now is the time.

June 16 – New Moon in Gemini

Your soap-box awaits you and now is the time to manifest your ideas into a system that has been waiting to hear what you have to say. Write that book, start a blog, update your Facebook page. Make your ideas known.

June 16 – The Moon, Sun, and Mars are Tripled in Gemini

Don't miss this chance to get your word out. According to this moon, it will manifest into something fruitful. Sound it out and direct your intentions toward your target. Now is the time!

June 21 – Summer Solstice – The Sun Moves into Cancer

Half the year has passed. Now is the time to look at what you have manifested in your prosperity garden during 2015. Begin by acknowledging what good you have done and add energy, where needed, to encourage growth.

June 24 – Mars Moves into Cancer

Expect a steam-cleaning of your feelings. Look and see what needs to be changed in your home and in your family.

June 25 – Venus and Jupiter Dance Together in Leo

Celebrate love for life and for each other. Be adored and adoring. The bliss pocket is activated – don't delay!

Super-Sensitivity – June 2-3

Keep your thoughts to yourself and work on your inner-self on these days. Stay grounded; explosive action could be in the air.

Low-Vitality – June 15-16, 19-26

Earth changes are prevalent on these days. Stay close to home and rest.

Aries	Cancer	Sagittarius	Moon	Saturn	North Node	V/C Void-of-Course
Taurus	Leo	Capricorn	Mercury	Uranus	South Node	Super-Sensitivity
Gemini	Virgo	Aquarius	Venus	Neptune	Enters	Low-Vitality
	Libra	Pisces	Mars	Pluto	Retrograde	
	Scorpio	Sun	Jupiter	Chiron	Stationary Direct	

June

Sunday	Monday	Tuesday	Wednesday	Thursday	Friday	Saturday
	1 ☿♄♀R ☽ V/C 4:01AM ☽→♐ 11:39AM 10. See beyond the obvious.	**2** ☿♄♀R ▲ ☽ V/C 10:58PM ○11°♐49′ 9:18AM 2. Grounding is balanced focus.	**3** ☿♄♀R ▲ ☽→♑ 5:50PM 3. Playing changes your viewpoint.	**4** ☿♄♀R 4. Practicality leads to calmness.	**5** ☿♄♀R ☽ V/C 3:53AM ☽→♒ 10:01PM ♀→♌ 8:34AM 5. Exercise adds to your vitality.	**6** ☿♄♀R 6. Beautify your environment.
7 ☿♄♀R ☽ V/C 7:30AM 7. Learning happens with humor.	**8** ☿♄♀R ☽→♓ 1:16AM 8. Everybody manifests differently.	**9** ☿♄♀R ☽ V/C 11:08AM 9. Education is a Divine tool.	**10** ☿♄♀R ☽→♈ 4:13AM 10. Truth is in the now, not for later.	**11** ☿♄♀R ☽ V/C 4:42PM ☿D-4°♊34 3:34PM 2. Combining ideas puts you in balance.	**12** ♄♆♀R ☽→♉ 7:16AM ♆R-9°♓49′ 2:10AM 3. Creativity requires receptivity.	**13** ♄♆♀R ☽ V/C 3:06PM 4. For efficiency, prioritize.
14 ♄♆♀R Flag Day ☽→♊ 10:50AM ♄→♏ 5:39PM 5. Move beyond resistance.	**15** ♄♆♀R ▼ 6. Add love to your relationships.	**16** ♄♆♀R ▼ ☽ V/C 7:05AM ☽→♋ 3:50PM ●25°♊07′ 7:05AM 7. A bigger picture opens thinking.	**17** ♄♆♀R 8. Avoid having to "be right."	**18** ♄♆♀R ☽ V/C 10:52PM ☽→♌ 11:22PM 9. Spiritual energy maintains vitality.	**19** ♄♆♀R ▼ 10. Truth is relative to the situation.	**20** ♄♆♀R ▼ 2. Drop "perfect" — just do your best.
21 ♄♆♀R ▼ Father's Day ☉→♋ 9:39AM Summer Solstice ☽ V/C 9:09AM ☽→♍ 9:58AM 3. Find a pocket of joy every day.	**22** ♄♆♀R ▼ 4. Structure isn't rigid - it's organized.	**23** ♄♆♀R ▼ ☽ V/C 10:12PM ☽→♎ 10:40PM 5. Take a different route today.	**24** ♄♆♀⚷R ▼ ♂→♋ 6:34AM ⚷R- 21°♓33′ 4:37AM 6. Love others' self-expression.	**25** ♄♆♀⚷R ▼ ☽ V/C 4:22PM 7. Use the ability to reason and discern.	**26** ♄♆♀⚷R ▼ ☽→♏ 10:56AM 8. Receiving is the key to abundance.	**27** ♄♆♀⚷R 9. Communicate verbally with Spirit.
28 ♄♆♀⚷R ☽ V/C 6:50PM ☽→♐ 8:21PM 10. Make planning a trip fun.	**29** ♄♆♀⚷R 2. Deciding to harmonize works.	**30** ♄♆♀⚷R ☽ V/C11:17 AM 3. Life's recipe: live-love-laugh.				

June 2nd
9:18 AM

Full Moon in Sagittarius

Degree Choice Points
   11° Sagittarius 48'

Motivation Transcendent Discovery

Resistance Controversy

Gift Find a new healing method or healer.

Statement I Seek
   Body Thighs
   Mind Philosophical
   Spirit Inspiration

Element
   Fire – Gives rise to the expression of the ego, the ability to stand up for yourself, the initiation of projects, enthusiasm, and warmth.

Fifth House Moon
   24° Scorpio 46'

Fifth House Umbrella Theme
   I Love/I Seek – The way you love and how you want to be loved.

Motivation
   Investigation/Research

Resistance No Alternatives

Gift Your third eye gets a rest while using your ability to feel, hear, smell, or taste.

The Sun is Opposite the Moon

Full Moons are always in opposition to the Sun. This creates a feeling of tension between where you want to shine and how your feelings are flowing on a sensory level about the Sun's directive. The two forces seem like they are working against each other, yet they are on the same team displaying different techniques to obtain the same mission. The Sagittarius/Gemini polarity creates tension between the quest for higher knowledge and the need for academic accolades.

Sagittarius Goddess

Iris, the goddess of the rainbow, is a symbol of multi-colored and multi-dimensional consciousness. She weaves many mysteries into the garment of life with her colors. The Rainbow Bridge gave Iris access to travel between Heaven and Earth. She was Hera's messenger, bringing visions and messages for greater awareness to those who needed insight. For this reason, part of the eye was named after her. The Rainbow is a symbol of a fortunate future and reminds us that we have the potential to manifest in all spheres and circumstances. One of Iris' jobs is to cut the cord of life to those crossing over to the other side and open the directive for the pathway of light. When the Moon is full in Sagittarius, we may find ourselves lost or directionless. It is time to call on the power of Iris to bring a new vision.

On Your Altar

Colors Deep purple, turquoise, royal blue

Numerology 2 – Grounding is balanced focus

Tarot Card Temperance – Balancing the present with the past, updating yourself

Gemstone Turquoise

Plant remedy Madia – Seeing and hitting the target

Fragrance Magnolia – Expanded beauty

Meditation

The freedom themes are provided by the zodiac sign and can be from this lifetime or other lifetimes. These meditations assist in dissolving blocks and opening pathways to new frontiers.

When the Moon is in Sagittarius, it is a time to become aware of dependency on rituals and philosophies. Look for perceptions of loyalty, fidelity, and ethics that keep you stuck in the past. Close your eyes and take in a few breaths. Ask for nighttime instructions from the Angel of Records to assist you in discovering a time when you became dependent on a practice that no longer serves you, your truth, your reality, and your daring. The Angel of Ritual will connect you to the new rituals that need to be reawakened at this time to empower your growth in the moment.

Sagittarius Challenges and Victories

Say all of the statements in this section out loud. Then, underline the phrase that means the most to you. Use the phrase as your special affirmation for manifesting and co-creating throughout this phase of the moon.

Today, I blend my old self with my new self, my physical reality with my spiritual awareness, my positive thoughts with my negative thoughts, my past with my present, my feminine with my masculine, my rewards with my losses, my ups with my downs, and my higher self with my lower self. It is a day for me to refine and fine tune my life by looking at my extremes. I recognize what inspires me and what keeps me stuck. I find my center today by acknowledging my extremes. I am aware that balance comes to those who are able to locate the space in the center of these opposite energy fields. When I am in my center, my polarities are in motion. Healing cannot occur unless my polarities are moving and I know that healing is motion.

I am ready for a healing today and know that by visiting my opposites and determining their vast opposition to each other, I can find the paradoxes that I have chosen for myself and begin to heal. I am willing to experiment with this blending of opposites and become the alchemist of my own life. When I blend all aspects of myself, rather than separating them, I can truly become whole. Today is a day to integrate, rather than separate, in order to release the spark of light that stays prisoner when my polarities are in operation. When I find balance, motion occurs and the Law of Harmony takes over, putting paradoxical energies to rest, thus breaking the crystallization of polarity. The Law of Harmony is beauty in motion, promoting the flow of color, light, sound, and movement into form. Balance is a condition that keeps my spark in motion. I become the vertical line in the center of polarity today and carry the secret of balance. Balance cannot be my goal, motion is my goal today. When I am in motion, I can take action to evolve and to express all of myself freely.

Sagittarius Homework

Now is the time to use your physical body to release the feeling of being caged in by people or circumstances. Choose an activity that burns away confinement and allows you to feel the power of your passion.

The Sagittarius Moon awakens us to know the spark of light that lives in our heart, thus elevating love in ourselves and in our world. This is when we come to realize what is in our highest and best good and we can begin to become free from all that is not lovable in our lives.

June 2nd
9:18 AM

Full Moon in Sagittarius

Clearing the Slate for Freedom

Remember a time when you experienced the following trigger points. Write down what happened, forgive yourself, release it, and let it go to clear your slate for freedom.

Unfiltered Language

- Forgive
- Release
- Let Go

Bluntness

- Forgive
- Release
- Let Go

Exaggerating

- Forgive
- Release
- Let Go

Excess

- Forgive
- Release
- Let Go

Gambling or Risk-Taking

- Forgive
- Release
- Let Go

My Freedom List

Say this statement out loud three times before writing your freedom list!

I am a free spiritual being and it is my desire to be free to think and to express myself fully.

I am now free and ready to make choices beyond survival!

Sagittarius Freedom List Ideas

Now is the time to set myself free from belief systems that no longer apply, attitudes that are not uplifting to me, addiction to excess and risk, the need to exaggerate based on low self-esteem, dishonest people, being too blunt, staying in the future and avoiding the NOW, overriding fear by being too optimistic, and preaching.

June 2nd
9:18 AM

Full Moon in Sagittarius

How to Use the Moon Book With Your Chart

Fill in the blanks on the Cosmic Check-In page. Then look up the degree of the moon on the chart below. Take note of the "I" statement on the outside of the wheel where the moon is located. Now, locate the same degree on your own chart and make a note of the house and corresponding "I" statement. Go back to the Cosmic Check-In page and circle the two statements from the charts and read what you wrote. This will give you an idea about what to expect from this moon phase on a personal level.

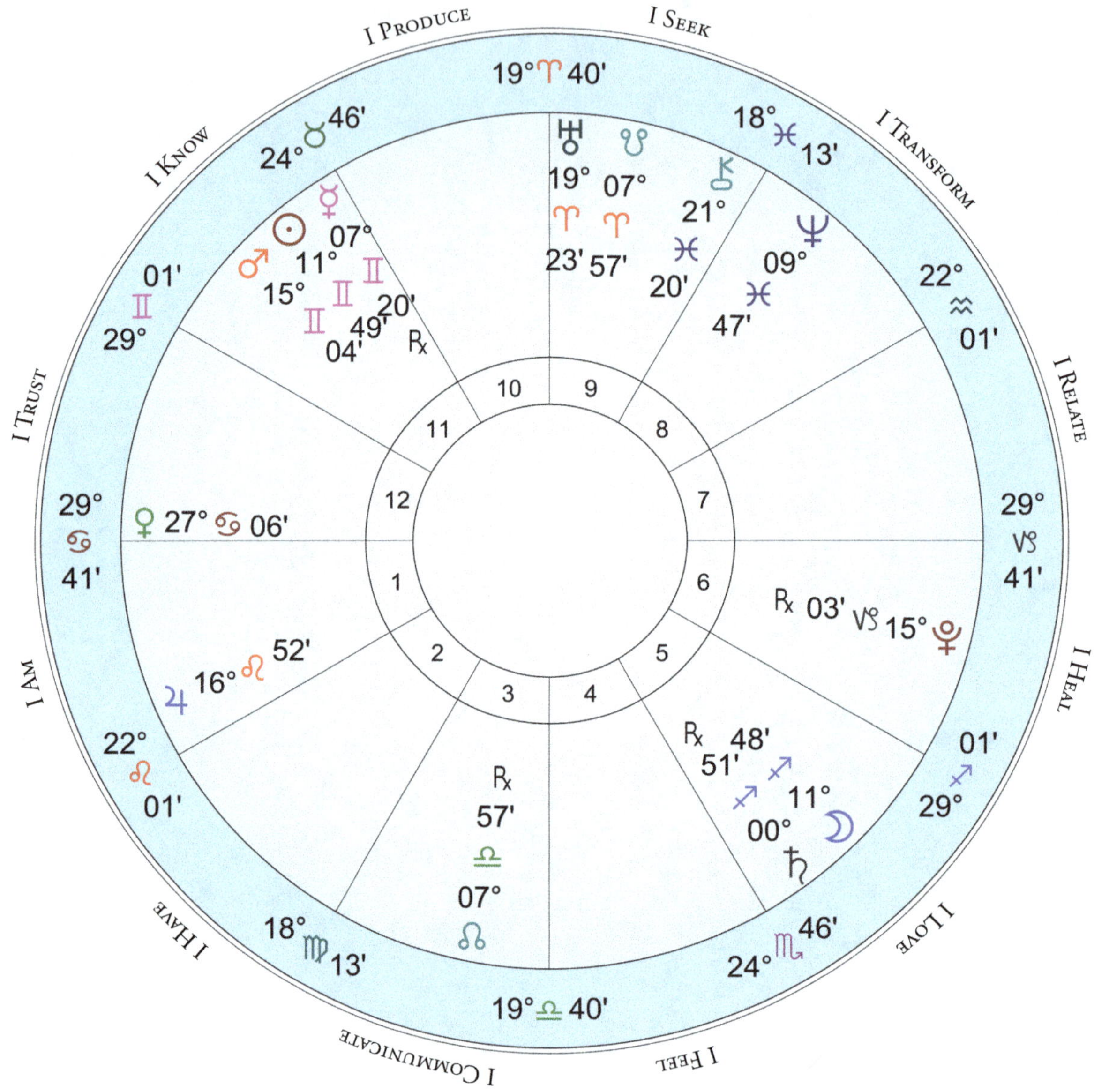

♈ Aries	♋ Cancer	♐ Sagittarius	☽ Moon	♄ Saturn	☊ North Node	V/C Void-of-Course
♉ Taurus	♌ Leo	♑ Capricorn	☿ Mercury	⛢ Uranus	☋ South Node	▲ Super-Sensitivity
♊ Gemini	♍ Virgo	♒ Aquarius	♀ Venus	♆ Neptune	➡ Enters	▼ Low-Vitality
	♎ Libra	♓ Pisces	♂ Mars	♇ Pluto	℞ Retrograde	
	♏ Scorpio	☉ Sun	♃ Jupiter	⚷ Chiron	SD Stationary Direct	

Cosmic Check-In

Take a moment to write a brief phrase for each "I" statement.
This activates all areas of your life for this creative cycle.

♐ I Seek

♑ I Produce

♒ I Know

♓ I Trust

♈ I Am

♉ I Have

♊ I Communicate

♋ I Feel

♌ I Love

♍ I Heal

♎ I Relate

♏ I Transform

June 16th
7:05 AM

New Moon in Gemini

Dropping Moon
This happens when a new or full moon peaks at the same time as it goes void. During a "dropping moon" it becomes very important for you to write your co-creation list or your freedom list half an hour before the designated time.

Degree Choice Points
25° Gemini 7'

Motivation	Natural Rhythms
Resistance	Halted Growth
Gift	Clear up any confusion that has occurred between yourself and another.
Statement	I Communicate
Body	Lungs and Hands
Mind	Intellect
Spirit	Intelligence

Element
Air – Freedom from attachment, curiosity, flexibility, active dreaming, bridge between the mundane and spiritual worlds.

Twelfth House Moon
10° Gemini 16'

Twelfth House Umbrella Theme
I Trust/ I Communicate – Determine how you deal with your karma, unconscious software, and what you will experience in order to attain mastery by completing your karma. It is also about the way your connect to the Divine.

Motivation	Fresh Starts
Resistance	Fickle
Gift	Share your ideas with community leaders.

Karmic Awakening: Aries/Libra
You may experience this karma if the need to initiate action comes up and you assert your own desire. Avoid the karma by sharing the need to maintain harmony with others. With Pisces on the cusp of Aries, it will become necessary to translate your idealism into action to avoid the karma. Virgo is on the cusp of Libra, demonstrating that analytical work must be put at the service of others to avoid the karma. Your lesson is to know that the results of your efforts must be shared.

When the Sun is in Gemini
This is a time when the ability to communicate is at the top of the priority list. Allow your thoughts to lead you to a formula for success so you can put your thoughts into action. Then, find the appropriate soapbox to stand on so your message can be heard. Right now is the time to make your message clear, enlightening, witty, and thought-provoking. Your bright mind is at its high throne and waiting for an audience. Try blogging, do a show on YouTube, join Toastmasters, write that screenplay, film yourself doing a travel show, start a discussion group, or write a newsletter for your neighborhood. Most of all, put your bright mind to work!

Gemini Goddess
Maya is the goddess of illusion. She tempts the mind into believing that what it thinks is always correct. She challenges you every step of the way to learn where the ego kicks in and leads you down pathways that are destructive. Her constant "mind chatter" sounds so convincing that you can spend your entire life living the illusion that thinking is better than experiencing. Maya will build this illusion so deep in the mind that you actually believe that your thoughts are worthy of accolades in the outer world. She distorts the value of inner work to keep you from knowing your personal truth.

On Your Altar

Colors Bright yellow, orange, multi-colors

Numerology 7 – A wider picture opens thinking

Tarot Card Lovers – Connecting to wholeness

Gemstones Yellow diamond, citrine

Plant Remedy Morning Glory – Thinking with your heart not your head

Fragrance Iris – The ability to focus the mind

My Co-Creation List

This or something better than this comes to me in an easy and pleasurable way, for the good of all concerned. Thank you, Universe!

Gemini Co-Creation Ideas

Now is the time to focus on manifesting communications, a promotion, technology, ideas, non-judgmental communication, thinking outside of duality, a quiet mind, charisma and charm, and flirting.

June 16th
7:05 AM

New Moon in Gemini

Gemini Challenges and Victories

Say all of the statements in this section out loud. Then, underline the phrase that means the most to you. Use the phrase as your special affirmation for manifesting and co-creating throughout this phase of the moon.

I am dark. I am light. I am day. I am night. The extremes in life exist within me, completing themselves in reality. The "I" that is "we" lives within me. I am one in the same. I am both.

I know that flow comes from accepting my opposite natures. Today, I accept my opposites and get into the flow. I am aware today of how my judgments separate me from people, events, experiences, and, most of all, from myself. Today, I am going to see where I have separated all of the parts of myself and begin to integrate into wholeness through acceptance and understanding. I begin by breathing. I breathe in wholeness and breathe out separation. I understand that breath is life and that life includes all facets of my experience to gain awareness. I know that I am Heaven. I know that I am Earth. I know that I am masculine. I know that I am feminine. Today, I become unified. Today, I integrate into wholeness. I breathe into all of these aspects of myself, knowing that in my totality I am connected to Oneness. The "I" that is "we" lives within me. I am one in the same. I am both.

Gemini Homework

The Gemini co-creates best through broadcasting and journalism, as a speech coach, comedian, political satirist, gossip columnist, negotiator, media specialist, manicurist, salesperson, teacher, or travel consultant.

Expect to awaken your will on seven levels…

- The will to direct – through the power of your original intention.
- The will to love – stimulating goodwill among humankind through cooperation.
- The will to act – by laying foundations for a happier world.
- The will to cooperate – the desire and demand for right relationships.
- The will to know – to think correctly and creatively so that every man/woman can find their outstanding characteristics.
- The will to persist – to be one with your light and represent the ideal standard for living.
- The will to organize – to carry forward direct inspiration through groups of goodwill.

Without Acknowledgment Progress Cannot Occur

Acknowledgement creates space for victory and gratitude, which automatically brings you to a level of completion so a new cycle of opportunity can occur in your life. When you celebrate your wins and acknowledge your victories with gratitude, you update your cells so that your ability to move forward is not hindered by a cellular holographic pattern that is stuck in the past. Cellular lag creates resistance and makes moving forward most difficult. The key is to stay continuously updated by acknowledging yourself for what you did do at the end of each day, rather than heading off to sleep thinning about what you did not do. By acknowledging what you did not do, you play into your karmic storage bank and keep your progress at bay. When you acknowledge yourself and your manifestations you are complete, and more cycles of opportunity become available to you in each new day. Be prepared for miracles!

Victory List

When a creation result is acknowledged it seals the deal. This makes room for more magnificence to expand into your life and increases your abundance factor adding to your ability to receive. As each aspect of your co-creation list arrives in your life, spend time allowing, acknowledging, and accepting it with the true gusto of gratitude! Keep your victory list active here.

Gratitude List

This fulfills the relationship between the giver and the receiver, which completes the cycle with the Universe so that a new beginning can be established.

June 16th
7:05 AM

New Moon in Gemini

How to Use the Moon Book With Your Chart

Fill in the blanks on the Cosmic Check-In page. Then look up the degree of the moon on the chart below. Take note of the "I" statement on the outside of the wheel where the moon is located. Now, locate the same degree on your own chart and make a note of the house and corresponding "I" statement. Go back to the Cosmic Check-In page and circle the two statements from the charts and read what you wrote. This will give you an idea about what to expect from this moon phase on a personal level.

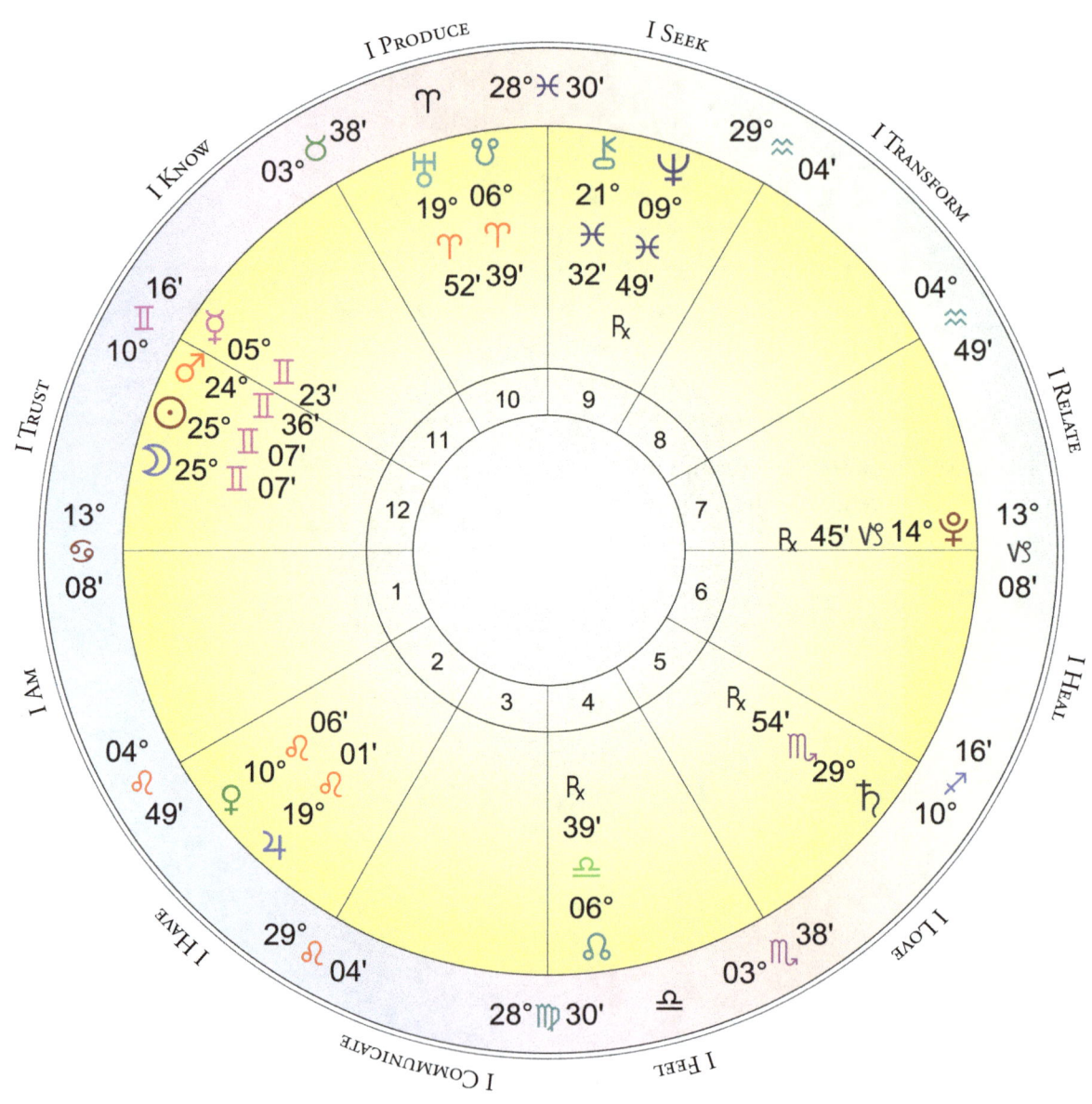

♈ Aries	♋ Cancer	♐ Sagittarius	☽ Moon	♄ Saturn	☊ North Node	V/C Void-of-Course
♉ Taurus	♌ Leo	♑ Capricorn	☿ Mercury	♅ Uranus	☋ South Node	▲ Super-Sensitivity
♊ Gemini	♍ Virgo	♒ Aquarius	♀ Venus	♆ Neptune	➡ Enters	▼ Low-Vitality
	♎ Libra	♓ Pisces	♂ Mars	♇ Pluto	℞ Retrograde	
	♏ Scorpio	☉ Sun	♃ Jupiter	⚷ Chiron	SD Stationary Direct	

116

Cosmic Check-In

Take a moment to write a brief phrase for each "I" statement.
This activates all areas of your life for this creative cycle.

♊ I Communicate

♋ I Feel

♌ I Love

♍ I Heal

♎ I Relate

♏ I Transform

♐ I Seek

♑ I Produce

♒ I Know

♓ I Trust

♈ I Am

♉ I Have

Planetary Highlights

Saturn is Retrograde in Scorpio Until August 1

The encore continues. Look to see if you feel like an authority is looking over your shoulder. If so, you are in need of more discovery – it is time to do a checklist on what you are avoiding.

Neptune Continues to be Retrograde in Pisces Until November 18

Do a check-in on feeling aimless or lost. There is a tendency here to daydream your life away. Use the Pisces pathway to ride above the timeline of your past to see where there is a cloud covering up what has been forgotten. Do some re-connection work and promise to find yourself again.

Pluto is Retrograde in Capricorn Until September 24

Your ego must give up its old ways and stop controlling you with lies. Find a moment of truth and make it grow, so that the ego can't control you anymore. Replace the old with something new and life will be easier.

Chiron is Retrograde in Pisces Until November 27

The healer must first accept the idea that healing can happen, even if there is long suffering attached to the healing challenge. It is time to say the serenity prayer to activate healing.

July 25 – Venus goes Retrograde in Virgo Until the end of the Month

Yikes! You could get crabby, especially if you let details get you down. Accept your commitment to raise the standard of excellence without complaining.

July 26 – Uranus goes Retrograde in Aries Until December 25

If you don't watch carefully, your explosive nature could take over. If you resist what is in front of you, the spontaneous nature of Uranus could play havoc with your stability.

July 1 – Full Moon in Capricorn is Conjunct with Pluto Retrograde

This moon will blast you into a total transformation! You may even see, within the deepest part of yourself, the most amazing system and structure for your success equation. Give up control and accept the gold that is being handed to you.

July 1 – Sun and Mars Conjunct in Cancer

Two hot, sizzling balls of fire are heating up the waters. If you relax and float, each wave of heat can take you to wondrous places. Dive in!

July 1 – Jupiter and Venus are Dancing in Leo Until July 25

Live love ... dance the dance of life ... have fun in the sun ... let your "kid" out and play like you never have before! Let someone know that you love them unconditionally in all her or his magnificence!

July 8 – Mercury Enters Cancer

This is a time to fully express your feelings, especially with those you love. Share what is new and what is good.

July 15 – New Moon in Cancer

It's time to manifest what you want in your home. Build a field of beauty that blasts from within, out the windows.

July 15 – Mercury and Mars are Coupled in Cancer

You may experience a very high voltage of energy. Let it work so that the cosmic architects can build you a lighted home and home life. If the urge to move comes over you, now is the time.

July 18 – Venus Enters Virgo

Details might catch you in a state of deep anticipation. Take time to go into Nature to expand your experience.

July 22 – The Sun Enters Leo

It's time to shine! Own your courage and roar, so you can become prosperous.

July 31 – Blue Moon in Aquarius

Re-calibration will be the theme for this moon. Open your heart to a new reality, accept the new and unusual.

July 31 – Mercury Enters Leo

Write love letters. Express your adorability. Focus on a better world where acceptance can rule.

Super-Sensitivity – July 1, 26-28

Let the chaos in the air do its work without your connection.

Low-Vitality – July 7-8, 12-13

The Earth is fragile; send love and healing. Beat your drum, send her a song.

♈ Aries	♋ Cancer	♐ Sagittarius	☽ Moon	♄ Saturn	☊ North Node	V/C Void-of-Course
♉ Taurus	♌ Leo	♑ Capricorn	☿ Mercury	♅ Uranus	☋ South Node	▲ Super-Sensitivity
♊ Gemini	♍ Virgo	♒ Aquarius	♀ Venus	♆ Neptune	➡ Enters	▼ Low-Vitality
	♎ Libra	♓ Pisces	♂ Mars	♇ Pluto	℞ Retrograde	
	♏ Scorpio	☉ Sun	♃ Jupiter	⚷ Chiron	S/D Stationary Direct	

July

Sunday	Monday	Tuesday	Wednesday	Thursday	Friday	Saturday
			1 ♄♆♇⚷℞ ▲ ☽→♑ 2:12AM ○ 9°♑55' 7:19PM 4. Keeping it simple avoids confusion.	**2** ♄♆♇⚷℞ 5. Set the pace that works best for you.	**3** ♄♆♇⚷℞ ☽ V/C 3:37AM ☽→♒ 5:20AM 6. Friendship is a two way street.	**4** ♄♆♇⚷℞ Independence Day 7. Your thinking process is flexible.
5 ♄♆♇⚷℞ ☽ V/C 5:31AM ☽→♓ 7:22AM 8. Celebrate your own success.	**6** ♄♆♇⚷℞ 9. Direct your prayer from the heart.	**7** ♄♆♇⚷℞ ▼ ☽ V/C 7:35AM ☽→♈ 9:37AM 10. Live today for what you desire.	**8** ♄♆♇⚷℞ ▼ ☿→♋ 11:53AM 2. Equal parts create wholeness.	**9** ♄♆♇⚷℞ ☽ V/C 6:46AM ☽→♉ 12:49PM 3. Lighten up with laughter.	**10** ♄♆♇⚷℞ 4. Start with a solid foundation.	**11** ♄♆♇⚷℞ ☽ V/C 2:52PM ☽→♊ 5:16PM 5. If you feel stuck, act a different way.
12 ♄♆♇⚷ ▼ 6. Support a healthy lifestyle.	**13** ♄♆♇⚷℞ ▼ ☽ V/C 8:31PM ☽→♋ 11:13PM 7. Take on a new way of learning.	**14** ♄♆♇⚷℞ 8. Success follows purpose.	**15** ♄♆♇⚷℞ ● 23°♋14' 6:24PM 9. Intention produce's results.	**16** ♄♆♇⚷℞ ☽ V/C 4:24AM ☽→♌ 7:14AM 10. Update something from the past.	**17** ♄♆♇⚷℞ 2. It's okay to choose again.	**18** ♄♆♇⚷℞ ☽ V/C 2:41PM ☽→♍ 5:46PM ♀→♍ 3:39PM 3. Go out and play today.
19 ♄♆♇⚷℞ 4. Reliability = Trustworthiness.	**20** ♄♆♇⚷℞ 5. Schedule a car repair.	**21** ♄♆♇⚷℞ ☽ V/C 3:06AM ☽→♎ 6:22AM 6. Provide a loving service for someone.	**22** ♄♆♇⚷℞ ☉→♌ 8:32PM 7. Accept your knowing.	**23** ♄♆♇⚷℞ ☽ V/C 11:11AM ☽→♏ 7:06PM ☿→♌ 5:15AM 8. Money is meant to be circulated.	**24** ♄♆♇⚷℞ 9. Keep body and Spirit connected.	**25** ♀♄♆♇⚷℞ ♀℞- 0°♍46' 2:30AM 10. Perseverance pays off.
26 ♀♄♆♇⚷℞ ▲ ☽ V/C 2:14AM ☽→♐ 5:24AM ♅℞- 20°♈30' 3:39AM 2. Act on the intuitive impulse.	**27** ♀♄♆♅♇⚷℞ ▲ 3. Joyful inspiration is yours today.	**28** ♀♄♆♅♇⚷℞ ▲ ☽ V/C 6:36AM ☽→♑ 11:47AM 4. Pay attention to details.	**29** ♀♄♆♅♇⚷℞ 5. Slow down and take your time.	**30** ♀♄♆♅♇⚷℞ ☽ V/C 11:49AM ☽→♒ 2:40PM 6. Have lunch with a family member.	**31** ♀♄♆♅♇⚷℞ ○ 7°♒56' 3:42AM ♀→♌ 8:28AM 7. You know how to get your answers.	

July 1st
7:19 PM

Full Moon in Capricorn

Degree Choice Points
  9° Capricorn 54'

Motivation Foster

Resistance Repress

Gift Be consistent.

Statement I Produce
  Body Knees
  Mind Authority Issues
  Spirit Self-Reliance

Element
  Earth – Determination, endurance, stability, structure, overly pragmatic, practical, stubborn.

First House Moon
  1° Capricorn 8'

First House Umbrella Theme
  I Am/I Produce – Your outer appearance, the way you present yourself, the way you dress, the way you enter a room, and what you leave behind when you leave the room.

Motivation Honor

Resistance Degrades

Gift Use intense energies to explore.

The Sun is Opposite the Moon

Full Moons are always in opposition to the Sun. This creates a feeling of tension between where you want to shine and how your feelings are flowing on a sensory level about the Sun's directive. The two forces seem like they are working against each other, yet they are on the same team displaying different techniques to obtain the same mission. The Capricorn/Cancer polarity creates tension between the quest for status and the need to feel secure.

Capricorn Goddess

Capricorn goddess, Kali, stands guard with her sword ready to slice away your demons of ignorance and resistance so you can move into your rightful position. She cuts away delusion and denial to assist you in creating beyond the limitations of your mind. Kali reminds you that every experience is an invitation to wake up. She will fight with you every step of the way until you accept your authority with integrity. When you accept her power and embrace Kali, your problems dissolve and you experience radiant bliss, freedom from limitation of the mind, and right use of your power.

On Your Altar

Colors Forest green, earth tones

Numerology 4 – Keep it simple to avoid confusion

Tarot Card Devil – Confinement, attachment to form, look at the broader view

Gemstones Smoky quartz, topaz, garnet

Plant remedy Rosemary – Activates appropriate memory

Fragrance Frankincense – Assists the Soul's entry into the body

Meditation

The freedom themes are provided by the zodiac sign and can be from this lifetime or other lifetimes. These meditations assist in dissolving blocks and opening pathways to new frontiers.

When the Moon is in Capricorn, begin by sitting down in a comfortable position, close your eyes and breathe in and out while asking for the Angel of Humility to show you the kernel of the heart of humility. Begin by releasing arrogance. Review the force of your thrusting will to determine the quality of your executive power. Release irritability and self-reproach. Renew the concept of true devotion and dedicate yourself to the Divine Master Plan of the Universe. This will set you free.

Capricorn Challenges and Victories

Say all of the statements in this section out loud. Then, underline the phrase that means the most to you. Use the phrase as your special affirmation for manifesting and co-creating throughout this phase of the moon.

I feel limited. I feel confined. I feel stuck. I feel there is no way out. Perhaps I am the target of someone's envy or jealousy, or perhaps I am jealous or I am envious. Maybe I am spending too much time in the outer world and putting too much value on material rewards, things, and possessions. Maybe I am trying to possess someone or limit their view or choice. I may feel there are no choices. Maybe I am living by someone else's rules and beliefs and forgot how to think for myself. I could also be overcome by fear and too terrorized to look at anything at all.

Today, I see and feel the limits of placing the source of love outside myself. I have tunnel vision and I seem to have forgotten to look at my options. I must ask myself today, "How many ways can I look at my life, my situation, or my perceived problems?" Today, I must expand my view to encompass 360-degrees instead of only 180-degrees. I begin by acknowledging to myself that today is the worst it is going to get. I know deep within me that if I allow myself to truly experience my bottom, the top will become visible to me. It is time to look at the brighter side. Begin by identifying the problem by writing it down on a piece of paper. Start with the phrase, "The problem is_____." Fill in the blank. Then, list as many solutions to the problem as you can. List at least three. Then, say these solutions out loud every day until the answer comes to you through a person, an idea, an event, or a choice.

Capricorn Homework

Put on a good pair of walking shoes and get ready to walk your blues away. It is time to get outside and feel the loving power of Mother Earth. The green of the trees refreshes your stagnant energy while you exhaust yourself to a point of vulnerability. Then, and only then, will you feel freedom. Give yourself permission to throw your watch away and learn to live in the moment.

The Capricorn moon is the reincarnation of Spirit emerging from the dark waters of our past emotions and releasing us from our fear of change and our fear of loss. Awaken your powerful and positive spiritual connection to be open to new possibilities. Ask yourself to release your emotional loyalty to the past. We are reminded of our need for material and emotional security at this time. In order to ensure this, we must learn to build a foundation for ourselves that is lit from within, made from the materials of love, goodwill, and intelligence.

July 1st
7:19 PM

Full Moon in Capricorn

Clearing the Slate for Freedom

Remember a time when you experienced the following trigger points. Write down what happened, forgive yourself, release it, and let it go to clear your slate for freedom.

Responsibility

- Forgive
- Release
- Let Go

Too Much Focus at Work

- Forgive
- Release
- Let Go

Too Much Focus on Status and Position

- Forgive
- Release
- Let Go

Lacking Compassion

- Forgive
- Release
- Let Go

Authority Challenges

- Forgive
- Release
- Let Go

My Freedom List

Say this statement out loud three times before writing your freedom list!

I am a free spiritual being and it is my desire to be free to think and to express myself fully.

From this day forward I resolve to be true – first to myself and my highest self, and then to the highest self in me which is the Source of Love That I Am.

Capricorn Freedom List Ideas

Now is the time to set myself free from obstacles to success, authority issues, sorrow and sadness, fear that blocks me, arrogance, irritability, limitations of time, priorities that are no longer valid, control and domination, the need to do it all alone, and responsibility.

July 1st
7:19 PM

Full Moon in Capricorn

How to Use the Moon Book With Your Chart

Fill in the blanks on the Cosmic Check-In page. Then look up the degree of the moon on the chart below. Take note of the "I" statement on the outside of the wheel where the moon is located. Now, locate the same degree on your own chart and make a note of the house and corresponding "I" statement. Go back to the Cosmic Check-In page and circle the two statements from the charts and read what you wrote. This will give you an idea about what to expect from this moon phase on a personal level.

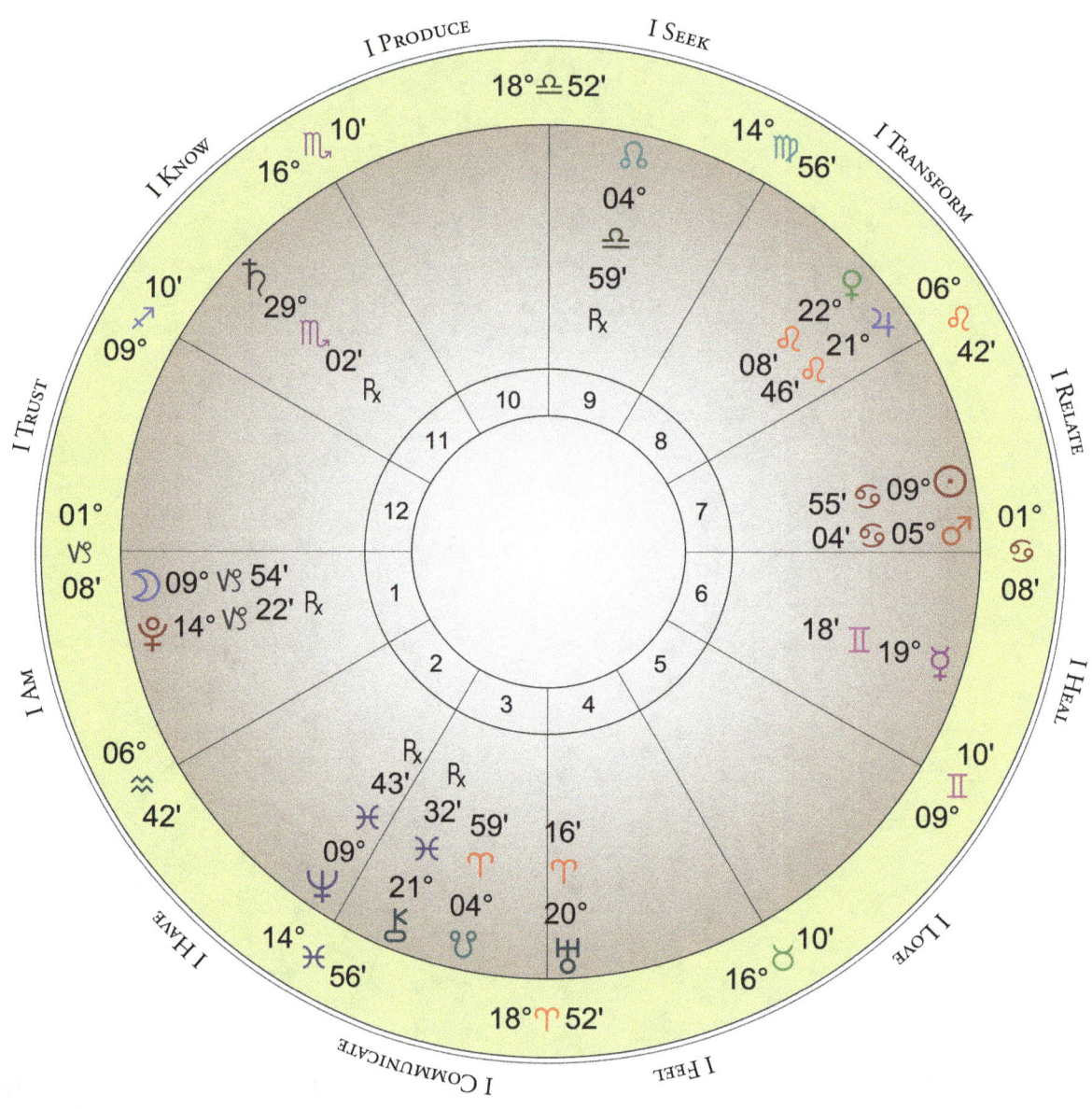

♈ Aries	♋ Cancer	♐ Sagittarius	☽ Moon	♄ Saturn	☊ North Node	V/C Void-of-Course
♉ Taurus	♌ Leo	♑ Capricorn	☿ Mercury	♅ Uranus	☋ South Node	▲ Super-Sensitivity
♊ Gemini	♍ Virgo	♒ Aquarius	♀ Venus	♆ Neptune	➡ Enters	▼ Low-Vitality
	♎ Libra	♓ Pisces	♂ Mars	♇ Pluto	℞ Retrograde	
	♏ Scorpio	☉ Sun	♃ Jupiter	⚷ Chiron	S/D Stationary Direct	

Cosmic Check-In

Take a moment to write a brief phrase for each "I" statement.
This activates all areas of your life for this creative cycle.

♑ I Produce

♒ I Know

♓ I Trust

♈ I Am

♉ I Have

♊ I Communicate

♋ I Feel

♌ I Love

♍ I Heal

♎ I Relate

♏ I Transform

♐ I Seek

July 15th
6:24 PM

New Moon in Cancer

Degree Choice Points
23° Cancer 14'

Motivation Choice of the Heart

Resistance Rivalry

Gift Your power is fueled by inspiration, revelation, compassion, and adaptation.

Statement I Feel
   Body Stomach
   Mind Worry
   Spirit Nurturing

Element
Water – Feelings, rhythm, cycles, supporting alignment, grace, creativity, receptivity, Divine Feminine.

Seventh House Moon
1° Cancer 9'

Seventh House Umbrella Theme
I Relate/I Feel – It's all about your people attraction and how you work in relationship with the people you attract.

Motivation Reflective

Resistance Longing for Magic

Gift Application of specific knowledge adds depth and detail.

When the Sun is in Cancer

It is now time to build our structure and foundation. Cancer holds the wisdom of the Great Cosmic Architect. Her statement is, "I build a lighted house and therein I dwell." The key is to use the materials of light, love, and wisdom to build your house and become the creator of form. Look within to see what lights your home and your body. Also check security systems, early environmental training, and mother/child relationships to see what materials you are using to build the structure for your life. Use this creating moon to build the structure you want.

Cancer Goddess

Birds are the symbol of expanded consciousness because they are born twice; once into the egg and once out of the egg. They are associated with rebirth and self-realization. Bird Woman is the Cancer goddess. She teaches us that, although we live in the illusion that security comes from our identity in the outer world, our true cosmic significance must be found within. Bird Woman directs us toward discovering our way home to our Soul, the place of lotus light. She has the ability to fly between Heaven and Earth, bringing communications from the angels and the spirit guides. She inspires souls to infuse matter with light – the true essence of co-creating.

On Your Altar

Colors Shades of gray, milky/creamy colors

Numerology 9 – Willingness and intention produce

Tarot Card Chariot – The ability to move forward, victory through action

Gemstones Pearl, moonstone, ruby

Plant Remedy Shooting Star – The ability to move straight ahead

Fragrance Peppermint – The essence of the Great Mother

My Co-Creation List

This or something better than this comes to me in an easy and pleasurable way, for the good of all concerned. Thank you, Universe!

Cancer Co-Creation Ideas

Now is the time to focus on manifesting being a good mother, new ways to be a mom, nurturing and self-love, the ability to see joy, a clutter-free home, your dream home, and inner and outer security.

July 15th
6:24 PM

New Moon in Cancer

Cancer Challenges and Victories

Say all of the statements in this section out loud. Then, underline the phrase that means the most to you. Use the phrase as your special affirmation for manifesting and co-creating throughout this phase of the moon.

Today I take advantage of my ability to take action and position myself for success. I clearly know that the road to success is before me, and all I need to do is move forward. I am aware that when I take action and move forward, the Universe fills in the dots. Whether I move left, right, or straight ahead doesn't matter—what matters is movement. Today, I release the indecisiveness that keeps me stuck. Today, I let go of vacillation that exhausts my mind. Today, I take my foot off of the brakes and find the gas pedal. I allow movement to occur, even if I don't know where I am going. When I take action, I trust that guideposts will appear. I am aware that action leads me to my new direction. So, today I know and GO! I remember that Karma comes to the space of non-action, while success comes through action. Action brings me to my victory. Standing still leads to regret, resentment, and chaos.

I am aware that action can be as simple as taking a walk on the beach, buying fresh flowers to add a new dimension to my home, or simply going to a new restaurant for lunch. I take action today to break up a crystallized pattern and, in so doing, my life begins to show me newfound awareness and light to guide me.

Cancer Homework

Cancer co-creates best when catering, writing cookbooks, marriage and family counseling, providing childcare, giving massage, or when engaged in genealogy, arts and crafts, architecture, and home-building.

During the Cancer New Moon cycle, we are asked to create light into form and turn it into beauty on four levels. Physically, we must feel nurtured and protected. Emotionally, we must set safe boundaries for the expression of our feelings. Mentally, we must release self-pity and embrace rightful thinking. Spiritually, we must hold the space for the infusion of light to shine inside all bodies on Earth.

Without Acknowledgment Progress Cannot Occur

Acknowledgement creates space for victory and gratitude, which automatically brings you to a level of completion so a new cycle of opportunity can occur in your life. When you celebrate your wins and acknowledge your victories with gratitude, you update your cells so that your ability to move forward is not hindered by a cellular holographic pattern that is stuck in the past. Cellular lag creates resistance and makes moving forward most difficult. The key is to stay continuously updated by acknowledging yourself for what you did do at the end of each day, rather than heading off to sleep thinning about what you did not do. By acknowledging what you did not do, you play into your karmic storage bank and keep your progress at bay. When you acknowledge yourself and your manifestations you are complete, and more cycles of opportunity become available to you in each new day. Be prepared for miracles!

Victory List

When a creation result is acknowledged it seals the deal. This makes room for more magnificence to expand into your life and increases your abundance factor adding to your ability to receive. As each aspect of your co-creation list arrives in your life, spend time allowing, acknowledging, and accepting it with the true gusto of gratitude! Keep your victory list active here.

Gratitude List

This fulfills the relationship between the giver and the receiver, which completes the cycle with the Universe so that a new beginning can be established.

July 15th
6:24 PM

New Moon in Cancer

How to Use the Moon Book With Your Chart

Fill in the blanks on the Cosmic Check-In page. Then look up the degree of the moon on the chart below. Take note of the "I" statement on the outside of the wheel where the moon is located. Now, locate the same degree on your own chart and make a note of the house and corresponding "I" statement. Go back to the Cosmic Check-In page and circle the two statements from the charts and read what you wrote. This will give you an idea about what to expect from this moon phase on a personal level.

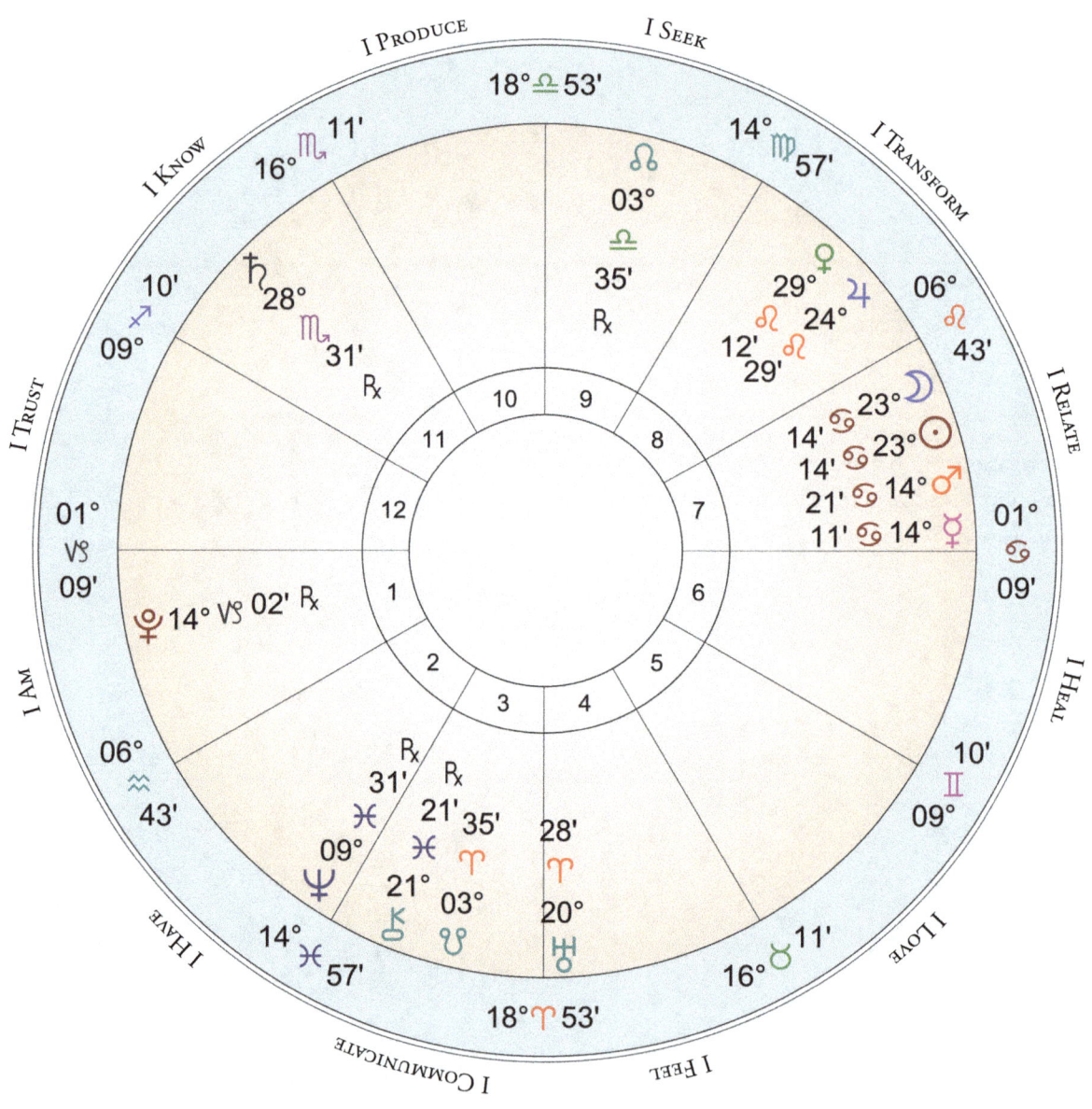

♈ Aries	♋ Cancer	♐ Sagittarius	☽ Moon	♄ Saturn	☊ North Node	V/C Void-of-Course
♉ Taurus	♌ Leo	♑ Capricorn	☿ Mercury	♅ Uranus	☋ South Node	▲ Super-Sensitivity
♊ Gemini	♍ Virgo	♒ Aquarius	♀ Venus	♆ Neptune	➡ Enters	▼ Low-Vitality
	♎ Libra	♓ Pisces	♂ Mars	♇ Pluto	℞ Retrograde	
	♏ Scorpio	☉ Sun	♃ Jupiter	⚷ Chiron	SD Stationary Direct	

Cosmic Check-In

Take a moment to write a brief phrase for each "I" statement.
This activates all areas of your life for this creative cycle.

♋ I Feel

♌ I Love

♍ I Heal

♎ I Relate

♏ I Transform

♐ I Seek

♑ I Produce

♒ I Know

♓ I Trust

♈ I Am

♉ I Have

♊ I Communicate

July 31st
3:42 AM

Full Moon in Aquarius

Degree Choice Points
7° Aquarius 55'

Motivation Director

Resistance Dated (Stuck)

Gift Update your wardrobe to match your new identity.

Statement I Know
Body Ankles
Mind True Genius
Spirit Vision

Element
Air – Curiosity, learning, flexibility, and directs consciousness towards manifesting form.

Eighth House Moon
7° Capricorn 29'

Eighth House Umbrella Theme
I Transform/I Know – How you share money and other resources, what you keep hidden.

Motivation Executive

Resistance Elitism

Gift Amplification of intelligence opens the gateway to elevated learning.

Karmic Awakening: Scorpio/Taurus

Karma will raise its head when you feel the need to get tangible results that produce something of value, rather than combining resources and having a transformational experience. In simpler terms, the karmic challenge will go head-to-head when the need to accumulate has trouble letting go of outcomes. Aries is on the cusp of Taurus, so you may be seen as a leader, but the Taurus side asks you to create something long-lasting. Libra on the cusp of Scorpio requires diplomacy and may overshadow your inner power and intensify karma that could rob you of the chance to create change.

The Sun is Opposite the Moon

Full Moons are always in opposition to the Sun. This creates a feeling of tension between where you want to shine and how your feelings are flowing on a sensory level about the Sun's directive. The two forces seem like they are working against each other, yet they are on the same team displaying different techniques to obtain the same mission. The Aquarian/Leo polarity creates tension between the quest for group interaction and the recognition of self.

Aquarius Goddess

Hera, the Queen of Heaven, was responsible for every aspect of existence. Her name means "Great Lady." Legend has it that she created the Milky Way from the milk in her breasts. When the drops of milk came to Earth, white lily fields manifested everywhere. Hera was the only goddess who accompanied women through every aspect of their lives. She was the great protector of their marriages, their children, and their welfare. She was an advocate for women until she married Zeus and had a complete personality change, cursing all women in whom Zeus was interested sexually. Scorned, she turned vindictive toward the women who were the objects of Zeus' desire, rather that placing her rage on Zeus, where it belonged. Her jealously became her trademark. When the Moon is full in Aquarius we must learn the Art of Detachment so we don't sell out to emotional entrapments.

On Your Altar

Colors Electric colors, neon, multi-colors, pearl white

Numerology 7 – You know how to get your answers

Tarot Card Star – Being guided by a higher source

Gemstones Aquamarine, amethyst, opal

Plant remedy Queen of the Night Cactus – The ability to see in the dark

Fragrance Myrrh – Healing the nervous system

Meditation

The freedom themes are provided by the zodiac sign and can be from this lifetime or other lifetimes. These meditations assist in dissolving blocks and opening pathways to new frontiers.

The Aquarius Full Moon promotes the rearrangement of plans. Sit quietly and close your eyes, breathe in and breathe out while watching for sudden changes in priorities and an urge to express yourself more freely. Watch out for hyperactivity and carelessness. The unexpected breakthrough in an ungratifying situation can occur, sparking the creation of a new pathway. Take time to connect to angelic forces to see the other side of frenzy and fantasy in order to know practical passion. Reconcile with times when your zeal has hurt others. Make contact with the magnetic energy currents of the atmosphere to recharge the body and behold the cosmic braille points of things to come. Receive instructions from the higher worlds to be the guardian of the unknown inventive treasures.

Aquarius Challenges and Victories

Say all of the statements in this section out loud. Then, underline the phrase that means the most to you. Use the phrase as your special affirmation for manifesting and co-creating throughout this phase of the moon.

Today my true potential can be realized. All I have to do is take a risk and know that my faith is in operation. My future is very bright and offers me a promise of things to come. Today is a day of destiny. I have chosen this day to determine a DESTINY PROMISE I MADE TO MYSELF BEFORE I CAME INTO THIS LIFE. All that is required of me is to move out of my comfort zone and take a risk. I am aware that faith cannot be determined without risk. I take the risk to move into the next space of creation in my life. I release fear and move into faith, knowing full well that my logic and reason are part of the fear that keeps me stuck.

I am reminded that the kingdom of heaven is open to the child. I find the child within me today to embrace what life has for me with open arms and a spirit of adventure. I know my true potential lives inside my magical child and she/he is willing to play and go for the gusto. I am here in this life to fulfill my promise to experience life to the fullest and to release the fear of judgment that has hounded me and kept me from playing full-out. I remember that when I experience, I gather a knowledge base within my Soul and keep my agreement with myself and the Universe. I connect to my super-consciousness and take on the bigger view of my life and all that it has to offer me when I risk reason and take a leap of faith. I know in the depth of my awareness that, if I jump off the diving board, there will be water in the pool. I am willing to risk reason for an experience. Everything I ever wanted is one step outside my comfort zone. I go for the GUSTO today! I release my fear today and turn it into faith. I trust in the promise of things to come. I know my potential is realized today, and that all I have to do is say "YES!" to life!

Aquarius Homework

The Aquarius moon reminds us of our connection to solar fire (the heart of the Sun) also known as the Heart of the Cosmos. During this time, we get our vitality recharged and our potent power comes into play motivating the masses to receive more energy to transmute into the new world. Voice all that you know to be true to the point of self-realization where your authentic purpose can be revealed to you. This is the moment where you have released all that has kept you from your true sense of freedom. Remember to replenish all the electrolytes in your system.

July 31st
3:42 AM

Full Moon in Aquarius

Clearing the Slate for Freedom

Remember a time when you experienced the following trigger points. Write down what happened, forgive yourself, release it, and let it go to clear your slate for freedom.

Stubborn

- Forgive
- Release
- Let Go

Spiritual Elitism

- Forgive
- Release
- Let Go

Frenzy and Chaos

- Forgive
- Release
- Let Go

Living in the Future

- Forgive
- Release
- Let Go

Rebellion

- Forgive
- Release
- Let Go

My Freedom List

Say this statement out loud three times before writing your freedom list!

I am a free spiritual being and it is my desire to be free to think and to express myself fully.

Freedom is mine when I live my Truth!

Aquarius Freedom List Ideas

Now is the time to set myself free from resistance to authority figures, blocks to living in the moment, unnecessary rebellion, non-productive frenzy and fantasy, the need to be spontaneous, and people who aren't team players.

July 31st
3:42 AM

Full Moon in Aquarius

How to Use the Moon Book With Your Chart

Fill in the blanks on the Cosmic Check-In page. Then look up the degree of the moon on the chart below. Take note of the "I" statement on the outside of the wheel where the moon is located. Now, locate the same degree on your own chart and make a note of the house and corresponding "I" statement. Go back to the Cosmic Check-In page and circle the two statements from the charts and read what you wrote. This will give you an idea about what to expect from this moon phase on a personal level.

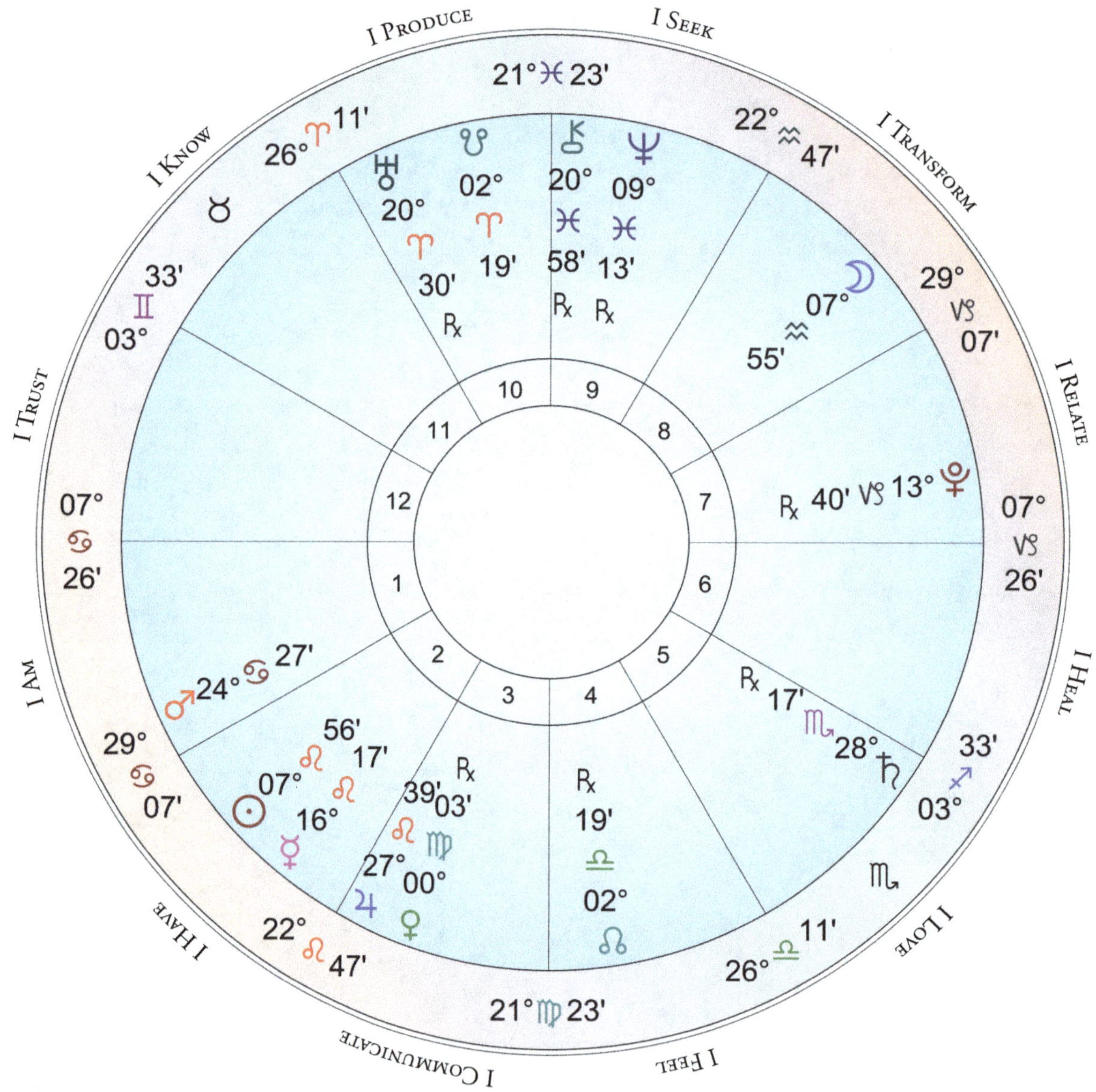

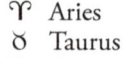

♈ Aries	♋ Cancer	♐ Sagittarius	☽ Moon	♄ Saturn	☊ North Node	V/C Void-of-Course
♉ Taurus	♌ Leo	♑ Capricorn	☿ Mercury	♅ Uranus	☋ South Node	▲ Super-Sensitivity
♊ Gemini	♍ Virgo	♒ Aquarius	♀ Venus	♆ Neptune	➡ Enters	▼ Low-Vitality
	♎ Libra	♓ Pisces	♂ Mars	♇ Pluto	℞ Retrograde	
	♏ Scorpio	☉ Sun	♃ Jupiter	⚷ Chiron	S/D Stationary Direct	

Cosmic Check-In

Take a moment to write a brief phrase for each "I" statement.
This activates all areas of your life for this creative cycle.

♒ I Know

♓ I Trust

♈ I Am

♉ I Have

♊ I Communicate

♋ I Feel

♌ I Love

♍ I Heal

♎ I Relate

♏ I Transform

♐ I Seek

♑ I Produce

Planetary Highlights

August 1 – Saturn in Scorpio goes out of Retrograde

This could help the mood swings a bit, making you feel less aggressive emotionally. Expect some future focus to capture your interest motivating a "full speed ahead" attitude.

Neptune is Retrograde in Pisces Until November 18

The process of escaping is in place. Avoidance is becoming your new name. See if you can get under this feeling and bring it up into the light. Otherwise you could sink into daydreaming your life away. If you can't catch it, regrets will come later.

Pluto is Retrograde in Capricorn Until September 24

Agony and ecstasy are simultaneously moving you towards a transformation. Let go and you will manifest your pot of gold.

Uranus is Retrograde in Aries Until December 25

If you are holding on to the old way of doing things, Uranus will knock your socks off and move you out of the confinement of your past. Allow the rules to float downstream, so you can arrive at a new place of freedom.

Chiron is Retrograde in Pisces Until November 27

The pain of your wound can leave you with a feeling of being cut off from the source of support, thus creating an emotional exile. Healing occurs when you accept unification.

August 7 – Mercury Enters Virgo

Mercury leaves the party behind to have the home court advantage in Virgo. The laser sharp mind can really get good mileage here matching up with the details of Virgo. Expect an accurate approach to be in line for some great manifesting.

August 8 – Mars Enters Leo

Expect to be unstoppable with the double fire expression. Dynamic Mars will activate all of the Leo qualities. Get ready to experience some abundant living. Grand style is the theme.

August 11 – Jupiter Enters Virgo

The broad strokes of Jupiter will be forced to face the details of the day. This could be confining and the expansion will be good for Virgos. The "Big Picture" may fade into the distance in exchange for excellence and a higher standard, adding quality to quantity.

August 14 – New Moon in Leo

Expect an increased growth spurt in passion, with a twist of drama, as it relates to marriage and banking laws.

August 14 – Neptune in Pisces Opposite Mercury in Virgo

This could force-feed Neptune into actualizing a dream with the influence of the sharp Mercury mind.

August 23 – The Sun Enters Virgo

The party is over, time to go to work.

August 27 – Mercury Enters Libra

This is a very favorable combination here as charm and wit enter conversations and negotiations. Expect positive results in all legal issues.

August 29 – Full Moon in Pisces

It's time to celebrate accomplishments, completions, finish up health treatments, and set yourself free. This moon is connected to the Sun, Jupiter, and dreamy Neptune. Many dreams could make it to reality this week.

August 29 – Venus Retrograde and Mars Conjunct in Leo

A blast from the past could throw a wrench on your path. Old lovers or banking issues could resurface – watch out!

August 29 – North Node and Mercury Coupled in Libra

Pay attention to what is said, especially as it applies to relationship. Something new is on the horizon and, if you listen, you may learn something from the heavens about relating.

Super-Sensitivity – August 23-24

The energies are moving fast on these days. Slow down to avoid accidents.

Low-Vitality – August 9-10

Take time out, rest, stay in bed, and nap. Do as little as possible in the physical department.

♈ Aries	♋ Cancer	♐ Sagittarius	☽ Moon	♄ Saturn	☊ North Node	V/C Void-of-Course
♉ Taurus	♌ Leo	♑ Capricorn	☿ Mercury	♅ Uranus	☋ South Node	▲ Super-Sensitivity
♊ Gemini	♍ Virgo	♒ Aquarius	♀ Venus	♆ Neptune	➡ Enters	▼ Low-Vitality
	♎ Libra	♓ Pisces	♂ Mars	♇ Pluto	℞ Retrograde	
	♏ Scorpio	☉ Sun	♃ Jupiter	⚷ Chiron	S/D Stationary Direct	

August

Sunday	Monday	Tuesday	Wednesday	Thursday	Friday	Saturday
						1 ♀♆♇♅⚷℞ ☽ V/C 3:02PM ☽→♓ 3:36PM ♄SD-28°♏17' 10:54PM 8. Verbalize what you desire to create.
2 ♀♆♇♅⚷℞ 9. Pray intently from your heart.	3 ♀♆♇♅⚷℞ ☽ V/C 1:35PM ☽→♈ 4:23PM 10. Live each day fully in the now.	4 ♀♆♇♅⚷℞ 2. Be sure to balance work with play.	5 ♀♆♇♅⚷℞ ☽ V/C 4:29PM ☽→♉ 6:29PM 3. See the cosmic joke.	6 ♀♆♇♅⚷℞ 4. Organize before you proceed.	7 ♀♆♇♅⚷℞ ☽ V/C 9:45PM ☽→♊ 10:39PM ☿→♍ 12:16PM 5. If it works, don't change a thing.	8 ♀♆♇♅⚷℞ ♂→♌ 4:33PM 7. Know what is best for you.
9 ♀♆♇♅⚷℞ ▼ 8. Helping someone manifest helps you.	10 ♀♆♇♅⚷℞ ▼ ☽ V/C 4:44AM ☽→♋ 5:08AM 9. Pray for a positive outcome.	11 ♀♆♇♅⚷℞ ♃→♍ 4:12AM 10. Envision a bright tomorrow.	12 ♀♆♇♅⚷℞ ☽ V/C 10:43AM ☽→♌ 1:52PM 2. Once you have decided, act.	13 ♀♆♇♅⚷℞ 3. Recycling serves a creative purpose.	14 ♀♆♇♅⚷℞ ☽ V/C 9:36PM ●21°♌31' 7:53AM 4. Be energized by your surroundings.	15 ♀♆♇♅⚷℞ ☽→♍ 12:45AM 5. Choose to eliminate toxins.
16 ♀♆♇♅⚷℞ 6. Use the logic your body provides.	17 ♀♆♇♅⚷℞ ☽ V/C 10:16AM ☽→♎ 1:22PM 7. Your knowledge helps others.	18 ♀♆♇♅⚷℞ 8. Celebrate achievements today.	19 ♀♆♇♅⚷℞ ☽ V/C 7:56PM 9. Your passion and mission relate.	20 ♀♆♇♅⚷℞ ☽→♏ 2:24AM 10. An end is a new beginning .	21 ♀♆♇♅⚷℞ 2. Slow down; find your balance.	22 ♀♆♇♅⚷℞ ☽ V/C 12:30PM ☽→♐ 1:40PM 3. Life is filled with creative purpose.
23 ♀♆♇♅⚷℞ ▲ ☉→♍ 3:38AM 4. If it's logical, it's probably right.	24 ♀♆♇♅⚷℞ ▲ ☽ V/C 3:03PM ☽→♑ 9:21PM 5. Change will suit your purpose.	25 ♀♆♇♅⚷℞ 6. The heart knows love.	26 ♀♆♇♅⚷℞ 7. The learning process never ends.	27 ♀♆♇♅⚷℞ ☽ V/C 12:19AM ☽→♒ 1:03AM ☿→♎ 8:46AM 8. Money is your friend.	28 ♀♆♇♅⚷℞ 9. Follow your intuition.	29 ♀♆♇♅⚷℞ ○6°♓6' 11:35AM ☽ V/C 12:02AM ☽→♓ 1:50AM 10. See each day as a new beginning.
30 ♀♆♇♅⚷℞ ☽ V/C 11:53PM 2. One decision may lead to another.	31 ♀♆♇♅⚷℞ ☽→♈ 1:32AM 3. Refine your creative expression.					

August 14th
7:53 AM

New Moon in Leo

Degree Choice Points
21° Leo 30'

Motivation Common Sense

Resistance Impractical

Gift Birth parents aren't necessarily your best nurturers.

Statement I Love
  Body Heart
  Mind Self-Confidence
  Spirit Generosity

Element
  Fire – Passion, enthusiasm, warmth, centered in personal identity.

Twelfth House Moon
13° Leo 45'

Twelfth House Umbrella Theme
  I Trust/I Love – Determine how you deal with your karma, unconscious software, and what you will experience in order to attain mastery by completing your karma. It is also about the way you connect to the Divine.

Motivation Inspired Manifestation

Resistance Lack of Interest

Gift Redecorate, rebuild, and renew your environment.

When the Sun is in Leo

This is the time when you feel the power from the Sun, the heart of the Cosmos. Leo has a direct relationship with the Sun's heart. The Sun rules your identity. Now is the time to shine and stand tall in the center of your life. Allow yourself to feel the power of your individual conscious Self. When you align with the power of the Sun, you become radiant. This radiance gives you the power to transmit energy into life. Personal fulfillment becomes a reality when you align your will with love. Remember to live love every day!

Leo Goddess

The Sun Goddess makes her appearance when the Sun is setting. She paints with the vast palette of colors available as the day turns to night. She infuses tomorrow's dreams and goals with vitality. She lives in the West where the feminine principle lives. She teaches you to express your creative power potential. She reminds you that the promise of tomorrow comes when you live in truth and integrity and follow the light of your awareness, even through the dark. When the flash of green appears to you at sunset, you know you have connected with the Sun Goddess.

On Your Altar

Colors Royal purple, royal blue, orange

Numerology 4 – Be energized by your surroundings

Tarot Card Sun – To stand tall in the center of life

Gemstones Peridot, emerald, amber

Plant Remedy Sunflower – Standing tall in the center of your garden

Fragrance Jasmine – Remembering your Soul's original intention

My Co-Creation List

This or something better than this comes to me in an easy and pleasurable way, for the good of all concerned. Thank you, Universe!

Leo Co-Creation Ideas

Now is the time to focus on manifesting new love or new ways of loving, new creative ways of expressing myself, bonding with those I love, quality time with those I love, knowledge of my Soul's intention, fun with my children, being a bright beaming light, and connecting to the hearts of humanity.

August 14th
7:53 AM

New Moon in Leo

Leo Challenges and Victories

Say all of the statements in this section out loud. Then, underline the phrase that means the most to you. Use the phrase as your special affirmation for manifesting and co-creating throughout this phase of the moon.

Today, I am at the center of bliss, happiness, abundance, and total celebration. It is my time to shine and feel the power of my true self blasting the Universe, the entire planet, and all of life with the light of my awareness. There is nothing that can stop me today, because I am free to be me. When I am free to be me, I can stand naked in the daylight and have nothing to hide. I truly know that all of life loves me and I love all of life. I feel the radiance and vibration of my being activating me with aliveness, vitality, and charisma. I know that I can make a difference because I celebrate life by infusing, sparking, and igniting matter with light. I am open and ready to embrace all that comes to me with joy. I say "YES!" to all opportunities today; knowing that today is my day. I am in the flow of abundance and I let abundance flow through me.

The child within me is open and ready to play full out; there is not a cloud in the sky today that can eclipse me or place a shadow on me and keep me from my true level of power. I am aware that the child state of being within me simply says yes to action and action is power. When I take action today, my possibilities are endless because they are generated from my true self and motivated by happiness, joy, and freedom. The child within me is able to play full out because I have birthed myself beyond my old perception of blocks. I know that in taking this true power, to be motivated by happiness, pathways on all levels and in all dimensions can open to the empowerment of joy. Empowerment is mine today because I am shining from within myself and I know my deepest self is connected to the source. Empowerment occurs when I live from the inside out. Today, I wave the banner of my being from within, feel the glow, and go.

Leo Homework

The Leo co-creates best through fashion and jewelry design, glamour, politics, super-modeling, movie stardom, child advocacy, fundraising, toy and game design, image consulting, authoring children's books, sales, and cardiology.

Leo gets you closer to your essential self, reminding you of your Soul's original intention. You become ready to receive the benefits of reflective light and radiating light at the same time, so that you can see your personality and your Soul connecting to love which constitutes a new level of fulfillment. Expect purification, transmutation, communication, and mastery to be part of your personal experience.

Without Acknowledgment Progress Cannot Occur

Acknowledgement creates space for victory and gratitude, which automatically brings you to a level of completion so a new cycle of opportunity can occur in your life. When you celebrate your wins and acknowledge your victories with gratitude, you update your cells so that your ability to move forward is not hindered by a cellular holographic pattern that is stuck in the past. Cellular lag creates resistance and makes moving forward most difficult. The key is to stay continuously updated by acknowledging yourself for what you did do at the end of each day, rather than heading off to sleep thinning about what you did not do. By acknowledging what you did not do, you play into your karmic storage bank and keep your progress at bay. When you acknowledge yourself and your manifestations you are complete, and more cycles of opportunity become available to you in each new day. Be prepared for miracles!

Victory List

When a creation result is acknowledged it seals the deal. This makes room for more magnificence to expand into your life and increases your abundance factor adding to your ability to receive. As each aspect of your co-creation list arrives in your life, spend time allowing, acknowledging, and accepting it with the true gusto of gratitude! Keep your victory list active here.

This fulfills the relationship between the giver and the receiver, which completes the cycle with the Universe so that a new beginning can be established.

Gratitude List

August 14th
7:53 AM

New Moon in Leo

How to Use the Moon Book With Your Chart

Fill in the blanks on the Cosmic Check-In page. Then look up the degree of the moon on the chart below. Take note of the "I" statement on the outside of the wheel where the moon is located. Now, locate the same degree on your own chart and make a note of the house and corresponding "I" statement. Go back to the Cosmic Check-In page and circle the two statements from the charts and read what you wrote. This will give you an idea about what to expect from this moon phase on a personal level.

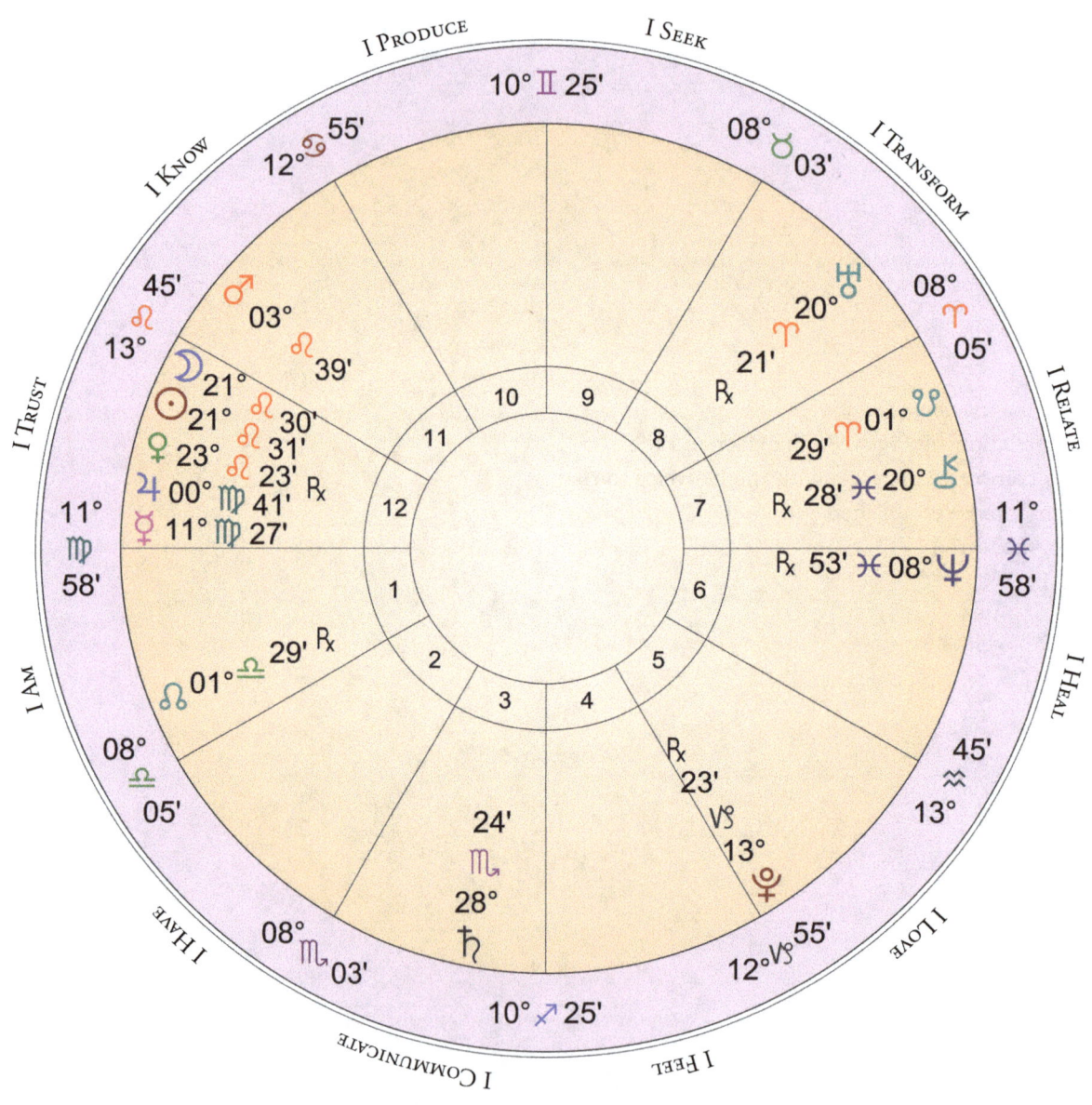

♈ Aries	♋ Cancer	♐ Sagittarius	☽ Moon	♄ Saturn	☊ North Node	V/C Void-of-Course
♉ Taurus	♌ Leo	♑ Capricorn	☿ Mercury	♅ Uranus	☋ South Node	▲ Super-Sensitivity
♊ Gemini	♍ Virgo	♒ Aquarius	♀ Venus	♆ Neptune	➡ Enters	▼ Low-Vitality
	♎ Libra	♓ Pisces	♂ Mars	♇ Pluto	℞ Retrograde	
	♏ Scorpio	☉ Sun	♃ Jupiter	⚷ Chiron	S/D Stationary Direct	

152

Cosmic Check-In

Take a moment to write a brief phrase for each "I" statement.
This activates all areas of your life for this creative cycle.

♌ I Love

♍ I Heal

♎ I Relate

♏ I Transform

♐ I Seek

♑ I Produce

♒ I Know

♓ I Trust

♈ I Am

♉ I Have

♊ I Communicate

♋ I Feel

August 29th
11:35 AM

Full Moon in Pisces

Degree Choice Points
6° Pisces 6'

Motivation
Sacrifice for the Many

Resistance Anti-Social

Gift Use a piece of golden tiger eye to lift your spirits.

Statement I Trust
Body Feet
Mind Super-Sensitive
Spirit Mystical

Element
Water – Feeling, rhythm, living by cycles, flowing, escapism from reality.

Fourth House Moon
16° Aquarius 47'

Fourth House Umbrella Theme
I Feel/I Trust – The way your early environmental training set your foundation for living and why you chose your mother.

Motivation Organizational Mastery

Resistance Distrustful

Gift Detach from the outcome.

The Sun is Opposite the Moon

Full Moons are always in opposition to the Sun. This creates a feeling of tension between where you want to shine and how your feelings are flowing on a sensory level about the Sun's directive. The two forces seem like they are working against each other, yet they are on the same team displaying different techniques to obtain the same mission. The Pisces/Virgo polarity creates tension between addiction and perfection.

Pisces Goddess

The Pisces goddess, Kuan Yin, is the embodiment of all that is compassionate. She guides you to the abyss, a place known as the "Great Unknown." It is here that the ego drops away and there is only the truth of your nature. Kuan Yin protects you and holds you when you let go, surrender, and evolve. She is the goddess of emptiness and helps you to constantly empty yourself of the limitations of the ego: fear, doubt, guilt, shame, and denial. In exchange, you gain beauty, light, and service. She is often pictured riding on the head of a dragon. It is the breath of the dragon that pierces the veil of illusion.

On Your Altar

Colors Greens, blues, amethyst, aquamarine

Numerology 10 – See each day as a new beginning

Tarot Card The Hanged Man – Learning to let go

Gemstones Opal, turquoise, amethyst

Plant remedy Passion flower – The ability to live in the here and now

Fragrance White lotus – Connecting to the Divine without arrogance

Meditation

The freedom themes are provided by the zodiac sign and can be from this lifetime or other lifetimes. These meditations assist in dissolving blocks and opening pathways to new frontiers.

When the Moon is in Pisces, take time out to sit quietly. Close your eyes and breathe in and out. Ask the Angel of Records to accompany you to see the chaotic regions in the matrix of your mind. See your hidden desires. Look with the eye of compassion to understand where these desires have hurt you or others. Expect a major healing by asking for grace to be given to you while visiting these sordid versions of your past. Make amends with yourself for romanticizing your past and release any escape fantasies that keep you from being present with yourself and with life. Allow yourself to be ignited with your power to heal. Visit hospitals and prisons; offer healings. Focus on your creative, spiritual self.

Pisces Challenges and Victories

Say all of the statements in this section out loud. Then, underline the phrase that means the most to you. Use the phrase as your special affirmation for manifesting and co-creating throughout this phase of the moon.

The best thing I can do for myself today is to get out of the way, so life can take its own course without the interference of my control drama. I take time out to let go and let things be. I have become too involved in the details and have lost sight of the vastness of the Universe, and the infinite possibilities that are available to me at all times and in every moment. I am aware that all I need is a different way of seeing what I have perceived as a problem, and that my view is limited by my needs, rather than by accepting things as they are. I trust that, when I get out of the way and give space to the power of NOW, all is in Divine Order and everything works out for the good of all concerned. This is the day when doing nothing gets me everything. I allow myself to experience the void. I empty myself of my rigidity, small-mindedness, racing thoughts, the need to be right, and to control outcomes. I know that non-action will present me with right action. I give the Universe a chance and trust the view to be larger than mine. When I accept myself as I am, I learn what I can become. I remove myself from all of the mind chatter and allow for silence to do its work. I am aware that a quiet mind brings me peace (the absence of conflict). In turning upside down, I see how right-side-up things really are. Acceptance brings me perspective. Acceptance sets me free. Acceptance brings me wholeness. Acceptance widens my mind.

Pisces Homework

Get a foot massage to bring your energy back to the ground. Feel the power of your path on the bottom of your feet. Now that you are back to your body, it is time to make a list of the ways your boundaries get breached. After the completion of your list, read it out loud and then throw it in the ocean. Now it is time to see the seed of life, the seed of love, and the seed of power that were planted into the womb of evolution.

August 29th
11:35 AM

Full Moon in Pisces

Clearing the Slate for Freedom

Remember a time when you experienced the following trigger points. Write down what happened, forgive yourself, release it, and let it go to clear your slate for freedom.

Unrealistic

- Forgive
- Release
- Let Go

Escape Dramas

- Forgive
- Release
- Let Go

Addictions

- Forgive
- Release
- Let Go

Emotionally Unreliable

- Forgive
- Release
- Let Go

Aimless

- Forgive
- Release
- Let Go

My Freedom List

Say this statement out loud three times before writing your freedom list!

I am a free spiritual being and it is my desire to be free to think and to express myself fully.

From this day forward I resolve to be true – first to myself and my highest self, and then to the highest self in me which is the Source of Love That I Am.

Pisces Freedom List Ideas

Now is the time to set myself free from addictions, illusions and fantasy, escape dramas, martyrdom, victimhood, and mental chaos.

August 29th
11:35 AM

Full Moon in Pisces

How to Use the Moon Book With Your Chart

Fill in the blanks on the Cosmic Check-In page. Then look up the degree of the moon on the chart below. Take note of the "I" statement on the outside of the wheel where the moon is located. Now, locate the same degree on your own chart and make a note of the house and corresponding "I" statement. Go back to the Cosmic Check-In page and circle the two statements from the charts and read what you wrote. This will give you an idea about what to expect from this moon phase on a personal level.

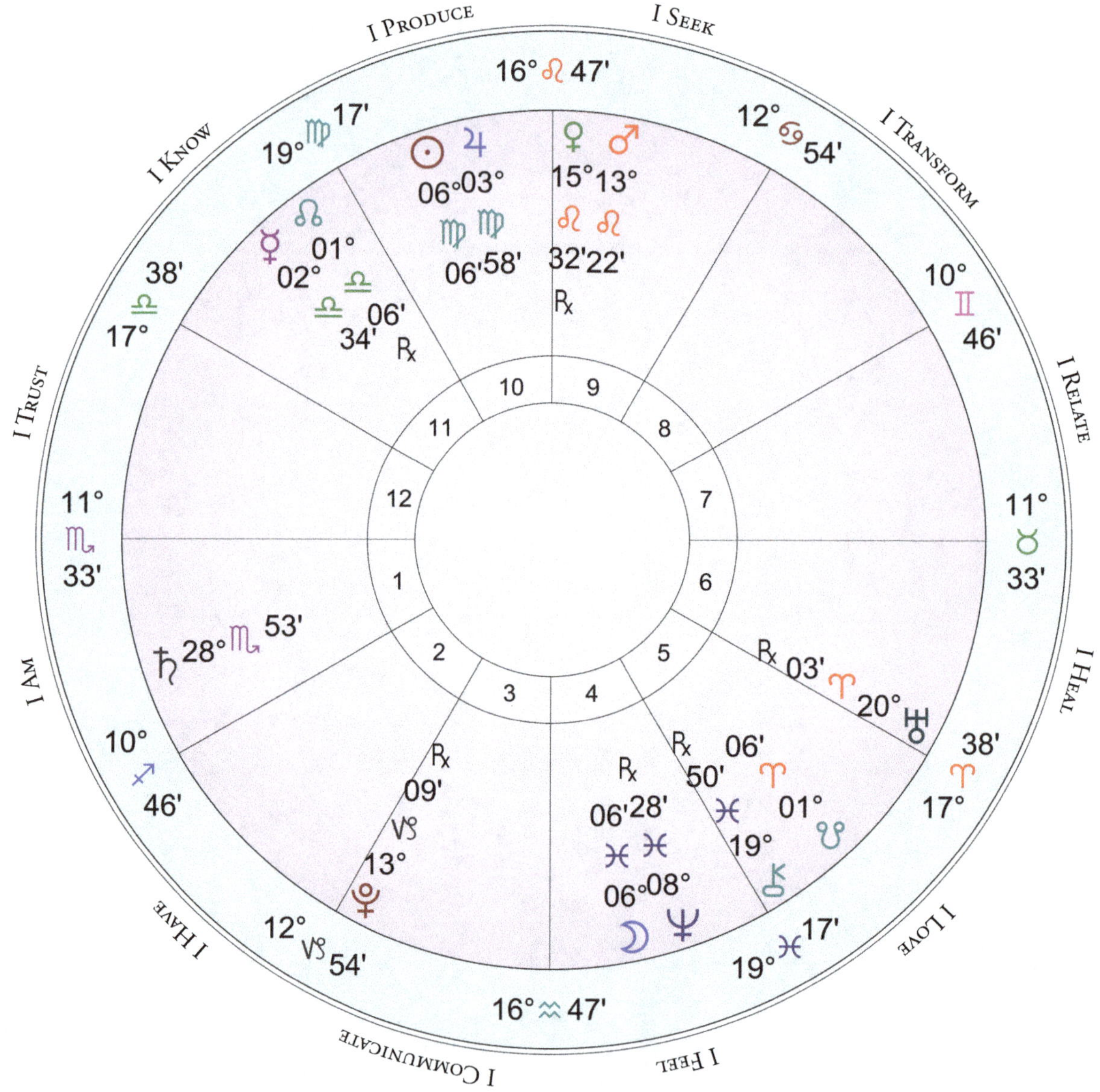

♈ Aries	♋ Cancer	♐ Sagittarius	☽ Moon	♄ Saturn	☊ North Node	V/C Void-of-Course
♉ Taurus	♌ Leo	♑ Capricorn	☿ Mercury	♅ Uranus	☋ South Node	▲ Super-Sensitivity
♊ Gemini	♍ Virgo	♒ Aquarius	♀ Venus	♆ Neptune	➡ Enters	▼ Low-Vitality
	♎ Libra	♓ Pisces	♂ Mars	♇ Pluto	℞ Retrograde	
	♏ Scorpio	☉ Sun	♃ Jupiter	⚷ Chiron	S/D Stationary Direct	

160

Cosmic Check-In

Take a moment to write a brief phrase for each "I" statement.
This activates all areas of your life for this creative cycle.

♓ I Trust

♈ I Am

♉ I Have

♊ I Communicate

♋ I Feel

♌ I Love

♍ I Heal

♎ I Relate

♏ I Transform

♐ I Seek

♑ I Produce

♒ I Know

Planetary Highlights

Venus Stays Retrograde in Leo Until September 6

Love, Live, and Laugh! Soak up all the love and playfulness you can right now.

Neptune Continues to be Retrograde in Pisces Until November 18

Do a check-up on yourself to see if you are still complaining about something in your past. If so, do what you can to stop! It's time to remember that complaining stops the creative process.

Pluto Continues to be Retrograde in Capricorn Until September 24

By now you should have advanced your abundance package by gathering enough courage to allow yourself to be prosperous! Test yourself by going "window shopping" to see where your mind is accepting or rejecting the idea of abundance.

Uranus Continues to be Retrograde in Aries Until December 25

How are you doing with reversals or change of events? It is Uranus' job to shake you up. Expect some people to enter your life temporarily to break you out of your old ways. Once their job is over, they will be gone.

Chiron Continues to be Retrograde in Pisces Until November 27

There is a tendency to try to heal yourself through relationships. Heal yourself from within to learn that the source of love is inside of you, not outside. This will help you avoid many years of suffering.

September 17 – Mercury goes Retrograde in Libra Until October 9

It's time to look back and re-interpret what you have said or heard from loved ones where there is a misunderstanding. Remember, Libra has a big tank of unresolved false accusations. It is time to add some reality to this issue and move on.

September 1-12 – Mars and Venus are Still Dancing

Make love, not war! This is a powerful choice point. I hope you choose love!

September 12 – Solar Eclipse – New Moon in Virgo

Release 19 years of habits that have not been operating at top speed. Then, write your new moon manifestation list about how the "healthier you" will live your life.

September 12 – Chiron in Pisces Opposing Sun and Moon in Virgo

This could be a major healing moment for you and for many of your lifetimes. Allow it to happen. Your memory bank and your souls are going to team up to reset your course. Suffering will no longer be an option.

September 17 – Saturn Enters Sagittarius

Oh my! Saturn leaves its three-year sojourn in Scorpio and will stay in Sagittarius until 2018. You have moved out of the dark, murky swamp and into the sunlight. Happy Trails!

September 23 – Autumn Equinox – The Sun Enters Libra

Equal light and dark are here to promote harmony.

September 24 – Mars Enters Virgo

A need for boundaries may come into play. Use this tight squeeze for healing and get focused on the inner strength that is required for your body.

September 27 – Lunar Eclipse – Full Moon in Aries

This is a major detox moon asking you to release your pockets of anger and get down to a base of love. The moon will present you with the shadow side of yourself that wants to be recognized and is afraid to ask. This source of anger will release 19 years of this pattern, due to the eclipse. Let it happen. It's time to clear the way for positive attention rather than passive aggression.

September 27 – Full Moon and South Node in Aries Opposing the Sun and North Node in Libra

This is a setup for a major breakthrough to let your truth out in a new way about how much attention you desire for yourself and from your partner.

Low-Vitality – September 5-6

Get rest ... pushing through will lead to regret.

Super-Sensitivity – September 20-21

Chaos is out there big time! Do what you can to stay out of it. Remember, it's global, not personal.

♈ Aries	♋ Cancer	♐ Sagittarius	☽ Moon	♄ Saturn	☊ North Node	V/C Void-of-Course
♉ Taurus	♌ Leo	♑ Capricorn	☿ Mercury	♅ Uranus	☋ South Node	▲ Super-Sensitivity
♊ Gemini	♍ Virgo	♒ Aquarius	♀ Venus	♆ Neptune	➡ Enters	▼ Low-Vitality
	♎ Libra	♓ Pisces	♂ Mars	♇ Pluto	℞ Retrograde	
	♏ Scorpio	☉ Sun	♃ Jupiter	⚷ Chiron	S/D Stationary Direct	

September

Sunday	Monday	Tuesday	Wednesday	Thursday	Friday	Saturday
		1 ♀♆♇♅⚷℞ ☽ V/C 9:37AM 4. Bring all the pieces together.	**2** ♀♆♇♅⚷℞ ☽→♉ 2:01AM 5. Adventure day. Get in your car.	**3** ♀♆♇♅⚷℞ 6. Love can't live where judgment is.	**4** ♀♆♇♅⚷℞ ☽ V/C 3:20AM ☽→♊ 4:47AM 7. Look for the bigger picture.	**5** ♀♆♇♅⚷℞ ▼ ☽ V/C 4:03PM 8. Be a leader without followers.
6 ♆♇♅⚷℞ ▼ ☽→♋ 10:39AM ♀D-14°♌24' 1:30AM 9. Trust that the Universe hears you.	**7** ♆♇♅⚷℞ Labor Day 10. Focus on a sunny tomorrow.	**8** ♆♇♅⚷℞ ☽ V/C 6:27PM ☽→♌ 7:35PM 2. Does your decision affect others?	**9** ♆♇♅⚷℞ 3. Having fun is good for the spirit.	**10** ♆♇♅⚷℞ 4. Play a board game you enjoy.	**11** ♆♇♅⚷℞ ☽ V/C 6:03AM ☽→♍ 6:55AM 5. Variety happens best by choice.	**12** ♆♇♅⚷℞ ● 20°♍10' 11:41PM Solar Eclipse 11:55PM 6. Check your dependability factor.
13 ♆♇♅⚷℞ Rosh Hashanah ☽ V/C 7:07PM ☽→♎ 7:40PM 7. Analyze carefully before acting.	**14** ♆♇♅⚷℞ 8. Success is the result of application.	**15** ♆♇♅⚷℞ ☽ V/C 9:21PM 9. When praying, focus on intent.	**16** ♆♇♅⚷℞ ☽→♏ 8:42AM 10. Choose not to hold on to the past.	**17** ☿♆♇♅⚷℞ ☿R-15°♎55' 11:11AM ♄→♐ 7:49PM 2. Balance is achieved by action.	**18** ☿♆♇♅⚷℞ ☽ V/C 12:48PM ☽→♐ 8:31PM 3. Playing is more vital than winning.	**19** ☿♆♇♅⚷℞ 4. Pick a room; bring in some order.
20 ☿♆♇♅⚷℞ ▲ 5. Add some variety in your cooking.	**21** ☿♆♇♅⚷℞ ▲ ☽ V/C 1:59AM ☽→♑ 5:32AM 6. Is it time to clean out your closet?	**22** ☿♆♇♅⚷℞ ☽ V/C 4:12PM 7. Be inspired to learn a new thing.	**23** ☿♆♇♅⚷℞ Autumn Equinox ☽→♒ 10:51AM ☉→♎ 1:22AM 8. Manifesting happens without limits.	**24** ☿♆♅⚷℞ ☽ V/C 9:01PM ♂→♍ 7:19PM ♇D 12°♑58' 11:56PM 9. Support a humanitarian cause.	**25** ☿♆♅⚷℞ ☽→♓ 12:43PM 10. Buy something new for your home.	**26** ☿♆♅⚷℞ ☽ V/C 9:32AM 2. Speak in a clear and concise manner.
27 ☿♆♅℞ ☽→♈ 12:28PM ○ 4°♈40' 7:50PM Lunar Eclipse 7:48 PM 3. Defense is not necessary.	**28** ☿♆♅℞ 4. Flexibility is forward movement.	**29** ☿♆♅℞ ☽ V/C 12:44AM ☽→♉ 11:56AM 5. A walk will create freedom.	**30** ☿♆♅℞ 6. Tell somebody you love them.			

Solar Eclipse
September 12th
11:41 PM

New Moon in Virgo

Degree Choice Points
 20° Virgo 10'

Motivation Respect

Resistance Easy Money

Gift Give your knowledge a practical application.

Statement I Heal
 Body Intestines
 Mind Critical
 Spirit Divinity in the Details

Element
 Earth – Family lineage and DNA healing, healing power from the plant kingdom, knowing nutrition and abundance, body awareness, connection to small animals.

Fourth House Moon
 3° Virgo 6'

Fourth House Umbrella Theme
 I Feel/I Heal – The way your early environmental training set your foundation for living and why you chose your mother.

Motivation Clever Responses

Resistance Anxiety

Gift You are not governed by concrete rules or traditions.

When the Sun is in Virgo

Virgo is called the "Womb of Time" in which the seeds of great value are planted, shielded, nourished, and revealed. It is the labor of Virgo that brings the Christ Principle into manifestation within individuals and humanity. This unification occurs when we feel the power within us to serve. When we serve, we give birth to Divinity. Virgo time is when we all have a chance to raise the standard of excellence in our lives and on the Earth. The Virgo intelligence stores and maintains light in a precise manner. Attention to detail is Virgo's great gift to life.

Virgo Goddess

The Virgo goddess, Cosmic Womb Woman, gives birth to Divinity. She is a symbol of the ability to give birth to the Self in order to serve, perfect, and purify. It is Cosmic Womb Woman who urges each human to fulfill the goal of evolution by planting seeds of love and power, sending the spark of light to each atom, plant, animal, and planet in the entire solar system.

On Your Altar

Colors Earth tones, blue, green

Numerology 6 – Check your dependability factor

Tarot Card The Hermit – Being a shining light for all of life

Gemstones Emerald, malachite, sapphire

Plant Remedy Sagebrush – The ability to hold and store light

Fragrance Lavender – Management and storage of energy

My Co-Creation List

This or something better than this comes to me in an easy and pleasurable way, for the good of all concerned. Thank you, Universe!

Virgo Co-Creation Ideas

Now is the time to focus on manifesting a high standard of excellence, a healthy lifestyle, self-acceptance, discernment without judgment, healing abilities, a contribution to nature, and a healthy body.

Solar Eclipse
September 12th
11:41 PM

New Moon in Virgo

Virgo Challenges and Victories

Say all of the statements in this section out loud. Then, underline the phrase that means the most to you. Use the phrase as your special affirmation for manifesting and co-creating throughout this phase of the moon.

Today, I recognize what I love most about myself. I am the source of my love, my life, and my experience. I will set aside time today to nurture myself. I allow myself to receive these gifts and know in my heart that it is natural for me to love myself. I discover, deep within myself, the knowing that the love I give myself is commensurate to the love I am willing to receive from others. I am aware that what I expect from others cannot be truly expressed or experienced if I cannot give to myself first. I can never be disappointed when I know that love is a natural resource for me today.

Today, I honor the Earth by acknowledging what she has given me. I take time out to walk in the woods or on the beach, to feel the power of the creative pulse of the creative forces flowing through my body with the energy of being alive. I spend time in my garden and plant flowers to enhance the idea of beauty today. I honor my body today and get a massage. I spend quality time sharing joyful moments with those who love to connect from the heart and realize the blessings that come from living my life with love.

Virgo Homework

Virgo co-creates best through working with herbology, folk medicine, environmental industries, organic farming, recycling, horticulture, acupuncture, healing arts, nutritional counseling, yoga instruction, and editing.

The Virgo moon cycle gives birth to Divinity in its own unique way, understanding the Soul's blueprint to be a temple of beauty. This creates what is known as the "crisis of perfection" within the minds of mankind during this time. We become aware of Spirit ascending and descending at the same time and must recognize that these contradicting energies are working within us in order to give birth to Divinity.

Without Acknowledgment Progress Cannot Occur

Acknowledgement creates space for victory and gratitude, which automatically brings you to a level of completion so a new cycle of opportunity can occur in your life. When you celebrate your wins and acknowledge your victories with gratitude, you update your cells so that your ability to move forward is not hindered by a cellular holographic pattern that is stuck in the past. Cellular lag creates resistance and makes moving forward most difficult. The key is to stay continuously updated by acknowledging yourself for what you did do at the end of each day, rather than heading off to sleep thinning about what you did not do. By acknowledging what you did not do, you play into your karmic storage bank and keep your progress at bay. When you acknowledge yourself and your manifestations you are complete, and more cycles of opportunity become available to you in each new day. Be prepared for miracles!

Victory List

When a creation result is acknowledged it seals the deal. This makes room for more magnificence to expand into your life and increases your abundance factor adding to your ability to receive. As each aspect of your co-creation list arrives in your life, spend time allowing, acknowledging, and accepting it with the true gusto of gratitude! Keep your victory list active here.

Gratitude List

This fulfills the relationship between the giver and the receiver, which completes the cycle with the Universe so that a new beginning can be established.

Solar Eclipse
September 12th
11:41 PM

New Moon in Virgo

How to Use the Moon Book With Your Chart

Fill in the blanks on the Cosmic Check-In page. Then look up the degree of the moon on the chart below. Take note of the "I" statement on the outside of the wheel where the moon is located. Now, locate the same degree on your own chart and make a note of the house and corresponding "I" statement. Go back to the Cosmic Check-In page and circle the two statements from the charts and read what you wrote. This will give you an idea about what to expect from this moon phase on a personal level.

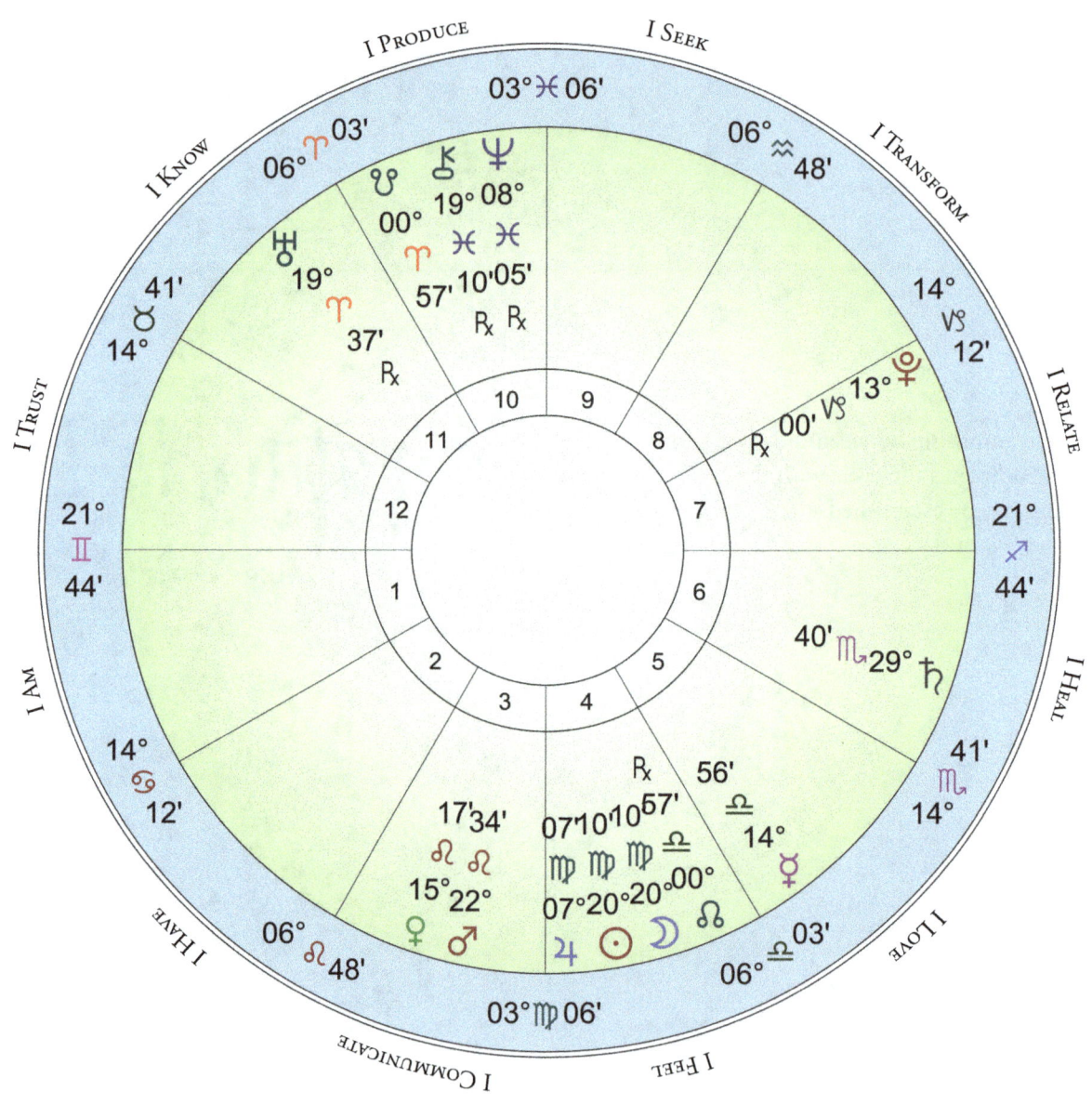

♈ Aries	♋ Cancer	♐ Sagittarius	☽ Moon	♄ Saturn	☊ North Node	V/C Void-of-Course
♉ Taurus	♌ Leo	♑ Capricorn	☿ Mercury	♅ Uranus	☋ South Node	▲ Super-Sensitivity
♊ Gemini	♍ Virgo	♒ Aquarius	♀ Venus	♆ Neptune	➡ Enters	▼ Low-Vitality
	♎ Libra	♓ Pisces	♂ Mars	♇ Pluto	℞ Retrograde	
	♏ Scorpio	☉ Sun	♃ Jupiter	⚷ Chiron	S/D Stationary Direct	

Cosmic Check-In

Take a moment to write a brief phrase for each "I" statement.
This activates all areas of your life for this creative cycle.

♍ I Heal

♎ I Relate

♏ I Transform

♐ I Seek

♑ I Produce

♒ I Know

♓ I Trust

♈ I Am

♉ I Have

♊ I Communicate

♋ I Feel

♌ I Love

Lunar Eclipse
September 27th
7:50 PM

Full Moon in Aries

Degree Choice Points
4° Aries 39'

Motivation
Self-Transcendence

Resistance
Oblivious

Gift
Learn through osmosis from extra-planetary intelligence.

Statement   I Am
    Body   Head and Face
    Mind   Ego
    Spirit   Awakening

Element
Fire – Inspiration, action, initiation, passion, enthusiasm, the Divine Masculine, "my way or the highway".

Twelfth House Moon
19° Pisces 13'

Twelfth House Umbrella Theme
I Trust/I Am – Determine how you deal with your karma, unconscious software, and what you will experience in order to attain mastery by completing your karma. It is also about the way you connect to the Divine.

Motivation   Gratification

Resistance   Self-Indulgence

Gift   Adjust your energy output to match that of the situation.

Karmic Awakening: Aries/Libra

You may experience this karma if the need to initiate action comes up and you assert your own desire. Avoid the karma by sharing the need to maintain harmony with others. With Pisces on the cusp of Aries it will become necessary to translate your idealism into action to avoid the karma. Virgo is on the cusp of Libra, demonstrating that analytical work must be put at the service of others to avoid the karma. Your lesson is to know that the results of your efforts must be shared.

The Sun is Opposite the Moon

Full Moons are always in opposition to the Sun. This creates a feeling of tension between where you want to shine and how your feelings are flowing on a sensory level about the Sun's directive. The two forces seem like they are working against each other, yet they are on the same team displaying different techniques to obtain the same mission. The Aries/Libra polarity creates tension between "I Am" and "We Are".

Aries God

Mars is the god of war. His statement is, "I fight." Before going into battle, Mars required something to be sacrificed on the eve of the battle. When he went into battle, he traveled with two gods: Deimos, god of terror, and Phobos, god of fear. They symbolized the unconscious elements of war. It never mattered to Mars on which side of the war he fought; it was the battle itself that seduced him. When the Moon is full in Aries, you are given the opportunity to examine your inner conflict. Where are you at war with yourself, your relationships, and your environment? Questions to ask yourself: Is my anger worth the sacrifice? What am I sacrificing in order to stay angry?

On Your Altar

Colors   Red, black, coral

Numerology   3 – Defense is not necessary

Tarot Card   Tower – Release from a stuck place, a major breakthrough

Gemstones   Diamond, red jasper, coral, obsidian

Plant remedy   Oak, pomegranate – Planting new life and rooting new life

Fragrance   Ginger – The ability to ingest and digest life

Meditation

The freedom themes are provided by the zodiac sign and can be from this lifetime or other lifetimes. These meditations assist in dissolving blocks and opening pathways to new frontiers.

When the Moon is in Aries, it is a time to face irritability issues relating to challenge, hostility, impatience, and war. Sit quietly and close your eyes, breathe in and breathe out, and look in the memory banks for times when you forced your will on others, and reconcile with the old warrior that you were. Open the pathway to becoming the peaceful warrior who expresses without impatience or the impulse of battle. Take action, be energized, and focus on yourself. Know that you have the power to work things out with clear self-expression. Continue to see yourself clearly, without the interfering definitions of others.

Aries Challenges and Victories

Say all of the statements in this section out loud. Then, underline the phrase that means the most to you. Use the phrase as your special affirmation for manifesting and co-creating throughout this phase of the moon.

Today, I let go. I trust that whatever breaks down or breaks through is a blessing in disguise for me. I make a commitment to allow myself to be spontaneous and live in the moment. I know the unexpected is a blessing for me and a way for me to make a breakthrough out of my limitations. I am aware that I am resistant to change. I know I must make changes and am too stubborn to take the appropriate action myself to change. I have built many walls of false protection around me, guarding me and blocking me from the reality that change is a constant. I have freeze-framed my life and desire support to update myself. I have allowed my fear of change to become my false motto and my life is at a standstill. I am unwilling use any more energy to perpetuate my resistance. I know that continuing to cling to the past is a waste of my energy. I can no longer put things off that delay my process. I feel the breaking down of form. I trust that all changes are in my favor. All changes lead me to golden opportunities. I release false pride. I release false foundations. I release false authorities. In so doing, I allow for everything to crumble around me so I can see that my true strength is within and I will build my life from the inside out.

I am ready for new experiences. I am ready for the unexpected. I am willing to have an event occur so I can become activated towards my breakthrough. I am ready for the power of now. I know being spontaneous will bring me to true joy. I know if I ride this carrier wave it will take me to a place far beyond my scope of limited thinking. I know the will of God works in my favor and knows more than I do in any given moment.

Aries Homework

Now you are ready to take a personal inventory on behaviors such as impatience, talking over people, brat attacks, and starting every sentence with "I."

This is a time when the light becomes a prisoner of polarized forces. This diminishing light begins its yearly sojourn beneath the surface asking us to balance light and dark by mastering the concept of equilibrium. Equilibrium is the Law of Harmony, where we attempt to reach a state of achievement by combining paradoxical fields that break the crystallization of polarity. Spend time looking for increasing and decreasing fields of light around you.

Lunar Eclipse
September 27th
7:50 PM

Full Moon in Aries

Clearing the Slate for Freedom

Remember a time when you experienced the following trigger points. Write down what happened, forgive yourself, release it, and let it go to clear your slate for freedom.

Anger

- Forgive
- Release
- Let Go

The Need to Be First

- Forgive
- Release
- Let Go

Arrogance

- Forgive
- Release
- Let Go

Impatience

- Forgive
- Release
- Let Go

Forcefulness

- Forgive
- Release
- Let Go

My Freedom List

Say this statement out loud three times before writing your freedom list!

I am a free spiritual being and it is my desire to be free to think and to express myself fully.

I am now free and ready to make choices beyond survival!

Aries Freedom List Ideas

Now is the time to set myself free from anger that is toxic, competition and comparison, irritation and struggle, the need to be first, overdoing it and not resting, impatience, impulsiveness, challenge, and hostility.

Lunar Eclipse
September 27th
7:50 PM

Full Moon in Aries

How to Use the Moon Book With Your Chart

Fill in the blanks on the Cosmic Check-In page. Then look up the degree of the moon on the chart below. Take note of the "I" statement on the outside of the wheel where the moon is located. Now, locate the same degree on your own chart and make a note of the house and corresponding "I" statement. Go back to the Cosmic Check-In page and circle the two statements from the charts and read what you wrote. This will give you an idea about what to expect from this moon phase on a personal level.

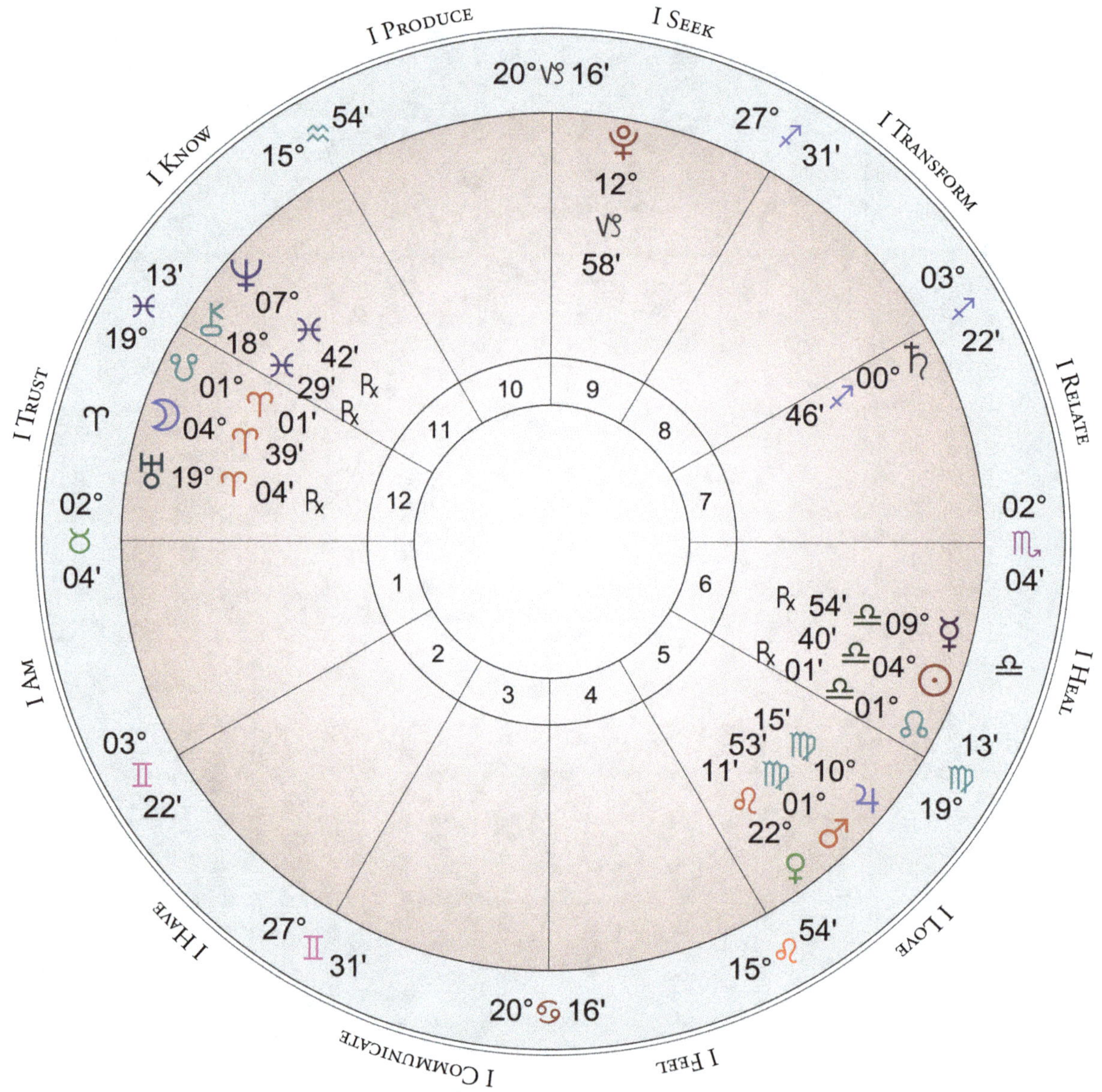

♈ Aries	♋ Cancer	♐ Sagittarius	☽ Moon	♄ Saturn	☊ North Node	V/C Void-of-Course
♉ Taurus	♌ Leo	♑ Capricorn	☿ Mercury	♅ Uranus	☋ South Node	▲ Super-Sensitivity
♊ Gemini	♍ Virgo	♒ Aquarius	♀ Venus	♆ Neptune	➡ Enters	▼ Low-Vitality
	♎ Libra	♓ Pisces	♂ Mars	♇ Pluto	℞ Retrograde	
	♏ Scorpio	☉ Sun	♃ Jupiter	⚷ Chiron	S/D Stationary Direct	

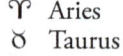

Cosmic Check-In

Take a moment to write a brief phrase for each "I" statement.
This activates all areas of your life for this creative cycle.

♈ I Am

♉ I Have

♊ I Communicate

♋ I Feel

♌ I Love

♍ I Heal

♎ I Relate

♏ I Transform

♐ I Seek

♑ I Produce

♒ I Know

♓ I Trust

Planetary Highlights

Mercury is Retrograde in Libra Until October 9

Use the Libra charm and ability to be diplomatic to resolve conflicts from the past, and move forward. Reconciliation is the goal here. Clean the slate now!

Neptune is Retrograde in Pisces Until November 18

You may notice the need to sleep or daydream in order to escape from reality. See if you can flip this pattern by using your creative talents and take on a project. Volunteer for a cause and save yourself from the loneliness that isolation creates during this transit. The cause will work better for you if it relates to the ocean.

Uranus is Retrograde in Aries Until December 25

Uranus is pushing you to face your deep need for recognition. This is hard to admit, yet very necessary for your future identity to be formed, repaired, and recalibrated in order for your peaceful warrior to be fully developed. Break down or break through, it's your choice!

Chiron is Retrograde in Pisces Until November 27

Chiron works to heal by bridging energy into matter, the spiritual into the mundane, and the cosmic into the ordinary. While visiting Pisces, Chiron dives into the deep waters of our unconscious software to bridge the unknown into the known in order to heal ourselves and the consciousness of the world from its denial of the possibility of peace. Pisces is a choice point between suffering and trusting the Divine. Let Chiron guide you over the bridge into being healed.

October 8 – Venus Moves into Virgo

The party is over ... time to get back to work. Instead of expressing love, getting massages, and buying diamonds, you will be focusing on perfecting your work, improving your health, and being of service. Remember, love comes in many avenues. See if you can try this one without a brat attack.

October 12 – New Moon in Libra Connected to Uranus

USUALLY Libra New Moons are all about politely working things out with your one-on-one relationships in diplomatic ways that bring hearts closer together. This time, Uranus is in the mix here adding a different quality to this manifesting moon. Instead of being diplomatic and doing conflict-resolution, you may just want to throw in the towel and walk away. If so, trust that there is plenty of support and strength to do so.

October 15 – Mars and Jupiter Conjoin in Virgo

This is an every other year reunion where action (Mars) meets optimism (Jupiter) for a blast of very positive energy. Expect to stretch and grow. Enthusiasm runs high; use it to your advantage. Later in the day, this dynamic duo makes a trine with transformational Pluto for an expansion of options. Go for it!

October 23 – The Sun Moves into Scorpio

This is an exchange from the harmonious mind of Libra into the intense and sometimes murky waters of Scorpio. The doors open for a deeper look into parts of ourselves that have been pushed aside to be dealt with at another time. The time is now.

October 27 – Full Moon in Taurus

It's time to get rid of things that no longer benefit your life. Remember, full moons are about completion. What do you need to do to complete yourself to gain personal value? The more you release now, the more magnetic you will become in the next lunar phase.

Low-Vitality – October 2-3, 30-31

Earth changes are possible. Some things might be coming to an end; if so, let it be. Get rest and stay close to home.

Super-Sensitivity – October 17-18

Chaos is in the air. Set strong mental boundaries so you don't plug into the thought pattern – it's not yours.

♈ Aries	♋ Cancer	♐ Sagittarius	☽ Moon	♄ Saturn	☊ North Node	V/C Void-of-Course
♉ Taurus	♌ Leo	♑ Capricorn	☿ Mercury	♅ Uranus	☋ South Node	▲ Super-Sensitivity
♊ Gemini	♍ Virgo	♒ Aquarius	♀ Venus	♆ Neptune	➡ Enters	▼ Low-Vitality
	♎ Libra	♓ Pisces	♂ Mars	♇ Pluto	℞ Retrograde	
	♏ Scorpio	☉ Sun	♃ Jupiter	⚷ Chiron	SD Stationary Direct	

October

Sunday	Monday	Tuesday	Wednesday	Thursday	Friday	Saturday
				1 ☿♆♅⚷℞ ☽ V/C 3:43AM ☽→♊ 1:03PM 7. Check a reliable resource.	**2** ☿♆♅⚷℞ ▼ 8. Spend freely, but don't be foolish.	**3** ☿♆♅⚷℞ ▼ ☽ V/C 10:18AM ☽→♋ 5:21PM 9 Give thanks for all that you have.
4 ☿♆♅⚷℞ 10. Be clear and the future will be bright.	**5** ☿♆♅⚷℞ ☽ V/C 4:04AM 2. Keep calm and carry on.	**6** ☿♆♅⚷℞ ☽→♌ 1:30AM 3. See yourself as creative.	**7** ☿♆♅⚷℞ ☽ V/C 2:10PM 4. Have a format and stay flexible.	**8** ☿♆♅⚷℞ ☽→♍ 12:50PM ♀→♍ 10:30AM 5. Making a change makes a difference.	**9** ♆♅⚷℞ ☽ V/C 3:12PM ☿SD-0°♎54' 7:59AM 6. True friends are to be cherished.	**10** ♆♅⚷℞ 7. It's time to reorganize your library.
11 ♆♅⚷℞ ☽→♎ 1:45AM 8. Be willing to be in charge.	**12** ♆♅⚷℞ Columbus Day ☽ V/C 5:05PM ● 19°♎20' 5:05 PM 9. See yourself fulfilling your dreams.	**13** ♆♅⚷℞ ☽→♏ 2:38PM 10. Make a space for something new.	**14** ♆♅⚷℞ ☽ V/C 5:57PM 2. Look at both sides of every issue.	**15** ♆♅⚷℞ 3. You are the creator of your desires.	**16** ♆♅⚷℞ ☽→♐ 2:18AM 4. In order to take charge, give up control.	**17** ♆♅⚷℞ ▲ 5. Self-perception changes easily.
18 ♆♅⚷℞ ▲ ☽ V/C 1:48AM ☽→♑ 11:52AM 6. Invite a friend to lunch.	**19** ♆♅⚷℞ 7. Donate your used books to a cause.	**20** ♆♅⚷℞ ☽ V/C 1:31PM ☽→♒ 6:37PM 9. Protect your spiritual well-being.	**21** ♆♅⚷℞ 10. Starting over is a new beginning.	**22** ♆♅⚷℞ ☽ V/C 9:21PM ☽→♓ 10:17PM 2. Share the middle.	**23** ♆♅⚷℞ ☉→♏ 10:48AM 3. Be the best you can be in all you do.	**24** ♆♅⚷℞ ☽ V/C 4:18AM ☽→♈ 11:21PM 4. Simplicity is the key to stay on track.
25 ♆♅⚷℞ 5. Don't "try" to do it - just do it!	**26** ♆♅⚷℞ ☽ V/C 5:24AM ☽→♉ 11:07PM 6. Do not assume - clarify to be sure.	**27** ♆♅⚷℞ ○ 3°♉45' 5:05 AM 7. Assess without judgment.	**28** ♆♅⚷℞ ☽ V/C 8:20AM ☽→♊ 11:24PM 8. Challenges aren't personal.	**29** ♆♅⚷℞ 9. When you find a solution, be grateful.	**30** ♆♅⚷℞ ▼ ☽ V/C 7:51PM 10. Release the old to open for new.	**31** ♆♅⚷℞ ▼ Halloween ☽→♋ 2:09AM 2. What serves you best is balance.

October 12th
5:05 PM

New Moon in Libra

Dropping Moon
This happens when a new or full moon peaks at the same time as it goes void. During a "dropping moon" it becomes very important for you to write your co-creation list or your freedom list half an hour before the designated time.

Degree Choice Points
19° Libra 20'

Motivation	Spiritual Translations
Resistance	Diluted Histories
Gift	Pass your wisdom on to others.
Statement	I Relate
Body	Kidneys
Mind	Social
Spirit	Peace

Element
Air – Promotes curiosity, insights, perspectives, bridges the mundane to the Divine.

Seventh House Moon
22° Virgo 58'

Seventh House Umbrella Theme
I Relate/I Heal – It's all about your people attraction and how you work in relationship with the people you attract.

Motivation
Professionalism

Resistance
Indispensability

Gift
Variety is important to your progress.

Karmic Awakening: Aries/Libra

You may experience this karma if the need to initiate action comes up and you assert your own desire. Avoid the karma by sharing the need to maintain harmony with others. With Pisces on the cusp of Aries it will become necessary to translate your idealism into action to avoid the karma. Virgo is on the cusp of Libra, demonstrating that analytical work must be put at the service of others to avoid the karma. Your lesson is to know that the results of your efforts must be shared.

When the Sun is in Libra

Libra energy gives us the opportunity to bridge the gap between the higher and lower mind; abstract thinking versus concrete thinking. During Libra time, the light and dark forces are in balance and you are given a chance to experience harmony. Harmony occurs when you keep your polarities in motion and put paradox to rest, thus breaking the crystallization of polarity. Now is the time to weigh your values through the light of your Soul. Libra asks you to look at what is increasing and decreasing in your life. Start with friendship, courage, sincerity, and understanding, and keep going until your scale is in motion.

Libra Goddess

The whole idea of Libra is to weigh and measure decreasing and increasing light. The goddess best known for the ability to measure light is Ma'at. Ma'at has the ability to weigh and measure frequencies of a light heart or a heavy one. According to Egyptian mythology, it is Ma'at who waits at the gateway to the other side and measures the lightness of being in order to determine the direction one is to take when entering the Underworld. Ma'at's symbol for measurement is an ostrich plume. Each heart that enters must be weighed and be in balance against her feather. If the heart is heavy, it is determined by Ma'at that the soul must transition to an area known as the darker world. If the heart is light and balanced with her feather, the soul is directed to the lighter world.

Because of this process, she began to make her contribution to civilization by holding the space for cosmic balance, right order, and natural law.

On Your Altar

Colors Pink, green

Numerology 9 – See yourself fulfilling your dreams

Tarot Card Justice – The Law of Cause and Effect

Gemstones Jade, rose quartz

Plant Remedy Olive trees – Stamina

Fragrance Eucalyptus – Clarity of breath

My Co-Creation List

This or something better than this comes to me in an easy and pleasurable way, for the good of all concerned. Thank you, Universe!

Libra Co-Creation Ideas

Now is the time to focus on manifesting relationships, wholeness, being loving, lovable, and loved, living life as an art form, balance and equality, integrity, accuracy, diplomacy, and peace.

October 12th
5:05 PM

New Moon in Libra

Libra Challenges and Victories

Say all of the statements in this section out loud. Then, underline the phrase that means the most to you. Use the phrase as your special affirmation for manifesting and co-creating throughout this phase of the moon.

I feel the call of the higher worlds awakening me to a new vibration. This call is to move beyond judgment and move to a place of acceptance, understanding, unconditional confidence, and love. I am at a place in my life where I can embrace the world of acceptance and wholeness, because I have birthed myself anew, beyond the imprisonment and crystallization of polarity and righteousness. My black and white worlds of right and wrong have integrated and blended into gray, the color of wisdom, where true knowledge exists. Knowledge simply is, and the need for proof does not exist where wisdom lives.

The only requirement is experience. I know that everything that comes before me is a direct reflection of my own experience and, in embracing this concept, I can now receive the gift of infinite awareness. I am in a place of awareness that came before and goes beyond where good and evil exist. I have within me, the presence of unconditional confidence to go where true love lives. I no longer need to prove myself.

I am now simply being myself. I release the need to be right and accept the right to BE. I no longer need to be forgiven, because I am neither wrong nor right. I no longer need to define myself. Acceptance has no reason for defense. I no longer need to be guilty; duty motivation is no longer a reality. I know that where there is judgment, there is separation. I know understanding unifies. I accept the call of the higher worlds and express myself freely and fully without fear of judgment. I accept myself as I am, so I can learn what I can become.

Libra Homework

Libra co-creates best through the legal industry, beauty industry, diplomatic service, match-making, urban development, mediation, feng shui, spa ownership, clutter-busting and space clearing, romance writing, wedding consulting, fashion design, and as a librarian.

It is time to weigh and measure the values of relationship, friendship, courage, sensitivity, sincerity, and understanding. Look at what is increasing and what is decreasing in these areas.

Without Acknowledgment Progress Cannot Occur

Acknowledgement creates space for victory and gratitude, which automatically brings you to a level of completion so a new cycle of opportunity can occur in your life. When you celebrate your wins and acknowledge your victories with gratitude, you update your cells so that your ability to move forward is not hindered by a cellular holographic pattern that is stuck in the past. Cellular lag creates resistance and makes moving forward most difficult. The key is to stay continuously updated by acknowledging yourself for what you did do at the end of each day, rather than heading off to sleep thinning about what you did not do. By acknowledging what you did not do, you play into your karmic storage bank and keep your progress at bay. When you acknowledge yourself and your manifestations you are complete, and more cycles of opportunity become available to you in each new day. Be prepared for miracles!

Victory List

When a creation result is acknowledged it seals the deal. This makes room for more magnificence to expand into your life and increases your abundance factor adding to your ability to receive. As each aspect of your co-creation list arrives in your life, spend time allowing, acknowledging, and accepting it with the true gusto of gratitude! Keep your victory list active here.

This fulfills the relationship between the giver and the receiver, which completes the cycle with the Universe so that a new beginning can be established.

Gratitude List

October 12th
5:05 PM

New Moon in Libra

How to Use the Moon Book With Your Chart

Fill in the blanks on the Cosmic Check-In page. Then look up the degree of the moon on the chart below. Take note of the "I" statement on the outside of the wheel where the moon is located. Now, locate the same degree on your own chart and make a note of the house and corresponding "I" statement. Go back to the Cosmic Check-In page and circle the two statements from the charts and read what you wrote. This will give you an idea about what to expect from this moon phase on a personal level.

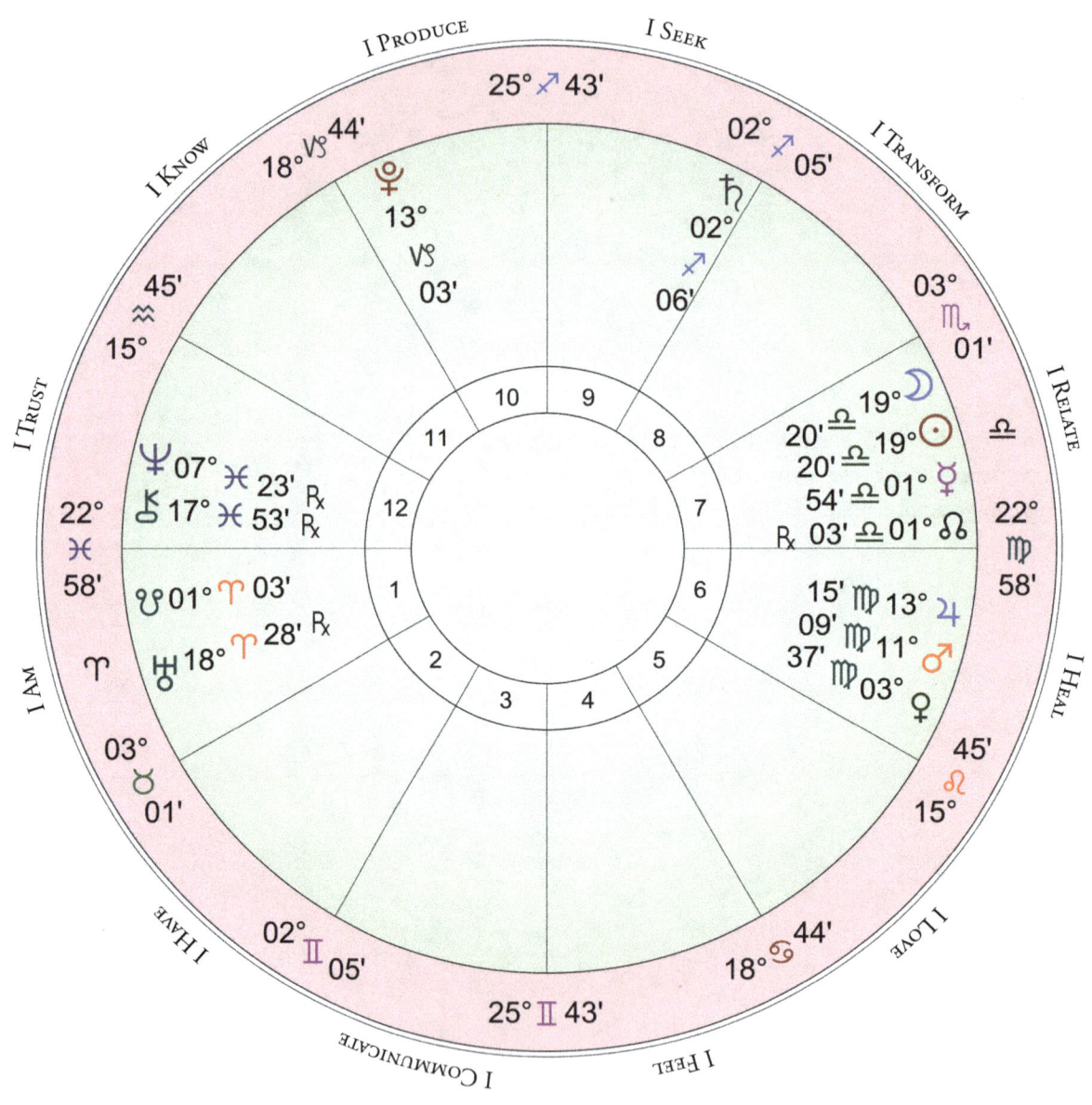

♈ Aries	♋ Cancer	♐ Sagittarius	☽ Moon	♄ Saturn	☊ North Node	V/C Void-of-Course
♉ Taurus	♌ Leo	♑ Capricorn	☿ Mercury	♅ Uranus	☋ South Node	▲ Super-Sensitivity
♊ Gemini	♍ Virgo	♒ Aquarius	♀ Venus	♆ Neptune	➡ Enters	▼ Low-Vitality
	♎ Libra	♓ Pisces	♂ Mars	♇ Pluto	℞ Retrograde	
	♏ Scorpio	☉ Sun	♃ Jupiter	⚷ Chiron	S/D Stationary Direct	

Cosmic Check-In

Take a moment to write a brief phrase for each "I" statement.
This activates all areas of your life for this creative cycle.

♎ I Relate

♏ I Transform

♐ I Seek

♑ I Produce

♒ I Know

♓ I Trust

♈ I Am

♉ I Have

♊ I Communicate

♋ I Feel

♌ I Love

♍ I Heal

October 27th
5:05 AM

Full Moon in Taurus

Degree Choice Points
3° Taurus 44'

Motivation Seeking

Resistance Pipe Dreams

Gift You are pregnant with creative energies that have to be expressed.

Statement I Have
   Body Neck
   Mind Collector
   Spirit Accumulation

Element
Earth – Self-value, abundant, aesthetic, business, sensuous, art, beauty, flowers, gardens, collector, and shopper.

Seventh House Moon
8° Aries 12'

Seventh House Umbrella Theme
I Relate/I Have – It's all about your people attraction and how you work in relationship with the people you attract.

Motivation Insightful

Resistance Side-Tracked

Gift You agreed to stand out from the crowd.

The Sun is Opposite the Moon

Full Moons are always in opposition to the Sun. This creates a feeling of tension between where you want to shine and how your feelings are flowing on a sensory level about the Sun's directive. The two forces seem like they are working against each other, yet they are on the same team displaying different techniques to obtain the same mission. The Taurus/Scorpio polarity creates tension between "my" money and "our" money.

Taurus God

Ganesh is the lord of wisdom and destroyer of all obstacles. He grants success, prosperity, and protection against adversity. He is the deity that rules merchants and their trading. He rules Dharma by creating and removing obstacles appropriate to each individual's pathway. He is called the Lord of Wisdom because when we have earned the right to have an obstacle removed, we have learned the lesson and gained wisdom. Ganesh always appears with a rat at his feet. The rat is a symbol of desire, and desire always presents us with an obstacle to overcome in order to attain our wish. The rat shows up in secret places, stealing what does not belong to him. When the Moon is full in Taurus, it is time to put Ganesh into operation. Ask Ganesh to set you free from obstacles in order to gain wisdom and fulfill your desires.

On Your Altar

Colors Scarlet, earth tones

Numerology 7 – Assess without judgment

Tarot Card Hierophant – Spiritual authority

Gemstones Red coral, red agate, garnet

Plant remedy Angelica – Connecting Heaven and Earth

Fragrance Rose – Opening the heart

Meditation

The freedom themes are provided by the zodiac sign and can be from this lifetime or other lifetimes. These meditations assist in dissolving blocks and opening pathways to new frontiers.

When the Moon is in Taurus, sit quietly, close your eyes, and breathe in and out. It is now time to search the Records of Stewardship to see where ownership of people and property may have been out of control. Look through the records to determine attitudes regarding possessions, objects of art, money, spending, lending, saving, and giving that may have been too extreme or impoverished. Ask for a guardian angel to show you where envy might be out of balance. Correct any dependency on others for their ability to acquire. Accept your own abundance factor.

Taurus Challenges and Victories

Say all of the statements in this section out loud. Then, underline the phrase that means the most to you. Use the phrase as your special affirmation for manifesting and co-creating throughout this phase of the moon.

Everything is possible for me today. My possibilities are endless. I have the power within me to make all of my dreams come true. I have the tools to make my talent a reality. I have the power to identify with my talent. Today, I focus my attention and intention on manifesting with my talent and, in so doing, I transform my ideas into reality. I recognize the part of me that is connected to the cosmic source of ideas, and I express that source within me to manifest my creative power. I see my possibilities and act on them today. I am the creative power. I am all-knowing. I am an individual. There is no one else like me. I can manifest anything I desire. I intend it. I allow it. So be it.

Rules for Manifesting ... know what you want, write it down, and say it out loud. Recognize that because you thought it, it can be so. Release your limiting beliefs. Override your limiting beliefs with power statements. Act as if you have already manifested your idea. Lastly, value yourself!

Taurus Homework

Newsflash for Taurus freedom process ... consumerism is not practicing abundance. Take a look at what you have accumulated over the last few days, months, and years. Eliminate what no longer resonates to the beauty of the now. Take some of these items to a charity of your choice or give gifts to admiring friends. Take the Taurus freedom test and go to the store where you made your last purchase and return the items. Do not buy anything else. Remember, quality not quantity, and take the pledge to become a wise steward of your resources.

It's time to transform priorities from the external world of the centralized self, into the depth and subtlety of the hidden forces below the surface that connect us to the vastness of existence.

October 27th
5:05 AM

Full Moon in Taurus

Clearing the Slate for Freedom

Remember a time when you experienced the following trigger points. Write down what happened, forgive yourself, release it, and let it go to clear your slate for freedom.

Hoarding

- Forgive
- Release
- Let Go

Stubborn

- Forgive
- Release
- Let Go

Greedy

- Forgive
- Release
- Let Go

Irresponsible Stewardship

- Forgive
- Release
- Let Go

Wasteful

- Forgive
- Release
- Let Go

My Freedom List

Say this statement out loud three times before writing your freedom list!

I am a free spiritual being and it is my desire to be free to think and to express myself fully.

From this day forward I resolve to be true — first to myself and my highest self, and then to the highest self in me which is the Source of Love That I Am.

Taurus Freedom List Ideas

Now is the time to set myself free from envy, financial insecurity, being stubborn, hoarding, addictive spending, not feeling valuable, and fear of change.

October 27th
5:05 AM

Full Moon in Taurus

How to Use the Moon Book With Your Chart

Fill in the blanks on the Cosmic Check-In page. Then look up the degree of the moon on the chart below. Take note of the "I" statement on the outside of the wheel where the moon is located. Now, locate the same degree on your own chart and make a note of the house and corresponding "I" statement. Go back to the Cosmic Check-In page and circle the two statements from the charts and read what you wrote. This will give you an idea about what to expect from this moon phase on a personal level.

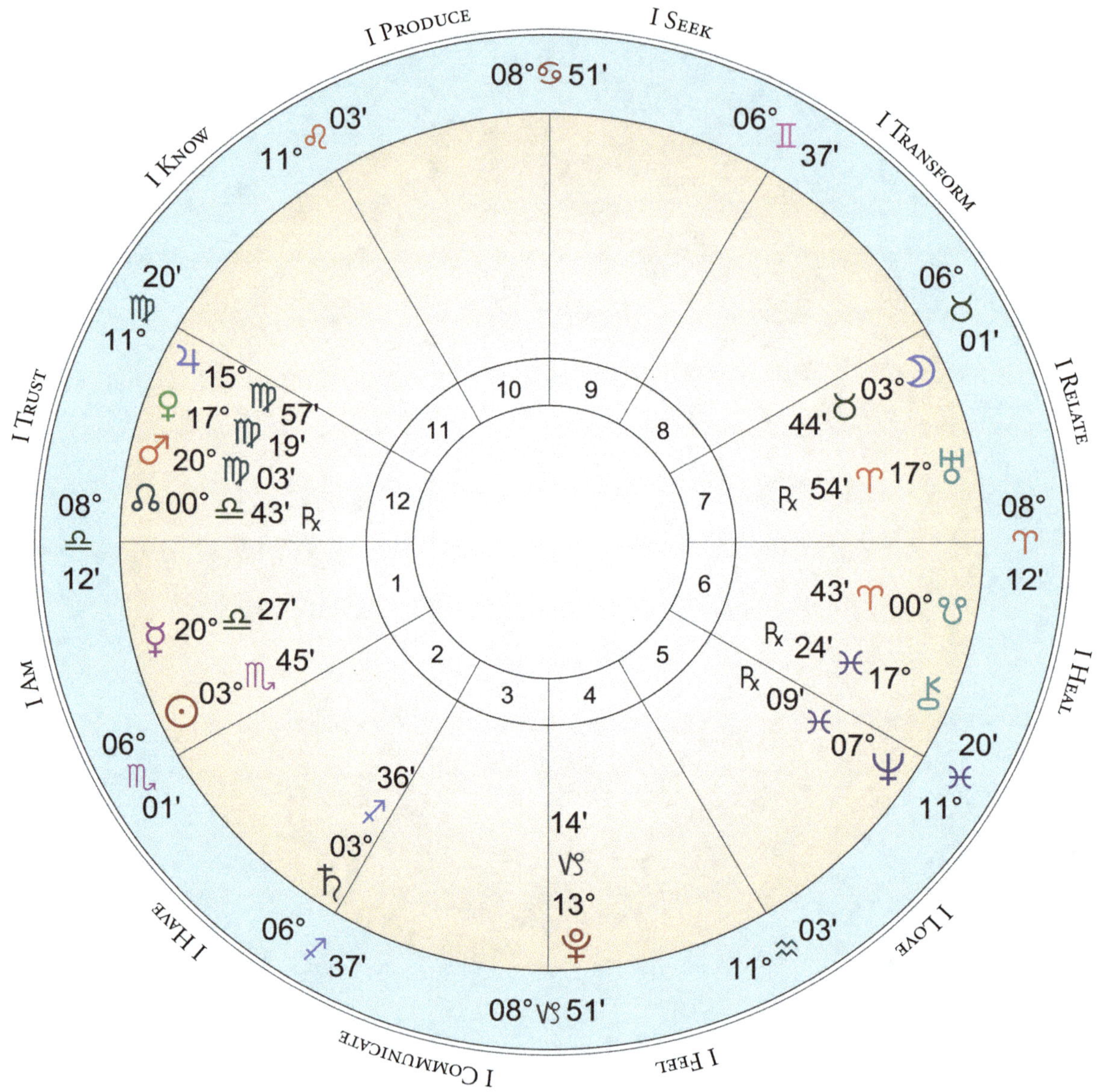

♈ Aries	♋ Cancer	♐ Sagittarius	☽ Moon	♄ Saturn	☊ North Node	V/C Void-of-Course
♉ Taurus	♌ Leo	♑ Capricorn	☿ Mercury	♅ Uranus	☋ South Node	▲ Super-Sensitivity
♊ Gemini	♍ Virgo	♒ Aquarius	♀ Venus	♆ Neptune	➡ Enters	▼ Low-Vitality
	♎ Libra	♓ Pisces	♂ Mars	♇ Pluto	℞ Retrograde	
	♏ Scorpio	☉ Sun	♃ Jupiter	⚷ Chiron	SD Stationary Direct	

Cosmic Check-In

Take a moment to write a brief phrase for each "I" statement.
This activates all areas of your life for this creative cycle.

♉ I Have

♊ I Communicate

♋ I Feel

♌ I Love

♍ I Heal

♎ I Relate

♏ I Transform

♐ I Seek

♑ I Produce

♒ I Know

♓ I Trust

♈ I Am

Planetary Highlights

Neptune is Retrograde in Pisces Until November 18

Tune in and do what it takes to clear your vision. Your true spiritual path is before you and you don't want to let your foggy vision get in your way. Stay awake.

Uranus in Aries is Retrograde Until December 25

Uranus is working overtime to get us to accept the new paradigm and release an old competitive urge to win at all cost. It is time to face winning through cooperation and mutually beneficial win/win solutions.

November 11 – The North Node goes Retrograde into Virgo

Now is the time to contribute to a project and serve actively with others, especially in a way that you can focus on the details.

November 7 – Chiron goes Direct in Pisces

Move beyond your pain and let go of Soul Suffering, so your entire being can heal. Update your cells to feel the power of the present moment.

November 1 – Mercury Moves into Scorpio

Now is the time to go deep and begin to understand the value of boundaries. You may find that your focus on investigation has gotten out of hand. Use it to discover what you are keeping hidden, rather than searching into other people's secret gardens.

November 8 – Venus Moves into Libra

This can be very romantic, especially if you are willing to be intimate. Look around and discover where you can upgrade your life in beautiful and harmonious ways.

November 11 – New Moon in Scorpio

Get some new routines going for your body and focus on wellness. Look where habitual action has become non-productive. A new routine can make it fun. Remember, everything doesn't have to be hard work.

November 11 – Venus and North Node Conjunct in Libra

This is a great combination for allowing yourself to be in a relationship that can accept freedom of expression. Learn that being the same in everything can lead to boredom. Celebrate your differences and learn new tools for loving through acceptance, rather than comparison.

November 12 – Mars Moves into Libra

It's time to learn how to be diplomatic. Learn to negotiate by allowing yourself to see both sides of a situation.

November 20 – Mercury Moves into Sagittarius

A larger horizon will appear and expand your mind. Expect a new learning curve. You just might find yourself in a distant land, traveling to places you never thought would be possible.

November 22 – The Sun Moves into Sagittarius

Party time is here; time to have a blast and be outrageous! Generosity is part of this pattern; open your heart and play full out! Expect your Soul Goal to appear, write it down, and watch it manifest.

November 25 – Full Moon in Gemini

Time to blast out your judgments and integrate, rather than separate. Unification is the goal here.

November 25 – The Sun, Saturn, and Mercury in Sagittarius are Opposite the Moon

Expressions, pathways, and lessons appear in the reflection of this moon. See which one gets your attention and work to release it. Expect some shadow of limitation to appear in the reflection. Remember to look for options and all will be well.

Super-Sensitivity – November 13-14

An activation in the sky could be distracting right now. Do what you can to avoid it. This fragility is universal, not personal. Pace yourself. Stay away from thinking too much to avoid feeling depressed.

Low-Vitality – November 26-27

Earth changes are possible. Stay close to home. Get rest and stay out of resistance.

♈ Aries	♋ Cancer	♐ Sagittarius	☽ Moon	♄ Saturn	☊ North Node	V/C Void-of-Course
♉ Taurus	♌ Leo	♑ Capricorn	☿ Mercury	♅ Uranus	☋ South Node	▲ Super-Sensitivity
♊ Gemini	♍ Virgo	♒ Aquarius	♀ Venus	♆ Neptune	➡ Enters	▼ Low-Vitality
	♎ Libra	♓ Pisces	♂ Mars	♇ Pluto	℞ Retrograde	
	♏ Scorpio	☉ Sun	♃ Jupiter	⚷ Chiron	S/D Stationary Direct	

November

Sunday	Monday	Tuesday	Wednesday	Thursday	Friday	Saturday
1 ♆♅⚷℞ All Saint's Day Pacific Standard Time Begins ☽ V/C 7:34PM ☿→♏ 11:07PM 3. Don't take things too seriously.	**2** ♆♅⚷℞ ☽→♌ 7:47AM 4. Be flexible with your sense of form.	**3** ♆♅⚷℞ ☽ V/C 5:46PM 5. Let your curiosity out,	**4** ♆♅⚷℞ ☽→♍ 6:22AM 6. Always come from your heart.	**5** ♆♅⚷℞ 7. Clarify your ideas and move forward.	**6** ♆♅⚷℞ 8. Manifest through self-reliance.	**7** ♆♅⚷℞ ☽ V/C 4:47AM ☽→♎ 7:14AM 9. Keep your spiritual goals in focus.
8 ♆♅⚷℞ ☽ V/C 6:42PM ♀→♎ 7:32AM 10. Transformation happens in a blink.	**9** ♆♅⚷℞ ☽→♏ 8:02PM 2. Be kind to your shadow side.	**10** ♆♅⚷℞ 3. Have the ability to laugh at yourself.	**11** ♆♅⚷℞ Veteran's Day ● 19°♏01′ 9:47AM ☊℞→♍ 4:59PM 4. Get ready to organize.	**12** ♆♅⚷℞ ☽ V/C 6:54AM ☽→♐ 7:13AM ♂→♎ 1:42PM 5. Cells know before a change happens.	**13** ♆♅⚷℞ ▲ ☽ V/C 7:18PM 6. Your best greeting is a smile.	**14** ♆♅⚷℞ ▲ ☽→♑ 4:21PM 7. Keep your thinking process flexible.
15 ♆♅⚷℞ 8. Be willing to spend graciously.	**16** ♆♅⚷℞ ☽ V/C 12:52PM ☽→♒ 11:24PM 9. Infuse Spirit into the body.	**17** ♆♅⚷℞ 10. Integrate a new technology.	**18** ♅⚷℞ ♆SD-7°♓01′ 8:33AM 2. Balance comes from self-kindness.	**19** ♅⚷℞ ☽ V/C 12:19AM ☽→♓ 4:21AM 3. Whatever you are doing, make it fun.	**20** ♅⚷℞ ☿→♐ 11:44AM 4. Even bridges need firm foundations.	**21** ♅⚷℞ ☽ V/C 5:22AM ☽→♈ 7:12AM 5. Help a friend making changes.
22 ♅⚷℞ ☽ V/C 11:15AM ☉→♐ 7:26AM 6. Sincerity comes from the heart.	**23** ♅⚷℞ ☽→♉ 8:25AM 7. A flexible mind is Divinely directed.	**24** ♅⚷℞ ☽ V/C 5:25PM 8. With pure intent, you can manifest.	**25** ♅⚷℞ ☽→♊ 9:15AM ○ 3°♊20′ 2:44PM 9. Donate to a humanitarian cause.	**26** ♅⚷℞ ▼ Thanksgiving Day ☽ V/C 7:35PM 10. A bright tomorrow begins today.	**27** ♅℞ ▼ ☽→♋ 11:26AM ⚷SD-16°♓56′ 10:42PM 2. Make decisions joyfully.	**28** ♅℞ 3. A sense of humor works wonders.
29 ♅℞ ☽ V/C 4:45AM ☽→♌ 4:47PM 4. Wholeness is a completed job.	**30** ♅℞ 5. Add variety to your rituals.					

November 11th
9:47 AM

New Moon in Scorpio

Degree Choice Points
19° Scorpio 0'

Motivation
Revealing Mysteries

Resistance
Polarity

Gift
Have compassion for the rigors of physical life.

Statement	I Transform
Body	Reproductive organs
Mind	Investigation
Spirit	Transformation

Element
Water – Intense, passionate, sexual, powerful, focused, controlling, deep, driven, and secretive.

Eleventh House Moon
18° Scorpio 44'

Eleventh House Umbrella Theme
I Know/I Transform – How you share money and other resources, what you keep hidden regarding sex, death, real estate, and regeneration.

Motivation Broadcasting

Resistance Infringement

Gift Gaze at a clear night sky to ease inner turmoil.

When the Sun is in Scorpio

Scorpio is the symbol of darkness which heralds the decline of the Sun in Autumn. Scorpio embodies the Law of Nature, which decrees that even the strongest will must bow to the body's mortality. As we watch all of nature going through a slow death, we begin to recognize the qualities of Scorpio's subtlety and depth, and the hidden forces that threaten those who live only on the surface. Scorpio rules all of the things that you try to keep hidden: death, taxes, power, money, sex, resentment, revenge, ambition, pride, and fear. When you face these self-imposed limits on yourself, you take on the true power of transformation. Transformation establishes pathways for you to decentralize the ego in the interest of higher humanitarian work.

Scorpio Goddess

Persephone, the goddess of the Underworld, is assigned to Scorpio. During the time of Scorpio, all of nature begins its sojourn into darkness in preparation for the void that comes in winter. Persephone is the harbinger of the Sun's decline. It is Persephone who asks you to release the idea of living on the surface in order to quest for the depth of your hidden forces, to recharge, rejuvenate, transform, and let go. Persephone rules your intuition, your inner beauty, the occult arts, and your ability to accept the cycles in nature that support your fertility, even when the cycle feels like death. Her domain comes alive in you every time you close your eyes. When the Moon is new in Scorpio, ask Persephone to guide you below the surface.

On Your Altar

Colors Deep red, black, deep purple

Numerology 4 – Get ready to organize

Tarot Card Death – The ability to transform, transmute, and transcend

Gemstones Topaz, smoky quartz, obsidian, jet, onyx

Plant Remedy Manzanita – Being open to transforming cycles

Fragrance Sandalwood – Awakens your sensuality

My Co-Creation List

This or something better than this comes to me in an easy and pleasurable way, for the good of all concerned. Thank you, Universe!

Scorpio Co-Creation Ideas

Now is the time to focus on manifesting transformation on all levels, bringing light to the dark, knowing and living cycles, knowing trust as an option, accepting change, accepting my sexuality, knowing sex is natural, knowing sex as good, and knowing sex as creative.

November 11th
9:47 AM

New Moon in Scorpio

Scorpio Challenges and Victories

Say all of the statements in this section out loud. Then, underline the phrase that means the most to you. Use the phrase as your special affirmation for manifesting and co-creating throughout this phase of the moon.

"When the student needs to learn, the teacher appears." Today, I recognize that the Law of Reflection is in operation. I have become aware of this through my over-indulgence of judgment and criticism of other people. I am aware that when my judgment is running rampant, I am in need of a teacher who can interpret this judgment as reflection, so I can see my judgments as my teachers and use them to re-interpret myself. I seek counsel with someone who has the ability to listen to me, hear me, and give me the space I need to see myself. I have become confused by spending too much time looking outside of myself for the answers. Perhaps my authority systems, like my religion or my family traditions, no longer serve me and I need to use this confusion to become aware of a new, more self-reliant way to live my life.

The Law of Reflection

Whatever I judge is what I am, what I fear, or what I lack. I make a list of my judgments:

I rewrite each judgment in the form of a question: Am I _____? Do I fear _____? Do I lack _____?

Example 1: I judge Mary's wealth. Do I fear wealth? Do I lack wealth? Am I wealthy in my own way and forgetting to acknowledge my own ability to manifest?

Example 2: I judge John's "be perfect" attitude. Do I fear perfection? Do I lack perfection? Have I forgotten to recognize my own perfection?

In moving through this process, I reconnect to myself and find my own authority today. I send blessings to others whose reflection has so beautifully shown me myself today. I now know and cherish my judgments as my greatest teachers and set myself free today.

Scorpio Homework

Scorpio co-creates best by being a private investigator, detective, probate attorney, mystery writer, mythologist, tarot reader, symbolist, hospice worker, transition counselor, mortician, sex surrogate, or in forensic medicine.

The Scorpio moon cycle asks you to transform. In order to do this you must transmute sex drive into creativity, physical comfort into serving the greater good, money into higher value, fear into light, animosity into understanding, ambition into service to beauty, pride into humility, separation into unity, control into harmony, and power into empowerment.

Without Acknowledgment Progress Cannot Occur

Acknowledgement creates space for victory and gratitude, which automatically brings you to a level of completion so a new cycle of opportunity can occur in your life. When you celebrate your wins and acknowledge your victories with gratitude, you update your cells so that your ability to move forward is not hindered by a cellular holographic pattern that is stuck in the past. Cellular lag creates resistance and makes moving forward most difficult. The key is to stay continuously updated by acknowledging yourself for what you did do at the end of each day, rather than heading off to sleep thinning about what you did not do. By acknowledging what you did not do, you play into your karmic storage bank and keep your progress at bay. When you acknowledge yourself and your manifestations you are complete, and more cycles of opportunity become available to you in each new day. Be prepared for miracles!

Victory List

When a creation result is acknowledged it seals the deal. This makes room for more magnificence to expand into your life and increases your abundance factor adding to your ability to receive. As each aspect of your co-creation list arrives in your life, spend time allowing, acknowledging, and accepting it with the true gusto of gratitude! Keep your victory list active here.

Gratitude List

This fulfills the relationship between the giver and the receiver, which completes the cycle with the Universe so that a new beginning can be established.

November 11th
9:47 AM

New Moon in Scorpio

How to Use the Moon Book With Your Chart

Fill in the blanks on the Cosmic Check-In page. Then look up the degree of the moon on the chart below. Take note of the "I" statement on the outside of the wheel where the moon is located. Now, locate the same degree on your own chart and make a note of the house and corresponding "I" statement. Go back to the Cosmic Check-In page and circle the two statements from the charts and read what you wrote. This will give you an idea about what to expect from this moon phase on a personal level.

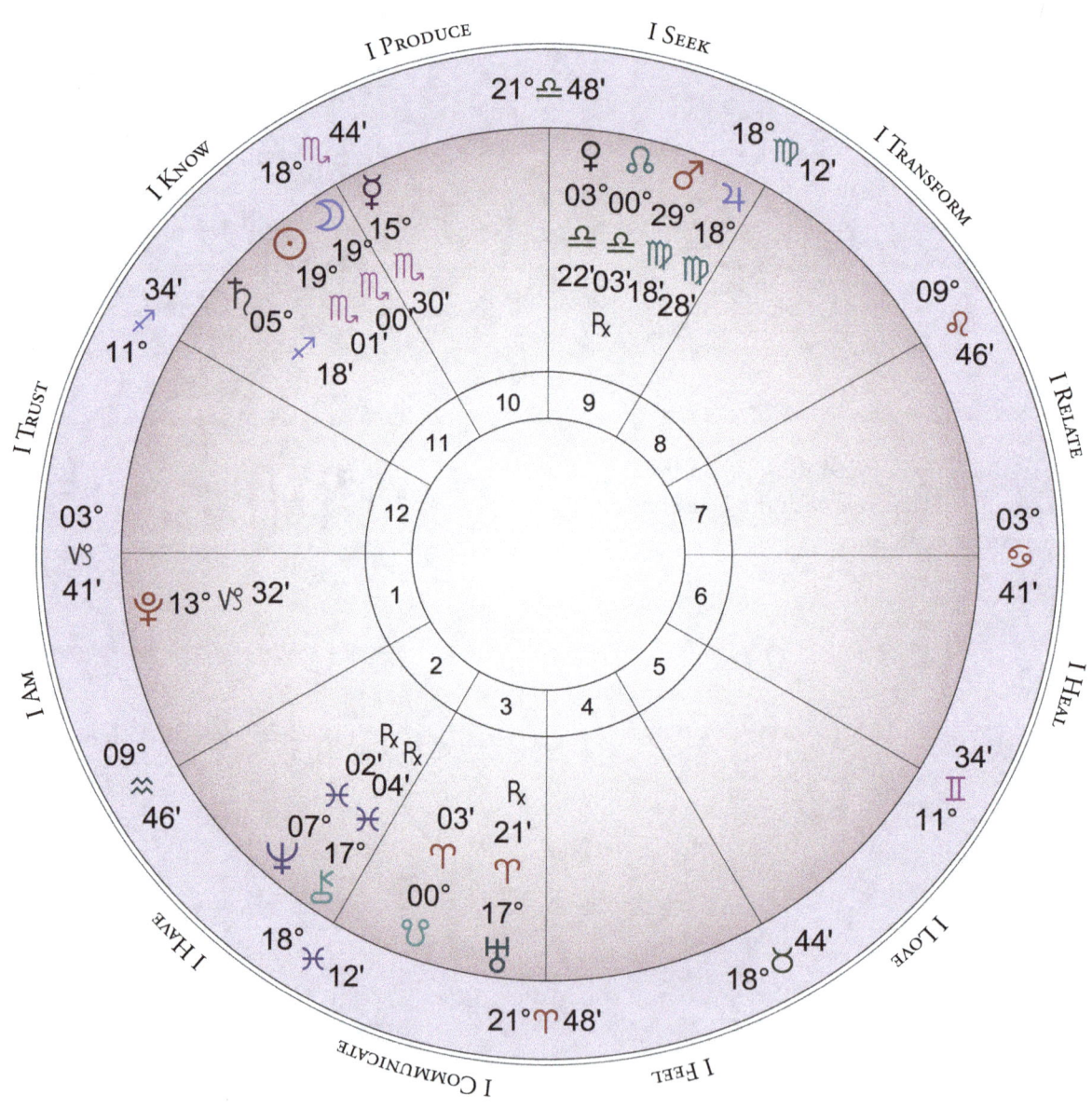

♈ Aries	♋ Cancer	♐ Sagittarius	☽ Moon	♄ Saturn	☊ North Node	V/C Void-of-Course
♉ Taurus	♌ Leo	♑ Capricorn	☿ Mercury	♅ Uranus	☋ South Node	▲ Super-Sensitivity
♊ Gemini	♍ Virgo	♒ Aquarius	♀ Venus	♆ Neptune	➡ Enters	▼ Low-Vitality
	♎ Libra	♓ Pisces	♂ Mars	♇ Pluto	℞ Retrograde	
	♏ Scorpio	☉ Sun	♃ Jupiter	⚷ Chiron	S/D Stationary Direct	

206

Cosmic Check-In

Take a moment to write a brief phrase for each "I" statement.
This activates all areas of your life for this creative cycle.

♏ I Transform

♐ I Seek

♑ I Produce

♒ I Know

♓ I Trust

♈ I Am

♉ I Have

♊ I Communicate

♋ I Feel

♌ I Love

♍ I Heal

♎ I Relate

November 25th
2:44 PM

Full Moon in Gemini

Degree Choice Points
3° Gemini 20'

Motivation
Cultural Bonds

Resistance
Restricted Emotion

Gift
Only those teachings necessary to keep you on your path remain focused.

Statement   I Communicate
     Body   Lungs and Hands
     Mind   Academic
     Spirit   Intelligence

Element
Air – Brings change, promotes curiosity, insight, and concepts.

Second House Moon
29° Taurus 39'

Second House Umbrella Theme
I Have/I Communicate – The way you make your money and the way you spend your money.

Motivation   Joy in Accomplishments

Resistance   Ostentatious

Gift   Cultivate tolerance for diversity.

The Sun is Opposite the Moon

Full Moons are always in opposition to the Sun. This creates a feeling of tension between where you want to shine and how your feelings are flowing on a sensory level about the Sun's directive. The two forces seem like they are working against each other, yet they are on the same team displaying different techniques to obtain the same mission. The Gemini/Sagittarius polarity creates tension between community ideas and global thinking.

Gemini Goddess

Echo means, "one who loves her own voice." Echo was a very talkative nymph who lived in the garden of Bacchus. Zeus visited this garden often to survey the desirable nymphs. He was enchanted by the gregarious Echo and began his conquest for her. Hera, Zeus' wife, arrived just as he was about to consummate his passion for Echo. Hera was so jealous that she punished the talkative Echo for flirting with her husband. She took away Echo's ability to converse, leaving her to repeat the last three words of other people's sentences. When the Moon is full in Gemini, it is time to look at your mindless chatter and release repeating thoughts that echo in the chamber of your mind.

On Your Altar

Colors   Bright yellow, orange, multi-colors

Numerology   9 – Donate to a humanitarian cause

Tarot Card   Lovers – Connecting to wholeness

Gemstones   Yellow diamond, citrine, yellow jade, yellow topaz

Plant remedy   Morning Glory – Thinking with your heart, not your head

Fragrance   Iris – The ability to focus the mind

Meditation

The freedom themes are provided by the zodiac sign and can be from this lifetime or other lifetimes. These meditations assist in dissolving blocks and opening pathways to new frontiers.

When the Moon is in Gemini, it is a time to review the split between your spiritual nature and your worldly nature. Sit down and close your eyes. Breathe in and breathe out. Ask for the Angel of Blending to bring you awareness of your double-mindedness, double-speaking, criticism of others, discontent, and mental unrest. Become aware of separation issues that divide you from your personal truth and be a unifier, rather than a divider.

Gemini Challenges and Victories

Say all of the statements in this section out loud. Then, underline the phrase that means the most to you. Use the phrase as your special affirmation for manifesting and co-creating throughout this phase of the moon.

Today, I blend my old self with my new self, my physical reality with my spiritual awareness, my positive thoughts with my negative thoughts, my past with my present, my feminine with my masculine, my rewards with my losses, my ups with my downs, and my higher self with my lower self. It is a day for me to refine and fine tune my life by looking at my extremes. I recognize what inspires me and what keeps me stuck. I find my center today by acknowledging my extremes. I am aware that balance comes to those who are able to locate the space in the center of these opposite energy fields.

When I am in my center, my polarities are in motion. Healing cannot occur unless my polarities are moving and I know that healing is motion. I am ready for a healing today. I know that by visiting my opposites, and determining their vast opposition to each other, I can find the paradoxes that I have chosen for myself and begin to heal. I am willing to experiment with this blending of opposites and become the alchemist of my own life. When I blend all aspects of myself, rather than separating them, I can truly become whole. Today is a day to integrate, rather than separate, in order to release the spark of light that stays prisoner when my polarities are in operation. When I find balance, motion occurs and the Law of Harmony takes over, putting paradoxical energies to rest, thus breaking the crystallization of polarity. The Law of Harmony is beauty in motion and promotes the flow of color, light, sound, and movement into form. Balance is a condition that keeps my spark in motion. I become the vertical line in the center of polarity today and carry the secret of balance. Balance cannot be my goal; motion is my goal today. When I am in motion, I can take action to evolve and to express all of myself freely.

Gemini Homework

Sit still and invite silence into your space. Stay quiet and still for at least 5 minutes. During this time take an inventory and see where you have interrupted people in the middle of their sentences. Now is the time to make a conscious effort to allow others the space to express their thoughts. Keep sitting there in silence and feel the frustration, while embracing the power of silence.

November 25th
2:44 PM

Full Moon in Gemini

Clearing the Slate for Freedom

Remember a time when you experienced the following trigger points. Write down what happened, forgive yourself, release it, and let it go to clear your slate for freedom.

Gossiping

- Forgive
- Release
- Let Go

Omitting the Truth

- Forgive
- Release
- Let Go

Not Listening/Talking Too Much

- Forgive
- Release
- Let Go

Hyperactivity

- Forgive
- Release
- Let Go

Over-Marketing

- Forgive
- Release
- Let Go

My Freedom List

Say this statement out loud three times before writing your freedom list!

I am a free spiritual being and it is my desire to be free to think and to express myself fully.

From this day forward I resolve to be true – first to myself and my highest self, and then to the highest self in me which is the Source of Love That I Am.

Gemini Freedom List Ideas

Now is the time to set myself free from unfinished business, shallow communication, old files and office clutter, lies I tell myself, broken communication devices, temptation to gossip, restlessness, over-thinking, and vacillation.

November 25th
2:44 PM

Full Moon in Gemini

How to Use the Moon Book With Your Chart

Fill in the blanks on the Cosmic Check-In page. Then look up the degree of the moon on the chart below. Take note of the "I" statement on the outside of the wheel where the moon is located. Now, locate the same degree on your own chart and make a note of the house and corresponding "I" statement. Go back to the Cosmic Check-In page and circle the two statements from the charts and read what you wrote. This will give you an idea about what to expect from this moon phase on a personal level.

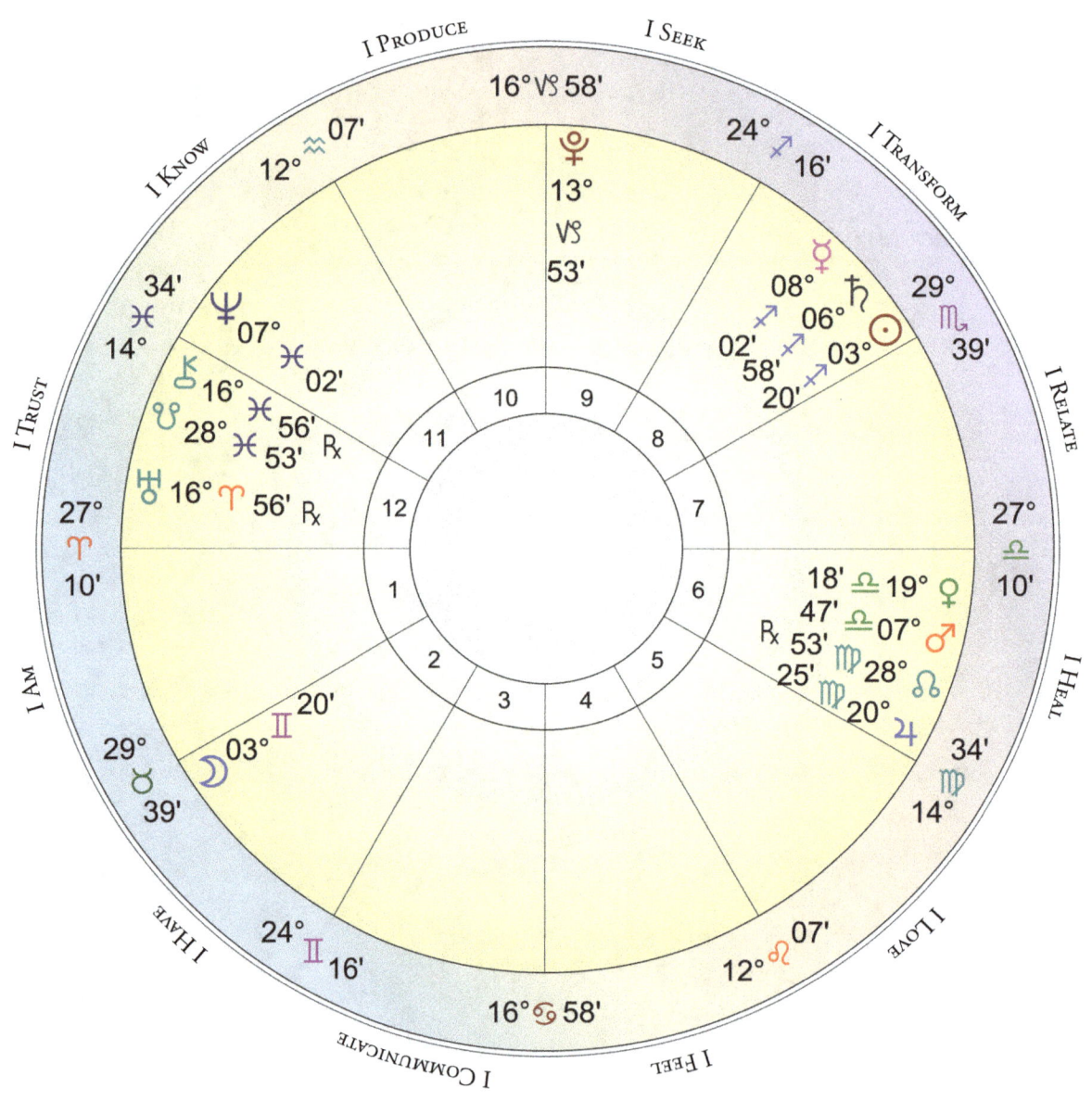

♈ Aries	♋ Cancer	♐ Sagittarius	☾ Moon	♄ Saturn	☊ North Node	V/C Void-of-Course
♉ Taurus	♌ Leo	♑ Capricorn	☿ Mercury	♅ Uranus	☋ South Node	▲ Super-Sensitivity
♊ Gemini	♍ Virgo	♒ Aquarius	♀ Venus	♆ Neptune	➡ Enters	▼ Low-Vitality
	♎ Libra	♓ Pisces	♂ Mars	♇ Pluto	℞ Retrograde	
	♏ Scorpio	☉ Sun	♃ Jupiter	⚷ Chiron	S/D Stationary Direct	

214

Cosmic Check-In

Take a moment to write a brief phrase for each "I" statement.
This activates all areas of your life for this creative cycle.

♊ I Communicate

♋ I Feel

♌ I Love

♍ I Heal

♎ I Relate

♏ I Transform

♐ I Seek

♑ I Produce

♒ I Know

♓ I Trust

♈ I Am

♉ I Have

Planetary Highlights

December 25 – Uranus in Aries Goes Out of Retrograde

The "wild child" of the solar system wakes up after a five-month rest. Prepare for some shaking and a rousing turns of events. Expect to feel a new kind of freedom expressing who you are.

December 4 – Venus Enters Scorpio

This could create some bumps in the road. Expect to become intense and secretive. You may even find yourself wanting to be right, instead of happy. Another way to look at this; Venus symbolizes peace and love, while Scorpio thrives on crisis.

December 9 – Mercury Enters Capricorn

This is a major shift from optimism into pessimism. Expect to be more logical and practical for the next three weeks, which is good for business and presenting to the marketplace.

December 11 – New Moon in Sagittarius

This is a major growth spurt toward being optimistic and inspired. It is time to think big and go out of bounds with your manifesting attitudes and ideas. Take a broad stroke on the canvas of your life and bring in some major treats for yourself.

December 11 – North Node is Conjunct with Jupiter in Virgo

This could indicate that good fortune and blessings will come to those who provide a loving service in some area of life. Pick a place to volunteer that inspires you, and watch it grow far beyond your intention.

December 21 – Winter Solstice – The Sun Enters Capricorn

The Earth's birthday is here! When the first light emerges from the long night of sleep, it's time to celebrate and birth yourself anew.

December 25 – Full Moon in Cancer

Celebrate with your family by the light of the full moon and allow this light to set you free from worry. The glowing will last all night and send warmth to nurture you.

December 25 – Jupiter and North Node in Virgo

Do something that makes a contribution to a cause; like feeding the homeless or bringing toys to kids in need. Great gifts will come from doing this – beyond your wildest dreams!

December 29 – Venus Enters Sagittarius

Venus leaving Scorpio will be a great escape. Time to celebrate entering the adventurous realm of the Sagittarius pathway. Follow Mark Twain's rule, "Sing like no one's listening, love like you've never been hurt, dance like nobody's watching, and live like it's Heaven on Earth."

Super-Sensitivity – December 8-11, 19-21

Combining the electricity in the atmosphere with the excitement of the holidays might put you on overload. Set your priorities in order and do what is in front of you to determine your peaceful approach to this busy time of year.

Low-Vitality – December 23-24

Taking a nap can be the answer on these days. A pattern interrupt may be necessary to keep you properly energized for the holidays. Go easy on yourself, knowing that everyone around you is in the same state of mind.

♈ Aries	♋ Cancer	♐ Sagittarius	☽ Moon	♄ Saturn	☊ North Node	V/C Void-of-Course
♉ Taurus	♌ Leo	♑ Capricorn	☿ Mercury	♅ Uranus	☋ South Node	▲ Super-Sensitivity
♊ Gemini	♍ Virgo	♒ Aquarius	♀ Venus	♆ Neptune	➡ Enters	▼ Low-Vitality
	♎ Libra	♓ Pisces	♂ Mars	♇ Pluto	℞ Retrograde	
	♏ Scorpio	☉ Sun	♃ Jupiter	⚷ Chiron	S/D Stationary Direct	

December

Sunday	Monday	Tuesday	Wednesday	Thursday	Friday	Saturday
		1 ♅℞ ☽ V/C 7:09PM 6. Make your holiday shopping list.	**2** ♅℞ ☽→♍ 2:09AM 7. Get the book you have been wanting.	**3** ♅℞ ☽ V/C 8:59PM 8. Abundance manifests now.	**4** ♅℞ ☽→♎ 2:33PM ♀→♏ 8:16PM 9. Embrace the joy of the season.	**5** ♅℞ 10. See the holidays in a new way.
6 ♅℞ ☽ V/C 6:02PM 11. Bring all the loose ends together.	**7** ♅℞ ☽→♏ 3:25AM 3. Save some time to play today.	**8** ♅℞ ▲ ☽ V/C 10:38PM 4. Make your plans simple and clear.	**9** ♅℞ ▲ ☽→♐ 2:25PM ♀→♑ 6:35PM 5. Be curious and adaptable.	**10** ♅℞ ▲ 6. Get your home ready for the season.	**11** ♅℞ ▲ ● 19°♐03′ 2:29AM ☽ V/C 8:05AM ☽→♑ 10:46PM 7. Learn a new thing about the computer.	**12** ♅℞ 8. Make all your purchases count.
13 ♅℞ ☽ V/C 3:07PM 9. Buy tickets for a holiday concert.	**14** ♅℞ ☽→♒ 4:58AM 10. Update your holiday décor.	**15** ♅℞ ☽ V/C 11:16PM 2. Gather opinions of trusting people.	**16** ♅℞ ☽→♓ 9:44AM 3. If it can't be fun, why do it?	**17** ♅℞ 4. To be safe, build from the bottom up.	**18** ♅℞ ☽ V/C 7:14AM ☽→♈ 1:26PM 5. Be open to last minute changes.	**19** ♅℞ ▲ 6. Happily do someone a favor.
20 ♅℞ ▲ ☽ V/C 2:00PM ☽→♉ 4:12PM 7. Recommend a good book.	**21** ♅℞ ▲ Winter Solstice ☉→♑ 8:49PM 8. If it is on sale, is it really worth it?	**22** ♅℞ ☽ V/C 6:26AM ☽→♊ 6:30PM 9. Enjoy the essence of the season.	**23** ♅℞ ▼ 10. Transform your holiday experience.	**24** ♅℞ ▼ ☽ V/C 12:03PM ☽→♋ 9:26PM 11. Things are coming together.	**25** Christmas Day ○ 3°♋20′ 3:11AM ♅D 16°♈33′ 7:54PM 3. Laugh at your own antics.	**26** ☽ V/C 7:35PM 4. Too much structure can ruin fun.
27 ☽→♌ 2:30AM 5. Variety, flexibility, travel. Be ready.	**28** 6. With love, everything works.	**29** ☽ V/C 9:37AM ☽→♍ 10:58AM ♀→♐ 11:18PM 7. Ask what you learned this year.	**30** 8. Prosperity opens the path to give.	**31** New Year's Eve ☽ V/C 9:33PM ☽→♎ 10:40PM 9. Celebrate joyfully and carefully.		

December 11th
2:29 AM

New Moon in Sagittarius

Degree Choice Points
19° Sagittarius 2'

Motivation Foresight

Resistance Superficial Reform

Gift Turn your healing energies inward.

Statement I Seek
Body Thighs
Mind Philosophical
Spirit Inspiration

Element
Fire – Inspiring, leadership, charisma, igniting, adventure.

Second House Moon
23° Scorpio 54'

Second House Umbrella Theme
I Have/I Transform – The way you make your money and the way you spend your money.

Motivation
Ground Instruction

Resistance
Condensation

Gift
Great a new experience with art, music, sex, or writing.

Karmic Awakening: Leo/Aquarius

Karma arises when the need for creative self-expression and recognition overshadow the inspiration to serve social concerns (beyond ego concerns). When Cancer is on the cusp of Leo, it may not feel that it is enough for you to care and nurture others, your will and creative strength need a more visible outlet. More karma could arise with Capricorn on the cusp of Aquarius. You may feel that it is not enough for you to be a respected part of social structure; your individuality must be given a chance to shine.

When the Sun is in Sagittarius

Now is the time for greater expansion of consciousness. Sagittarius is about exterminating all of the man-eating symbols of our illusions, harmful thoughts, inertia, prejudices, and superstitions that hide behind our excuses. It is truth time, so that the Soul Goal of the Sagittarius can come into being and direct its light toward greater aspiration. Questions to ask yourself at this time are: What is my goal for myself? What is my goal for my nation? What is my goal for humanity? All goals get stimulated during this time.

Sagittarius Goddess

The Sagittarius goddess, Saraswati, is in charge of fusing your personality with the light of your inner divinity. When this fusion occurs, the Law of Sound is made available to you and you have the power to manifest by directing your vision through the resonance of your own tone, note, or voice. The power of speech reaches a high level with Saraswati, the goddess of speech and knowledge. The activation of sound sheds light on your path, directing you toward the magnetic matrix of your future, and your goals. Saraswati reminds you that everything you put to sound ultimately manifests. It's best to avoid harmful speech, gossip, and your story, in order to be present with the power of the moment. Call on Saraswati to deliver you to your point of experience that provides the knowledge you are here to gain.

On Your Altar

Colors Deep purple, deep blue, turquoise

Numerology 7 – Learn a new thing about the computer

Tarot Card Temperance – Blending physical and spiritual

Gemstones Turquoise, lapis

Plant Remedy Madia – Seeing the target and hitting it

Fragrance Magnolia – Expanded beauty

My Co-Creation List

This or something better than this comes to me in an easy and pleasurable way, for the good of all concerned. Thank you, Universe!

Sagittarius Co-Creation Ideas

Now is the time to focus on manifesting truth, teaching and study, understanding advanced ideas, optimism and inspiration, bliss, goals, travel and adventure, and philosophy and culture.

December 11th
2:29 AM

New Moon in Sagittarius

Sagittarius Challenges and Victories

Say all of the statements in this section out loud. Then, underline the phrase that means the most to you. Use the phrase as your special affirmation for manifesting and co-creating throughout this phase of the moon.

Destiny is in my favor today. I know, without a doubt, that I cannot make a wrong turn today. I access my blueprint to ensure perfect timing for all opportunities to be open to me today. I promise to be open to these opportunities, knowing full well that today is my day. I am on time and in time today. My destiny is here and working in my favor. I see all that is available to me today and claim my pathway to success. I pay attention to what comes my way today and know that it is an opening for good fortune to be my reality. I am ready to accept my good fortune now. All I have to do is move in the direction of my truth. I know that my truth is my good fortune. I trust in coincidence and synchronicity to provide me with direction to my destiny. All points of action lead me to my true expression. I can see clearly into my future today with great optimism. I intend it. I allow it. So be it. All is in Divine Order.

Mantra during this Time *(repeat this 10 times out loud)*

"My truth is my good fortune. My timing is perfect. I trust that all that comes to me today is in my highest and best good. I am open to optimism. The drum of destiny beats in my favor. So be it!"

Sagittarius Homework

Sagittarius co-creates best through teaching, publishing and writing, travel, spiritual adventures, and as tour group leaders, airline and cruise ship personnel, evangelical ministers, philosophers, anthropologists, linguists, and translators.

The Sagittarius moon cycle creates a magnetic matrix that stimulates us to take direction towards becoming one with a goal and then sheds light on the path. In the ancient mystery schools, Sagittarius moons were used to set the stage for candidates to reach higher levels of awareness by inspiring their desire to reach a goal and then to step toward the goal. It is time now to become one with my goal.

Without Acknowledgment Progress Cannot Occur

Acknowledgement creates space for victory and gratitude, which automatically brings you to a level of completion so a new cycle of opportunity can occur in your life. When you celebrate your wins and acknowledge your victories with gratitude, you update your cells so that your ability to move forward is not hindered by a cellular holographic pattern that is stuck in the past. Cellular lag creates resistance and makes moving forward most difficult. The key is to stay continuously updated by acknowledging yourself for what you did do at the end of each day, rather than heading off to sleep thinning about what you did not do. By acknowledging what you did not do, you play into your karmic storage bank and keep your progress at bay. When you acknowledge yourself and your manifestations you are complete, and more cycles of opportunity become available to you in each new day. Be prepared for miracles!

Victory List

When a creation result is acknowledged it seals the deal. This makes room for more magnificence to expand into your life and increases your abundance factor adding to your ability to receive. As each aspect of your co-creation list arrives in your life, spend time allowing, acknowledging, and accepting it with the true gusto of gratitude! Keep your victory list active here.

This fulfills the relationship between the giver and the receiver, which completes the cycle with the Universe so that a new beginning can be established.

Gratitude List

December 11th
2:29 AM

New Moon in Sagittarius

How to Use the Moon Book With Your Chart

Fill in the blanks on the Cosmic Check-In page. Then look up the degree of the moon on the chart below. Take note of the "I" statement on the outside of the wheel where the moon is located. Now, locate the same degree on your own chart and make a note of the house and corresponding "I" statement. Go back to the Cosmic Check-In page and circle the two statements from the charts and read what you wrote. This will give you an idea about what to expect from this moon phase on a personal level.

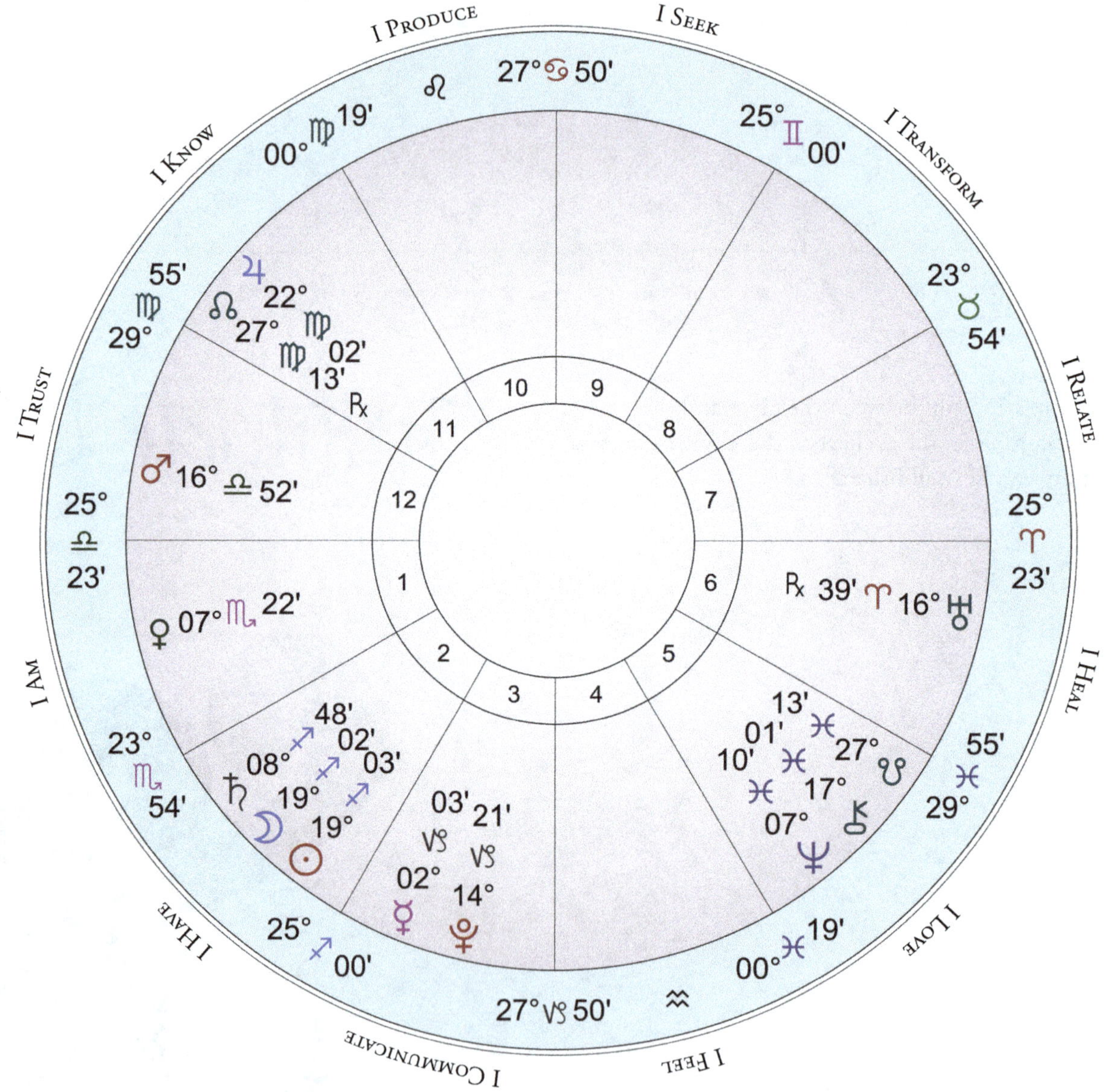

♈ Aries	♋ Cancer	♐ Sagittarius	☽ Moon	♄ Saturn	☊ North Node	V/C Void-of-Course
♉ Taurus	♌ Leo	♑ Capricorn	☿ Mercury	♅ Uranus	☋ South Node	▲ Super-Sensitivity
♊ Gemini	♍ Virgo	♒ Aquarius	♀ Venus	♆ Neptune	➡ Enters	▼ Low-Vitality
	♎ Libra	♓ Pisces	♂ Mars	♇ Pluto	℞ Retrograde	
	♏ Scorpio	☉ Sun	♃ Jupiter	⚷ Chiron	S/D Stationary Direct	

Cosmic Check-In

Take a moment to write a brief phrase for each "I" statement.
This activates all areas of your life for this creative cycle.

♐ I Seek

♑ I Produce

♒ I Know

♓ I Trust

♈ I Am

♉ I Have

♊ I Communicate

♋ I Feel

♌ I Love

♍ I Heal

♎ I Relate

♏ I Transform

December 25th
3:11 AM

Full Moon in Cancer

Degree Choice Points
  3° Cancer 19'

Motivation Predator/Prey

Resistance Harassment

Gift A breakthrough experience will enhance your life.

Statement I Feel
  Body Stomach
  Mind Worry
  Spirit Nurturing

Element
  Water – Motion without resistance, gateway to all things hidden (conscious and unconscious), a need for emotional nourishment.

Eighth House Moon
  15° Gemini 10'

Eighth House Umbrella Theme
  I Transform/I Feel – How you share money and other resources, what you keep hidden.

Motivation Activist

Resistance Underdog

Gift Disregard the old belief.

The Sun is Opposite the Moon

Full Moons are always in opposition to the Sun. This creates a feeling of tension between where you want to shine and how your feelings are flowing on a sensory level about the Sun's directive. The two forces seem like they are working against each other, yet they are on the same team displaying different techniques to obtain the same mission. The Cancer/Capricorn polarity creates tension about being at home with family or being at work positioning yourself for success.

Cancer Goddess

Demeter is the Goddess of Nature's Abundance. When her family was disrupted and her child taken, she withheld nourishment from the Earth, and Nature stopped producing. The people weren't nourished and withheld their honoring of the Gods. As a result, an agreement was struck between Heaven and Earth. Demeter agreed to let go and release full control of her child and restored Nature's abundance in exchange for a new, balanced relationship with her daughter. When the Moon is full in Cancer it is time to look at your mother/child issues and release what is no longer nurturing you.

On Your Altar

Colors Shades of gray and milky, creamy colors

Numerology 3 – Laugh at your own antics

Tarot Card The Chariot – The ability to move forward

Gemstones Pearl, moonstone, ruby

Plant remedy Shooting Star – The ability to move straight ahead

Fragrance Peppermint – The essence of the Great Mother

Meditation

The freedom themes are provided by the zodiac sign and can be from this lifetime or other lifetimes. These meditations assist in dissolving blocks and opening pathways to new frontiers.

When the Moon is in Cancer, it is time to reconcile with past events. Sit quietly and breathe, in and out, until you are settled. Ask for an Angel of Records to show you a time when your need was not fulfilled. It is important to listen to your emotional nature and take time out to be nurtured. Reflection and illumination are the main themes while sinking deeply into the subconscious memory. During the Cancer moon, it is time to research your Soul's records to release past memories of wrongs enacted against you so you can move beyond any attachment to self-pity.

Cancer Challenges and Victories

Say all of the statements in this section out loud. Then, underline the phrase that means the most to you. Use the phrase as your special affirmation for manifesting and co-creating throughout this phase of the moon.

Today, I take advantage of my ability to take action and position myself for success. I clearly know that the road to success is before me, and all I need to do is move forward. I am aware that when I take action and move forward, the Universe fills in the dots. Whether I move left, right, or straight ahead doesn't matter—what matters is that I am in movement. Today, I release indecisiveness that keeps me stuck. Today, I let go of vacillation that exhausts my mind. Today, I take my foot off of the brakes and find the gas pedal. I allow movement to occur, even if I don't know where I am going. When I take action, I trust the guideposts will appear. I am aware that action leads me to my new direction. Today, I know and GO! I remember that Karma comes to the space of non-action, while success comes through action. Action brings me to my victory. Standing still leads to regret, resentment, and chaos. I am aware that action can be as simple as taking a walk on the beach, buying fresh flowers to add a new dimension to my home, or simply going to a new restaurant for lunch. I take action today to break up a crystallized pattern and, in so doing, my life begins to show me newfound awareness and light to guide me.

Cancer Homework

It's now time to conquer pride and ambition, overcome fear of loneliness, release the need for money, security, and possessions, discover the value of emotions, and connect to beauty. Submerge yourself in a tub of water, relax, and let the clean water flow through your cells to wash away all of your hurts, resentments, and history that keep you trapped in the past. Pull the plug and let the spiral of water carry away your pain. Be prepared to boldly claim your presence in the present. Look around your kitchen and throw away the pots and pans that continue to feed your past, rather than vitalizing your life now.

December 25th
3:11 AM

Full Moon in Cancer

Clearing the Slate for Freedom

Remember a time when you experienced the following trigger points. Write down what happened, forgive yourself, release it, and let it go to clear your slate for freedom.

Blame

- Forgive
- Release
- Let Go

Attachment to Things

- Forgive
- Release
- Let Go

Emotional Attachment to the Past

- Forgive
- Release
- Let Go

Self-Pity

- Forgive
- Release
- Let Go

Broken Promises

- Forgive
- Release
- Let Go

My Freedom List

Say this statement out loud three times before writing your freedom list!

I am a free spiritual being and it is my desire to be free to think and to express myself fully ∽ to move about my life toward Truth and Wisdom ∽ to accept and enjoy all good which is mine in living my Truth

I am now free and ready to make choices beyond survival!

Cancer Freedom List Ideas

Now is the time to set myself free from self-pity, defensive behavior, nurturing everyone else but me, living in the past, being a mother, and having a mother.

December 25th
3:11 AM

Full Moon in Cancer

How to Use the Moon Book With Your Chart

Fill in the blanks on the Cosmic Check-In page. Then look up the degree of the moon on the chart below. Take note of the "I" statement on the outside of the wheel where the moon is located. Now, locate the same degree on your own chart and make a note of the house and corresponding "I" statement. Go back to the Cosmic Check-In page and circle the two statements from the charts and read what you wrote. This will give you an idea about what to expect from this moon phase on a personal level.

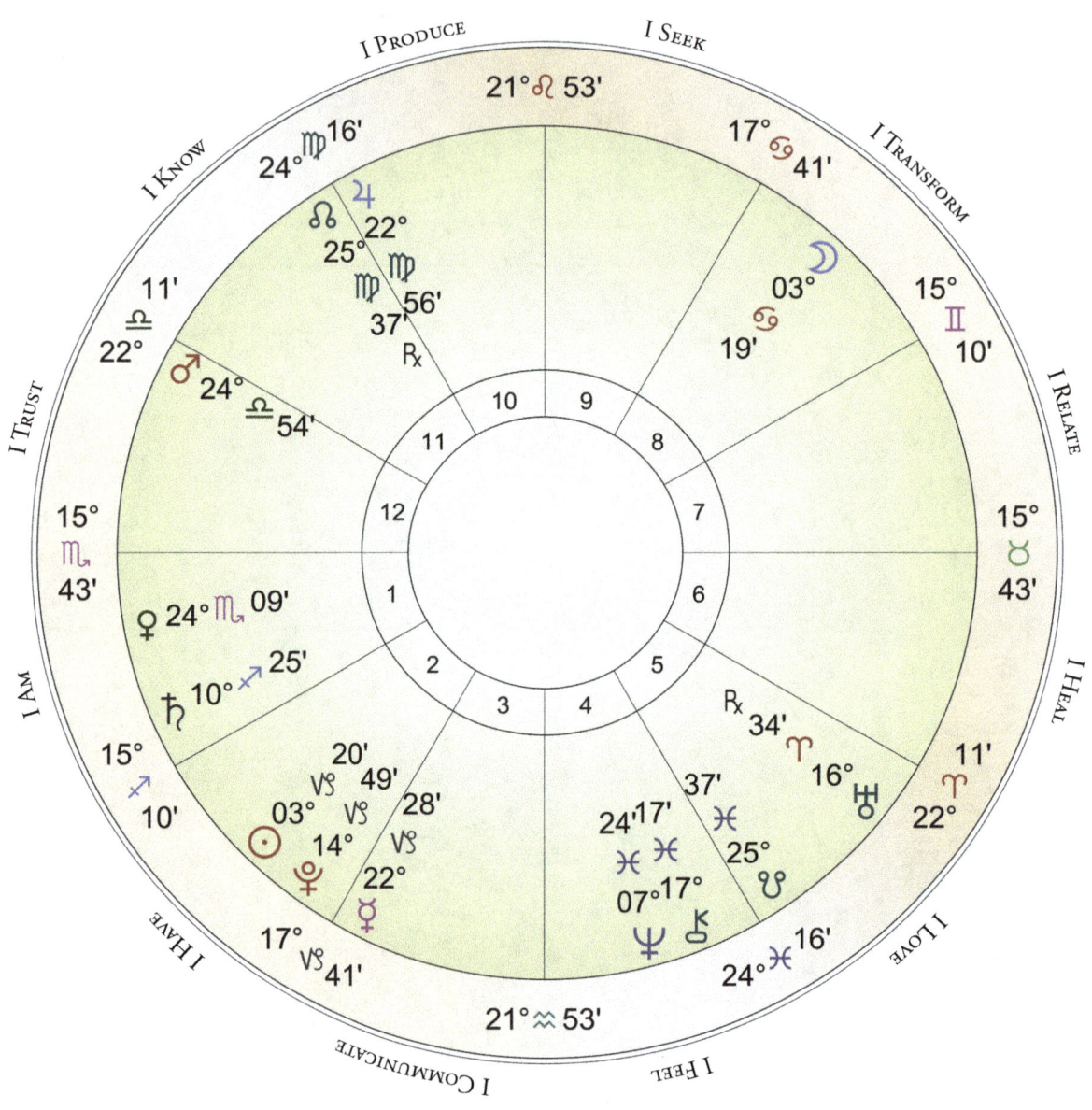

♈ Aries	♋ Cancer	♐ Sagittarius	☽ Moon	♄ Saturn	☊ North Node	V/C Void-of-Course
♉ Taurus	♌ Leo	♑ Capricorn	☿ Mercury	♅ Uranus	☋ South Node	▲ Super-Sensitivity
♊ Gemini	♍ Virgo	♒ Aquarius	♀ Venus	♆ Neptune	➡ Enters	▼ Low-Vitality
	♎ Libra	♓ Pisces	♂ Mars	♇ Pluto	℞ Retrograde	
	♏ Scorpio	☉ Sun	♃ Jupiter	⚷ Chiron	S/D Stationary Direct	

232

Cosmic Check-In

Take a moment to write a brief phrase for each "I" statement.
This activates all areas of your life for this creative cycle.

♋ I Feel

♌ I Love

♍ I Heal

♎ I Relate

♏ I Transform

♐ I Seek

♑ I Produce

♒ I Know

♓ I Trust

♈ I Am

♉ I Have

♊ I Communicate

About the Author

Beatrex Quntanna

is a dynamic teacher devoted to the growth and development of the human potential. She inspires, motivates, and stimulates growth with her ever-present zest for life and the human experience. Beatrex is an author, lecturer, symbolist, and tarot expert. She has been counseling and teaching for the past thirty years using the Tarot as an enhancement for personal and intuitive development. Her students find her workshops and books inspiring, enlightening, full of wise truths, and helpful in pursuing the most positive outcome in their own lives.

Beatrex is also the author of *Tarot: A Universal Language*, an easy-to-use approach to understanding the symbolism of tarot and applying it to daily life.

Interested in ongoing Moon Classes and workshops with Beatrex? Contact her at beatrex@cox.net or visit www.beatrex.com

Visit www.MyMoonBook.Com for Moon-related products created by Beatrex

2015 The Year of Prosperity

Wall Calendar

By Beatrex Quntanna & Michael Makay

Astrological Calculations by Katherine Sale

Follow Mark Twain's rule, "Sing like no one's listening, love like you've never been hurt, dance like nobody's watching, and live like it's Heaven on Earth."

Yes! The tide turns this year as we move beyond the polarized forces that have haunted us since 2012 began. We can now open ourselves to good fortune, universal love, expansion, community spirit, inspired thinking, and the courage to accept abundance. Get ready to take a standing ovation for exchanging the restriction of polarity for the ability to combine power with opportunity.

When we do this, we experience the Year of Prosperity and have the ability to multiply beauty, quality, laughter, and ideas—life is fulfilling! We are energized, we are vital, we are healthy, we trust support systems, we are happy, and WE ARE LOVE!

Often we confuse manifesting with money, and in so doing, we deny and limit the idea of prosperity. The Earth is filled with all that is required for abundant living. Be open to receive all that life has to offer.

The number eight is the umbrella energy for 2015; it is all about manifestation. At long last you can stand tall in the garden of life and be your authentic self, realizing every dream you have ever had has the possibility to come true. Put on your dancing shoes and get ready to party through the year with bliss in your heart living love every day!

This calendar is designed as a complete support system to enhance your understanding of how to best work with the planetary movements and numerological influences in the coming year.

This calendar offers many tools and modalities to guide us through the entire year including…

- Astrological Highlights
- Tibetan Numerology of the Day
- Planetary Retrogrades listed monthly
- New Moons and Full Moons, referred to by time, astrological sign, and degree
- Super-Sensitivity Days and Low-Vitality Days
- The times at which the Sun enters a new Zodiac Sign

To order, call 1-760-944-6020 or go to www.mymoonbook.com

Tarot: A Universal Language

Experiencing the Road of Life Through Symbols

By Beatrex Quntanna

Embark on this fascinating journey through the unfolding Story of Life as told by the Universal Language of the Tarot. This book contains innovative avenues to understand the tarot through the author's in-depth knowledge of symbology.

Learn how to quickly read and interpret the tarot by following this simple, informative, and illustrated guide. Use the expanded symbology section to understand each symbol depicted on the Minor and Major Arcana cards.

This book includes an interpretation of all 78 tarot cards, plus readings created by this nationally-known tarot teacher, reader, and symbolist.

To order, call 1-760-944-6020 or go to www.Beatrex.com

"Brilliantly Engineered."

"Amazingly Accurate."

"A refreshing, uncluttered approach to learning the tarot."

"Her exceptional background in symbology and numerology as well as her extraordinary psychic insight makes this book unique among tarot books, and a must-have reference for the tarot novice and professional alike."

www.ingramcontent.com/pod-product-compliance
Lightning Source LLC
Chambersburg PA
CBHW082316230426
43666CB00036B/2733